Delivering Customer Value Through Marketing

CIM Coursebook: Delivering Customer Value Through Marketing

Edited by: Colin Linton

and

Authored by: Ray Donnelly

ELSEVIER

AMSTERDAM • BOSTON • HEIDELBERG • LONDON • NEW YORK
OXFORD • PARIS • SAN DIEGO • SAN FRANCISCO •
SINGAPORE • SYDNEY • TOKYO
Butterworth-Heinemann is an imprint of Elsevier

Butterworth-Heinemann is an imprint of Elsevier
Linacre House, Jordan Hill, Oxford, OX2 8DP, UK
30 Corporate Drive, Suite 400, Burlington, MA 01803, USA

First published 2009

British Library Cataloguing in Publication Data
A catalogue record for this book is available from the British Library

Library of Congress Cataloging-in-Publication Data
A catalog record for this book is available from the Library of Congress

ISBN: 978-1-85617-718-4

For information on all Butterworth-Heinemann publications
visit our web site at www.elsevierdirect.com

Typeset by Macmillan Publishing Solutions
www.macmillanpublishingsolutions.com

Printed and bound in Italy

09 10 11 12 13 14   10 9 8 7 6 5 4 3 2 1

Working together to grow
libraries in developing countries

www.elsevier.com | www.bookaid.org | www.sabre.org

ELSEVIER   BOOK AID
             International   Sabre Foundation

Contents

Don't forget to look at the extra online support at www.marketingonline.co.uk which includes more free mini case studies.

Preface

Welcome to the *Delivering Customer Value Through Marketing* CIM course text.

The subject focuses on a number of important marketing tools, concepts, models and activities, all of which can help organisations to achieve key business and marketing objectives. To satisfy the examiner in this subject, it is imperative that students not only understand the basic principles but can also apply what they have learnt.

Assessments for the subject will focus on different types of organisations that may operate in a number of different markets and in various geographic territories. As a result, students will be required to apply their knowledge in different organisational contexts and in domestic, international and global markets.

Questions will be highly practical in emphasis and students, therefore, to broaden their understanding, are urged to look at examples in the world around them. To this end, students should consider why organisations are making the kind of marketing decisions they are and how marketing activities are structured and executed by them in an integrated way. This course text contains numerous examples, but it is recommended that students supplement these with examples from their own markets.

The course text content is broken down into four sections that align with the subject syllabus. The first section focuses on a number of key areas, including why and how products (and services) are managed; how and why new products are developed; the importance of enhancing and rejuvenating existing products; how and why products are branded; the importance of positioning in product management; how products are priced and the factors that will influence pricing decisions.

Students must be able to examine product management both in the context of individual products and also in managing product portfolios. Some of the tools and techniques used in product management may have featured in previous studies. It is important that students recognise the academic level of this qualification and, as a result, that they will be expected to apply these tools and techniques, as well as understanding the limitations, where appropriate, of their use.

In the second section the text examines the topic of channel management. The effective delivery of products to customers is a key aspect of marketing and can have a major impact on revenues, profitability, customer satisfaction, positioning and so much more. Specifically, the text considers the importance of channel management strategy in achieving key business and marketing objectives; the factors, issues and challenges which influence channel management strategy; the choice of channels available in different organisational contexts and their application; the identification and management of key stakeholders in channel management; and the contractual aspects of channel management.

The third section focuses on arguably one of the most important aspects of marketing and a key element of the marketing mix – communications. Communicating the right message to the right people in the most cost-effective way is a key goal of marketers.

In this section, the text examines the development of communications strategy and objectives; the development and execution of communications plans; the importance of internal communications and the methods used; the application of the promotional mix; the role of creative agencies in marketing communications; and measuring the performance of marketing communications activities. This latter aspect is of particular importance as, very often, marketing communications activities account for a high proportion of marketing expenditure and so 'proving' the value that has been derived is an important task for the successful marketer.

The concluding section assesses customer service. In particular, the text concentrates on the importance of service to customers in different segments; understanding what constitutes 'good service' to different customers; measuring customer satisfaction; how to develop and implement customer service plans and customer care programmes; the identification and management of key account customers; and the crucial role of information in customer relationship management.

Customer service is critical in the achievement of important marketing goals, including customer retention, market share growth, building customer loyalty and achieving differentiation through the provision of a superior service proposition. This aspect, of course, is particularly relevant in services marketing where often the service itself (and the people who deliver it) are the main potential source of competitive advantage.

The content is highly relevant to marketer's in today's highly competitive and rapidly changing world. Marketing's contribution, not only to business success but also to economies around the globe, is potentially significant. It is hoped that students will enjoy studying this subject and will be able to benefit both themselves, in their careers, and their organisations through better planning, execution and performance measurement of aspects contained within the syllabus.

Colin Linton, Senior CIM Examiner – Delivering Customer Value
Through Marketing, 2009–2010

About the Authors

Colin Linton DipM MBA MCIPS FCIEA FCIM FCIB. Colin is a senior level marketing practitioner. He held a number of senior positions in a marketing career in financial services spanning more than twenty years, including four years as Marketing Director of RBS' UK Corporate Banking Division. He is CIM Senior Examiner for Delivering Customer Value Through Marketing. He is also Senior Assessor in Marketing for Purchasers for the Chartered Institute of Purchasing & Supply. In addition, he is Chief Examiner in Organisational Management in Financial Services and a Moderator in Marketing for the ifs School of Finance.

Ray Donnelly Author, trainer and academic who is also CIM Course leader, London Metropolitan Business School, London Metropolitan University.

Product Proposition and Brand Management

CHAPTER 1

New Product Development and Positioning

LEARNING OBJECTIVES

By the end of this chapter you will be able to:
- Examine the value and contribution of effective product management
- Apply the new product development process
- Assess product positioning and how it is applied

INTRODUCTION

Chapters 1 to 4 cover the part of the syllabus which relates to the role of products, the relationship with branding and the influence of pricing (product proposition and brand management). These are key tools available to a marketer when developing a product portfolio which meets the ever-changing needs of customers, and at the same time delivers corporate profitability.

The chapters of study will enable the reader to understand a number of techniques which have been tried and tested by a range of organisations to assist with effective strategic management of the product portfolio.

The reader will be introduced to a number of processes which enables you to develop a better understanding of the product and its key elements, the reasons for managing products to maximise customer value and the tools available to achieve this. Readers will be appraised of the advantages of strategic product management but at the same time will be asked to consider the limitations and how this might be managed.

A variety of different techniques will be explored including Product Life Cycle, BCG Matrix, GE Matrix and the new product development process. They will equip the reader with a number of options in achieving effective product management and this will be set in the context of opportunities both at home and abroad. The difficulties in developing products that eventually come to market and the key stages in the process will be explored and examples provided.

The marketing mix will be introduced as a concept which aids the strategic management of the product portfolio by developing an understanding of the role of the variable elements and the inter-relationship between them.

The role of branding will also be explored in the context of its critical role in shaping and positioning products with customers. Readers will be aware of a variety of strategies which can be explored with a view to maximising the attractiveness of the product range, the appeal to the customer and organisational profitability. Branding categories will also be considered and a view of how branding can be used to differentiate products explored. The role of branding in developing global products in overseas markets will be looked at particularly in relation to the degree of adaptation required.

The pricing variable will also be considered with a view to deepening the understanding of the impact that a variety of pricing strategies can have on the product position in the market. We will explore the ways in which pricing can be used to manage the product at various stages in its lifecycle in order to maximise the appeal of the product and profitability. Readers will be appraised of the importance of setting pricing objectives as a benchmark and to guide strategic product development. The role of the customers' view of different strategies will also be considered, particularly in terms of the perception of value for money over which pricing strategies have significant influence. The role of pricing in building market share will also be considered as a key element of the marketing mix.

By the end of Chapter 4 readers will have a greater understanding of the key variable of the marketing mix, a range of techniques available to manage product portfolios effectively and a variety of examples of how this has been achieved.

It must be remembered that the subject encompasses both the domestic and international markets and this is applicable across all the Chapters. Similarly the context of the material needs to be understood in terms of different organisations or sectors, e.g. B2B, B2C, public and the not-for-profit sectors.

WHAT IS A PRODUCT?

The terms 'product' and 'services' are used interchangeably but they do have precise definitions and implications which helps marketers be more effective in carrying out their roles.

Kotler (1999) defines a product as 'anything that is offered to the market for attention, acquisition, use or consumption that might satisfy a need or want'. He goes on to define a service as 'products that consist of activities, benefits, or satisfactions that are offered for sale that are essentially intangible and do not result in the ownership of anything'.

A product can be a physical good, service, idea or indeed a person. Leona Lewis, your favourite soup, or replacement parts for your car, all come within the definition of a product. In other words a product it is something which is capable of meeting customers' needs.

It can be the case that a product has tangible and non-tangible elements i.e. a combination of both product and service. Consider the purchase of a new software product by an organisation to streamline its payroll system. The software will be tangible, but its complexity means that an engineer needs to install it and then train staff on its use.

A product can be viewed from three levels:

- The core product

- The actual product

- The augmented product

These levels are used by marketers to offer a range of benefits that will have a different meaning for each customer.

The anatomy of a product (the different levels) is shown as a series of concentric rings as illustrated in Figure 1.1.

When marketers think about a product, its constitution is a little more complex than might be obvious and the various levels are summarised in Table 1.1.

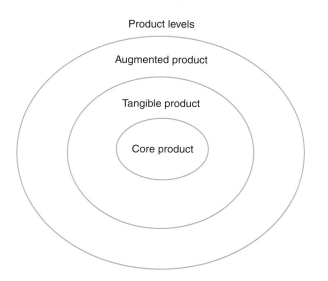

Product levels

Augmented product

Tangible product

Core product

FIGURE 1.1
Product levels.

Table 1.1	Summary of product levels
■ The core product	This is the basic product i.e. what the customer is buying. Marketers must define the core product elements in terms which are meaningful to the customer.
■ The actual product	Is composed of several characteristics such as styling, brand, quality, and packaging.
■ The augmented product	Additional consumer benefits and services are added. This could include things like warranties, guarantees, finance terms, dedicated help line.

It is at the augmented level that most competition takes place. For example, having made a decision to purchase a new car and narrowed the choice of vehicles to two manufacturers, it may be the case that the decision is swayed by the three years interest free credit deal offered by one of the brands. Organisations must constantly look to differentiate their product offers from the competition.

EXAMPLE

PC World will now sell you a laptop computer that comes as a basic product, or with security software added, and/or mobile broadband with a range of payment terms which in summary allow you to choose to pay (say) £400, or in fact nothing, depending on whether you select a broadband package.

PRODUCT CATEGORIES

Products can be categorised into consumer and business products. The key differentiator is the purpose for which the product is to be used. It is important for marketers to understand the different categories in order for the appropriate marketing mix to be developed. However, it is not always easy to differentiate between the two categories. For example, the owner of a company buys a laptop computer for home use. However, by clearly understanding the different purchasing intentions the marketing mix can be highly targeted.

Consumer products can be further subdivided into four categories and industrial products can be subdivided into seven categories (Dibb *et al.*, 2005) which are shown in Table 1.2.

NEW PRODUCT DEVELOPMENT PROCESS

The new product development process (NPD) can be considered as the development of an original product, improvement or innovation which goes through a series of processes prior to being launched in the market.

Table 1.2 Consumer products vs industrial products

Consumer products	Industrial products
Convenience products	Raw materials
Shopping products	Major equipment
Speciality products	Accessory equipment
Unsought products	Component parts
	Process materials
	Consumer supplies
	Industrial services

Developing new products is an essential process for any organisation if it is to be successful in delivering customer value. In particular, it:

- reduces the possibility of product obsolescence, so that a range of products to meet customer needs will always be available

- ensures a match with environmental conditions, as consumers become more 'green' organisations need to develop 'cleaner' products

- enables the organisation to compete in new and developing markets

- can reduce the dependence on vulnerable product sectors; a range of products can weather changing economic conditions

- can achieve long term growth and profit by ensuring a better fit with customer needs and expectations

- responds to changing customer needs and expectations

NPD is an expensive process and does not offer any guarantee that the product being developed will be financially successful, or will meet customer needs.

In a rapidly changing market, organisations sometimes seek to bring new products to market by buying a company which has the capability to launch quickly into market. This can be because the organisation does not have the internal capability itself, but senses the gap in the market which it then fills by buying in the resources.

Sometimes failure can be down to timing, i.e. the market isn't yet ready for the product, or the product simply is not right for the market and insufficient research has been undertaken for an effective launch into the market.

There are many phases in the NPD process and the seven key ones are described in Figure 1.2.

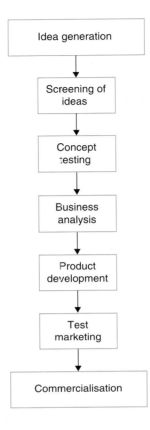

Idea Generation

This is the first stage of the NPD process and there should be formal channels within the organisation to collect and collate the ideas generated. Organisations will receive ideas from many sources, which need to be evaluated and moved on to the next phase or discarded.

Ideas can come from customers, who may have identified weaknesses in existing products or have made suggestions for new ones. Monitoring the competition through a sales team or research can also be helpful. Market research commissioned by the organisation will suggest gaps in the product range and possible product, or product features, that customers would be interested in. Staff who are in regular contact with customers can often offer useful market intelligence.

A number of organisations employ staff suggestion schemes where any member of staff can suggest a new idea which is rewarded in some way.

All the ideas received must be centrally collated and evaluated. It is usually the case that a significant number of ideas are generated, but very few move through to be commercially developed.

Screening

The second stage is to 'screen' the ideas. It is here that the ideas generated are assessed to see if they should be taken forward. A systematic process should be in place to ensure that only ideas which match the organisation's vision and objectives should be developed. Most ideas are rejected as being unsuitable when properly screened and analysed. Organisations have finite resources and only those products with the greatest potential for success can be developed.

Concept Testing

Having got to this stage, it is necessary to establish what potential customers think of the idea, which now needs to be translated into a concept which can be visualised. This can take the form of samples, 'mock-ups' of the final product, a simulation, or simply a presentation. The concept can be tested with a focus group(s), or individuals can be invited to test the concept.

The idea of concept testing is to ensure the organisation is moving in the right direction and customers see the appeal of the product and recognise the benefits. Depending on the feedback at this stage, adjustments can be made before costs are incurred later in the development process.

Business Analysis

The organisation fully costs out the financial benefits to be derived from the product. Break-even costs can be established with some certainty and sales will be estimated, taking into consideration the affects of any cannibalisation of any other products in the portfolio. Costs will be established and this will need to account for any new facilities, such as premises or equipment which maybe needed for launch. Additional staff, or those with different skills, may be required and all of these costs must be fully explored.

Once the full financial picture has been established, an organisation must seek approval from senior management to gain the necessary high level commitment to proceed.

This is a crucial stage as if the organisation proceeds and it subsequently transpires the estimates made were wrong, it could potentially bring financial ruin to the organisation, or negatively impact on future development opportunities.

Product Development

Once financial agreement has been obtained, the organisation can now develop the concept into reality. What was presented as an idea at the concept testing stage must now be developed and a prototype or model produced. This not only gives consumers a clear picture of the product, but also allows the organisation to test whether the production costs (or similar) previously estimated were realistic.

The organisation will now start to outline a marketing strategy and be considering the deployment of the marketing mix (using the 7Ps where a service is involved).

Test Marketing

Prior to full roll out of the product, organisations will often undertake a 'test' in the real environment in a defined geographical area. This allows the organisation to fully roll out a sample of its marketing programme. The scale of the test depends on the importance of the product and the costs already invested.

Customer response to the product and the marketing activity are evaluated and if any changes are needed they can be introduced now, rather then incur a costly launch only to make subsequent changes which could be embarrassing.

It is important that this stage is concluded quickly as there is some vulnerability from the competition who can see what is being planned. Also if the test runs for a long period of time consumers may get the impression that the product will never actually launch and lose interest.

Commercialisation

Any changes needed will have been identified in the previous phase. The decision has been made to launch and now not only must the production and technical plans be fully developed and approved, the marketing programme must also be developed and the entire roll out plans coordinated.

Any investments identified and approved in the business analysis stage will have been initiated. Production commences and should be at such a level that demand can be met. An organisation launching a new product will need to ensure its call centre can handle the volume of customer calls, or that its website will not crash.

Boeing, when it launched the 747, virtually risked the future of the company on the success of the launch. Procter and Gamble (P&G) spent $1bn on marketing the new Fusion six-blade razor, Ford typically spends millions of dollars on a new product launch.

It is estimated that only 8% of new products launched by major organisations are successful (Dibb *et al.*, 2005). The rigour of the NPD process must be sound to maximise the chances of commercial success.

TYPES OF NEW PRODUCT

The parameters of a product have been outlined. The characteristics of a new product have been explained. We have previously defined a product, but there are different types of 'newness'. Brassington and Pettitt (2006) suggest four types:

- *New to company and market*: this is a totally new product which has never been offered before. At one time mobile phones would have come under this category.

- *New to company, significant innovation for market*: the core product is familiar to the consumer, but an additional feature has been added. As an example, historically a DVD player would have been separate from the TV, now they can be incorporated within the TV as one appliance.

- *New to company, minor innovation for market*: the burden now is on the company and the launch of the product is unlikely to have a significant impact on the market, but it may be important for the company in order to fill a gap in its product range and therefore retain customers.

- *New to company, no innovation for market:* 'me too' products often when a market follower launches a product into the market.

Sony is generally regarded as an innovator in the electronics sector. Bush on the other hand is a follower who doesn't invest significantly in NPD leaving that to the market innovators.

PRODUCT STANDARDISATION OR ADAPTATION

Organisations that operate outside their domestic market must consider the implications for standardising or adapting its products to meet the needs of the market it intends to serve.

Where the product is standardised, the organisation will offer the same product in each of the markets it serves, whereas with adaptation the product will be changed according to the needs of each market. So which way is best?

Before exploring the two options the different types of organisations involved in overseas activities are summarised in Table 1.3.

Having decided to enter an overseas market, an organisation needs to adopt the 'best' strategy to serve the target market and there are three product strategies an organisation could employ which are summarised in Table 1.4.

Table 1.3	Different types of organisations involved in overseas activities
Organisation	**Summary**
International	Domestic marketing mix applied to all countries in which it operates
Multinational	Each overseas market is regarded as a discrete area which reports into the home country head office
Global	Organisations which have a single marketing mix. A global rather than country approach is taken

Table 1.4	Three product strategies an organisation could employ in an overseas market
Strategy	**Summary of strategy**
Keep product the same worldwide (standardisation)	The product is exactly the same worldwide, there is no product development.
Adapt the product for each market (adaptation)	The product is changed for each market to meet the local needs.
Invent a new product	Create a new product for overseas markets. This could take the form of an entirely new product, or t could be adapted from an earlier product.

Product Standardisation

An organisation may prefer to offer the same product, because it can be cheaper in terms of production and because the cost of adapting the product cannot be justified in terms of the potential income. Equally the costs of product development and research are reduced through standardisation. Sometimes the overseas market may prefer the product not to be adapted e.g. HP sauce which is quintessentially British. IKEA is a good example of an organisation that offers the same product across each of its markets.

Keeping the product the same worldwide has some advantages, such as no additional product development or research because no changes are anticipated or implemented. The ability to actually achieve this may be restricted because the product name does not translate well (may cause offence), or simply has a different meaning. Therefore it is not always possible to export a brand in its existing form.

Adaptation

Here it is assumed the product would benefit from being tailored to the needs of the local market.

A product's size and packaging may have to be modified to facilitate shipment or to conform to possible differences in engineering or design standards in a country or regional markets. Product adaptations may even include changes in one or more combinations of brand name, colour, size, taste, design, style, features, materials, warranties, after sale service, technological sophistication and performance.

On occasions there is no choice but to adapt the product to meet the differing needs of the market.

This can come about for legal, social, cultural or health and safety issues and concerns that will require careful market sensing to find the appropriate fit.

Car manufacturers have to produce the same model in left and right-hand-drive versions. Electronics companies need to produce products to accept different electricity voltages. McDonalds needs to offer Halal meat options. Beer manufacturers need to offer their products in pint and litre options. Soft drink manufacturers need to change the formulation to meet the needs of each market.

ACTIVITY 1.1

For your own organisation or an organisation of your choice, review its NPD process and evaluate how it could be improved.

PRODUCT POSITIONING

A product's position is 'the way the product is defined by consumers on important attributes-the place the product occupies in consumers' mind relative to competing products' (Kotler *et al.*, 1999). This suggests that there may be some element of chance when a consumer positions a product in their mind. Clearly this is not what an organisation wants and 'they must plan positions that will give their products the greatest advantage in selected markets (Kotler *et al.*, 1999). This means the product must be clearly positioned against the competition and have a distinct image in the market. Coca Cola is positioned as 'the real thing' which clearly helped it at the time when a number of organisations such as supermarkets and Virgin were developing cheaper alternatives. Gillett's slogan for its men's razors 'the best a man can get' again clearly positioned it in the mind of the consumer. Stella Artois is 'reassuringly expensive'.

Kotler *et al.* (1999) say that 'products are created in the factory, but brands are created in the mind'.

FIGURE 1.3

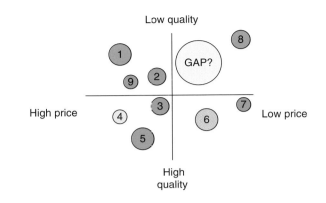

FIGURE 1.3

Perceived position mapped against quality and price.

How to Position New Products

Perception maps are used to show a consumer's perception of a brand and its perceived attributes. Each circle in Figure 1.3 shows a brand's perceived position mapped against two variables, in this case quality and price. The size of each circle represents the relative market share held by the brand. We can see that in the low price/high quality quadrant that two brands are competing and brand '6' has the higher market share. In the low price/low quality market only brand '8' is competing and there is potentially a gap in the market (big circle) where an organisation may potentially want to compete because there is no competition and it represents the ideal positioning i.e. relatively low price, with relatively low quality.

Dibb *et al.* (2005) suggests there are six options available when developing a positioning for a product:

1. Identify the product features or attributes that are superior or desirable and matched by few, if any, competitors, or

2. Identify the key benefits achieved as a result of using the product, or

3. Emphasise specific product occasions

4. Identify and depict user groups

5. Adopt a head-to-head positioning

6. Have a clear point of differentiation from the competition

PRODUCT ADOPTION

Product adoption refers to the various stages a consumer goes through as part of the process of adopting a new product.

Table 1.5	Production adoption stages
Product adoption stages	**Summary**
1. Awareness	At this stage the consumer becomes aware of the product, but lacks information on it.
2. Interest	The consumer now seeks information on the product and this could be around features and benefits.
3. Evaluation	Is the product worth trying? Will it meet the needs of the consumer?
4. Trial	The consumer will now try the product; this could be by free sample, special promotion or free trial.
5. Adoption	The consumer tries to make full use of the product, although this does not offer any guarantee of loyalty.

For the marketer it's important to understand the customer journey so the most effective communication strategies can be developed to move the consumer through each stage as rapidly as possible.

The journey consists of five stages as shown in Table 1.5.

Product Adoption Categories

Consumers do not take up a new product at the same rate and we can group them into categories reflecting the rate at which the product is adopted. However, not everybody takes up a new product and some people will adopt the product just at the time its replacement is being introduced.

Rodgers (1962) identified five separate categories reflecting the rate at which they adopt a product. It should be noted that because a person is an innovator for example in respect of mobile phones, it does not necessarily suggest they will be innovators across other categories.

Knowing where customers are in the 'model' shown in Figure 1.4 allows a marketer to develop an integrated marketing mix which is targeted at each stage.

Innovators

Innovators are the first people to try the product, they enjoy trying new things and they like adventure. They are a small group of people who help get the product launched. They are generally young, confident and well educated.

Early Adopters

Early adopters enter the market early and take their lead from the innovators who are taking the risk. Once the early adopters enter the market, the

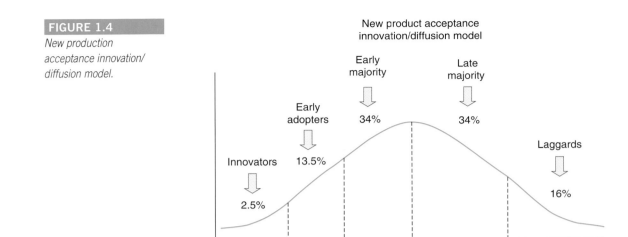

FIGURE 1.4

New production acceptance innovation/ diffusion model.

PLC can enter the growth stage. Although innovators are followers, they remain alert to new developments in the market.

Early Majority

At this stage the mass market is starting to build. The group is more risk adverse than previous ones and will seek reassurance that the product will work. Relatively well educated, they tend to have above-average incomes.

Late Majority

The late majority is content to watch and see how the market develops; competition may be building, so they will have a range of products to choose from. May have been hesitant for financial reasons. The product may be reaching maturity by the time the late majority take it up.

Laggards

Laggards are the last to be converted. They are adverse to change and may have attitude or economic issues preventing them from taking up the product. There is little risk now in taking up the product as others have dealt with this. Prices are now starting to fall and innovators are already purchasing the next product.

PRODUCT INNOVATION

The process and technical aspects of developing new products, managing their position in changing markets and the relationship with the dynamic needs of customers has been considered. However, innovation brings these processes to life and enables excellent NPD and management. Innovation comes from a variety of sources:

■ Customers

■ Front line staff

■ Executives

■ Advisers

Innovation is not just about bringing new products to the market. It is about reinventing business processes and building entirely new markets that meet untapped customer needs. Most important, as the Internet and globalization widen the pool of new ideas, it's about selecting and executing the right ideas and bringing them to market in record time (*Business Week*, April 2006).

There is some debate about what constitutes innovation and the following definition should offer some help.

> Innovation is 'not a single action but a total process of interrelated sub processes. It is not just the conception of a new idea, nor the invention of a new device, nor the development of a new market. The process is all these things acting in an integrated fashion.' Myers & Marquis (1969)

The innovation process cannot be left to chance and organisations must gear up to the opportunities for innovation and allow it to become the lifeblood of the organisation. Innovation comes from a wide variety of sources and needs. Research conducted by Business Week and Boston Consulting Group (2006) suggested some explanations for the innovative capacity of an organisation:

■ Cooperation with suppliers

■ Understanding of customers and cultures

■ Speed of product development

■ Design

■ Use of external technology

There are a number of ways to categorise innovation. Utterback (1994) suggested the following:

■ *Product innovation*; making changes to the products offered by the organisation: e.g. moving from CD to MP3 or MP4 players

- *Process innovation*; changing the way products are created and delivered, e.g. online payment for Car Tax, or online banking

- *Position innovation*: changes to the context in which products are introduced, e.g. mobile phones which combine email, internet, music, radio, satellite navigation and the ability to make phone calls!

- *Paradigm innovation*: changes in the underlying attitude of an organisation, e.g. Northern Rock which initially moved from a small Building Society to one of the largest mortgage lenders in the UK (now nationalised at the time of writing).

We can also add to the list:

- *Organisational innovation*, i.e. outsourcing or combining business function with other organisations

- *Management innovation*: business process re-engineering

- *Marketing innovation*: new delivery channels

As the definition above suggests, innovation is not to be regarded as a one-off process never to be repeated, it is ongoing and customers welcome new products. Equally organisations often have to stimulate demand to encourage purchase.

It has been noted that not all new product ideas survive, in fact most are rejected at some point in the NPD process and then for those that do get launched, the majority will be unsuccessful. Therefore organisations need to have a mechanism or criteria in place to encourage successful innovation. Hooley *et al.* (2008) suggest three conditions:

- *Closeness to customers*: i.e. understand their needs very well

- *Cross-functional communication*: i.e. an effective communications procedure is in place between the key functions within the organisation

- *Multi-functional team work:* most innovation comes about through teams working effectively together rather than people working alone

The Innovation Process

Innovation can be achieved through small incremental changes or a 'big bang' or radical changes. Most organisations will follow an incremental process, as the 'big bang 'approach requires a radical organisation.

Hooley *et al.* (2008) suggests six broad approaches that can be adopted by organisations to encourage and develop innovation, as seen in Table 1.6.

Table 1.6	Six broad approaches that can be adopted by organisations to encourage and develop innovation
Approach	**Commentary**
Functional approach	People from the different business units within the organisation undertake the requisite tasks with a representative from each unit meeting with the other units to progress development. This is usually an additional activity beyond the normal day to day tasks.
Taskforce	A group of individuals will be selected to progress development. The team should be selected on the basis of individual skills and it is likely that the individuals will be able to allocate more time to the project than with the functional approach. However, they will still have their normal duties to attend to.
Functional Matrix	Here team members will be expected to spend around 50% of their time on the project and the rest on their normal activities although insufficient time is usually available to undertake them.
Venture teams	People are released from their normal activities and spend their entire time on the project.
Spin-outs	Used by large organisations to support high risk projects which do not fit in with the organisations core activities.
Inside-outside venture	Teams from different organisations come together to develop the project combining the skills from both organisations.

Radical innovation, concerned with exploration of new technology, is fundamentally different from incremental innovation that is concerned with exploitation of existing technology. "Radical innovation is a product, process, or service with either unprecedented performance features or familiar features that offer potential for significant improvements in performance and cost." It creates such a dramatic change in processes, products, or services that they transform existing markets or industries, or create new ones.

Source: http://www.1000ventures.com/business_guide/innovation_radical.html

Table 1.7 shows the world's ten most innovative organisations in 2006.

Benefits of Innovation

To adapt and evolve, i.e. to be successful, an organisation must innovate. It is hard to find examples of successful companies where they have not been innovative. As we have seen, innovation can be incremental or radical, its benefit or purpose is to launch a new product into the market to gain a competitive and improve sales.

Table 1.7	The world's ten most innovative organisations in 2006		
Rank	**Company name**	**Company margin growth 1995–2005 (%)**	**Stock returns 1995–2005 (%)**
1	Apple	7.1	24.6
2	Google	N/A	N/A
3	3M	3.4	11.2
4	Toyota	10.7	11.8
5	Microsoft	2	18.5
6	General Electric	5.7	13.4
7	Procter & Gamble	4.4	12.6
8	Nokia	0	34.6
9	Starbucks	2.2	27.6
10	IBM	−0.7	14

Source: http://www.businessweek.com/magazine/content/06_17/b3981401.htm

In the 1990s, innovation was about technology and control of quality and cost. Today, it's about taking corporate organizations built for efficiency and rewiring them for creativity and growth. "There are a lot of different things that fall under the rubric of innovation," says Vijay Govindarajan, a professor at Dartmouth College's Tuck School of Business and author of *Ten Rules for Strategic Innovators: From Idea to Execution*. "Innovation does not have to have anything to do with technology."

http://www.businessweek.com/magazine/content/06_17/b3981401.htm

ACTIVITY 1.2

For an organisation that you are familiar with, consider the types of new product(s) it has launched and justify its choice.

QUESTIONS

1. Give examples of how a car manufacturer can compete at the augmented product level

2. Why is the development of new and innovative products essential to the ongoing success of an organisation?

3. Why would an organisation launch a new product into the market categorised as 'new to company, no innovation to market'?

4. Identify and explain the different stages of the NPD

5. Why do think the success rate for new products is low?

6. What do you understand by the term 'innovation'?

7. What are the five stages in the diffusion of innovation model?

8. What are innovators as identified in the model?

9. What is a product?

10. What are the two product categories?

SUMMARY

In this chapter the importance of defining what is a product has been established. Organisations can no longer offer customers a basic product which may satisfy their need. They must go beyond this and differentiate themselves and actively 'stand out' from the competition if they want to attract new customers, particularly at the augmented product level.

Organisations need to be continually developing new products to meet the changing needs of customers, as well as addressing potential gaps in the market. It is also necessary to evaluate different ways of delivering products to customers, recognising the opportunity this brings. New products are essential for an organisation if it wants to compete successfully for new business.

'Tired' products can be replaced and customers will see the organisation as being continually relevant to them. If the competition is allowed to launch new products, or their portfolio is perceived to be more attractive, customers will be lost. This not only affects revenue, but it also requires additional marketing spend to be focused on recruiting new customers. Most commentators agree it is more expensive to recruit new customers than it is to retain existing ones. Organisations that do not have processes in place to develop innovative new products will rapidly lose market share and ultimately may become irrelevant to their customers.

Throughout the NPD process many potential products will fail to be launched as they are continually evaluated through rigorous development. Even for those products eventually launched there is no guarantee of success as the failure rate is high.

Customers seeing a new product being launched into the market will purchase it at different timescales. We have seen that 'innovators' are the first to make the purchase and the other categories of purchasers follow later. Organisations who understand the purchasing categories of potential customers can develop a range of promotional activity and targeted messages to encourage purchase and move the product through its life cycle (see Chapter 2).

FURTHER STUDY/ADDITIONAL READING

http://www.1000ventures.com/business_guide/innovation_radical.html

http://www.businessweek.com/magazine/content/06_17/b3981401.htm

BIBLIOGRAPHY

Brassington, F. and Pettitt, S. (2006) *Principles of Marketing*. FT Prentice-Hall.

Business Week (2006) *The world's most innovative firms*, 24 April 2006. Online at: http://www.businessweek.com/magazine/content/06_17/b3981401.htm

Dibb, S., Simkin, L., Pride, W. and Ferrell, O. (2005) *Marketing: Concepts and Strategies*, 5th European edition. Houghton Mifflin.

Hooley, G., Saunders, J., Piercy, N.F. and Nicoulaud, B. (2008) *Marketing Strategy and Competitive Positioning*, 4th edition. FT Prentice-Hall.

Kotler, P., Armstrong, G., Saunders, J. and Wong, V. (1999) *Principles of Marketing*, 2nd European edition. Prentice Hall.

Myers, S. and Marquis, D.G. (1969) *Successful Industrial Innovation: a study of factors underlying innovation in selected firms*. National Science Foundation, Washington DC.

Rogers, E.M. (1962) *Diffusion of Innovation*. The Free Press.

Utterback, J. (1994) *Mastering the Dynamics of Innovation*. Harvard Business School Press.

CHAPTER 2

Managing and Developing an Organisation's Product Portfolio

INTRODUCTION

In this Chapter readers will be shown the advantages of strategic product management and, at the same time, will be asked to consider the limitations and how this might be managed. A variety of different techniques will be explored including Product Life Cycle, BCG Matrix, and the GE Matrix. They will equip the reader with a number of options in achieving effective product management and this will be set in various contexts.

PRODUCT MANAGEMENT PROCESS

Organisations generally try to offer customers a range of products suited to their particular needs based on their knowledge of the market. Very few organisations have just one product to offer their customers and a range of products allows for segmentation, targeting and positioning (STP) of the portfolio, leading to a greater market share, higher levels of customer satisfaction and increase resilience for the organisation.

Additional products cannot be added to the portfolio without considering the impact on other products and how they are performing (e.g. financially, or by market share) and therefore a range of portfolio management

Table 2.1	The seven marketing mix Ps
Marketing mix	**Commentary**
Product	The right product(s) available to meet current customer needs (added value). The product range can be expanded or collapsed as needs change.
Price	It is important to understand how customers perceive price, so the organisation must be clear on exactly how to price its products and the relationship with any other products within its portfolio.
Promotion	A range of tools is available to support the product, create customer satisfaction and loyalty through careful positioning in the customer's mind. Branding reinforces the product image with the consumer.
Place	It is necessary to get the products to customers where they want to purchase not where you would like them to purchase.
Physical evidence	Where services are concerned, some tangibility needs to be provided to support the overall proposition. This could range from brochures to the decor of the office where the service is delivered.
People	Arguably the most important element, who need to be consistent and professional and reflect the brand.
Processes	Important to train staff and have defined processes in place to support staff in delivering a consistent and a high quality service.

tools must be utilised to ensure the portfolio is effective. Products need to be managed effectively so that customers receive a best in class product and the organisation maximises its opportunities for profit.

Additional products must be added in a systematic and logical way.

Product management is integral in creating value for customers, it does this through the effective management of the marketing mix (4/7Ps) in order to satisfy customer needs – see Table 2.1.

Effective management of the marketing mix process allows an organisation to effectively meet a range of customer needs as categorised below.

Table 2.2, based on Blythe (2006), suggests 5 customer needs.

ACTIVITY 2.1

Which customer derives the most value in the following situation?

A busy businessman needs to fill up his car with petrol. From experience he can choose from two petrol stations which are the same distance from his current location. They are the local independent garage, where he will be served quickly, but petrol will be 2p per litre more expensive than the supermarket garage where he will have to wait 10 minutes to get served.

Table 2.2	Customer needs (Blyth, 2006)
Needs	**Summary**
Current product need	Identified through research are the key features and benefits of the product acceptable or they need to be enhanced?
Future needs	Identifying future demand levels and product functionality is difficult, but effective management of the PLC supported by on going research will assist.
Pricing levels	While customers may want to buy at the 'best' price, this is often based on quality v cost issues and the balance must be understood.
Information needs	What information does the customer need to commit to the purchase? How can this information be conveyed?
Product availability	Customers generally want the product available to them in a readily accessible way and therefore the choice of distribution channel and channels members is crucial.

Table 2.3	How an organisation's portfolios can be categorised
Product mix	This is the total of all products (and variants) that an organisation offers to its customers.
Product line	Here the product mix is divided and grouped into products which are related to each other for internal (production or technical reasons) or external reasons as they all offer a similar solution to the consumer.
Product item	The product line is further divided into individual products which meet a specific customer need.

New products cannot simply be added to the organisation's product portfolio in a random way; Table 2.3 sets out how an organisation's portfolios can be categorised.

Effective product management will develop sufficient product variants to meet the needs of the different groups of customers with specific needs which must be satisfied.

An example of a product mix for a typical university is shown below in Figure 2.1.

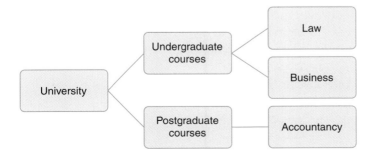

FIGURE 2.1

Product mix for a typical university.

The University may want to expand its law programmes, i.e. want to expand its product mix width and it may offer:

- Law with Spanish
- Law with French
- Criminal Law
- Child Law

And within each programme it could offer short course, foundation degrees, full degrees, etc. Consequently it has a larger product mix.

CUSTOMER VALUE

Customer value is derived from a customer-centric organisation that understands its customers. The better it understands them, the better value achieved through the deployment of the marketing mix. It is customers who define value, not the organisation, and organisations must stay close to the dynamic nature of this definition in order to keep the product portfolio relevant to customer needs.

Value is derived either directly or indirectly through better customer services, brand reputation, market coverage and technology, pricing or cost savings. Activity 2.1 earlier in this chapter asked you to consider whether price or convenience was more important. Often the value to be derived will take into consideration the value of the brand, so Shell petrol may convey more value because (for example) it cleans the engine and offers more miles per gallon. Tesco petrol on the other hand may simply offer all round good value without being specific.

STRATEGIC PLANNING TOOLS

Marketers have a range of tools available to them to help them make strategic choices when developing and managing a product portfolio. Strategic planning tools help marketing managers understand the current position or help to devise future strategies to improve efficiency, performance and profitability through a better understanding of customers.

Product Life Cycle (PLC)

Products are considered to have a finite life, this life is referred to as the PLC and the 'classic' view is shown in Figure 2.2. The PLC helps marketers

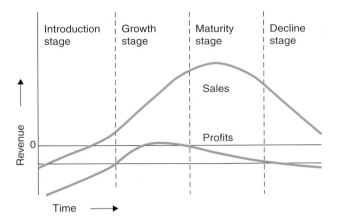

FIGURE 2.2

Product life cycle.

to develop their marketing strategies as well as monitoring the progress of the product from launch.

Marketers will want any newly launched product to have as long a life as possible in order to generate an accepted level of profit for the organisation after the costs of development have been recovered.

It is difficult to predict the life of the product and consequently the shape of the PLC can vary as modifications or changes are made to the product throughout its life.

A temporary period of unusually high sales volumes driven by consumer enthusiasm and immediate product or brand popularity (Kotler *et al.*,1999) otherwise known as a 'fad' or 'novelty' will shorten the PLC. A good example will be the 'must have' toy for Christmas. Parents will spend a considerable amount of money (and time) ensuring they get the product only to find that after Christmas it is being discounted and quickly moves off sale.

Marketers want to effectively manage each stage of the PLC and while the concept receives criticism it is undoubtedly a useful tool. As will be seen below each stage of the product's life will be monitored, so that the appropriate strategies can the developed. Pricing, product features, promotion (repositioning, rebranding) and distribution strategies will be reviewed at each stage and adjustments made as necessary.

Some organisations will find they have a majority of their products in the maturity stage and much time will be spent advertising the products, but with thought being given to rebranding, repositioning or product modification. The changes made at this stage can be quite dramatic, or subtle in delivery. As an example, Mercedes Benz changed the shape of the headlights on its modules to a 'tear drop' shape which attracted new sales.

The PLC in Figure 2.2 shows sales and revenue plotted against time.

There is a critical relationship between the analysis of a product's life cycle and the ability to develop, generate and maintain customer value through a deeper understanding of the customers changing needs over time.

The four key stages of the PLC are Introduction, Growth, Maturity and Decline. Let's look at these closer.

Introduction

Generally it takes time for a product to be accepted and sales can be slow at this stage. Depending on the investment, profit can be negative. However, the role of the marketer is to raise the level of sales with the target audience and widen distribution into the market to develop the product through to the next stage. Depending on the marketing objectives a skimming or penetration pricing strategy can be adopted.

Growth

Sales start to rise quickly, possibly because there are now competitors in the market and more consumer awareness. The original product may be improved through the addition of new product features to compete more effectively maximise profit.

Profit is starting to rise at the growth stage and promotional activity needs to focus on brand building to encourage customers to purchase with less focus on price.

Brand building needs to be effective to encourage customers from then organisation rather than the competition to build a strong position in the market and generate customer loyalty.

Maturity

Maturity tends to be the longest stage of the PLC, but sales now start to plateau and then fall. Profits come under pressure as the organisation focuses its marketing effort on countering competitive activity. However, the market becomes saturated and some of the weaker competitors will leave as profitability drops steeply. While many products at this stage remain unchanged, it is here that organisations develop enhanced versions of the product or launch new ones. Innovative use of the marketing mix can extend the maturity stage i.e. prolong the life of the product, but eventually it will move into decline.

Decline

The decline stage can be a little unpredictable; sales can drop off dramatically, or follow a slow but steady downturn. The marketer has to decide on the most effective way of dealing with this by slowing down sales decline or by withdrawing marketing support and letting the product 'die' i.e. milking it.

Depending on the product, there is always the possibility of repositioning it in the customers mind and develop new markets or customers. Take for example Lucozade which is the name for a range of energy and sports drinks. Originally a drink for people who were unwell, designed to provide a source of energy, it was sold in glass bottle with an orange cellophane wrapper. In 1983, the slogan was changed from 'Lucozade aids recovery' to 'Lucozade replaces lost energy' along with a change in packaging. The glass bottle and wrapper was replaced with plastic. The rebranding was deemed a success as sales over a 5 year period were reported as tripling.

The rapid development of technology increasingly forces manufacturers to consider letting the product die. We are currently seeing evidence of this in the demise of video players and video tapes, and with CD players being replaced by MP3 players.

Organisations do need to understand that a failing product not only affects the organisation's profitability, but can diminish the brand in the consumers' minds if competitors are launching 'newer' or more advanced products.

Product Enhancement

Careful management is necessary at all stages in the PLC, but particularly at the growth stage. Competition is increasing as more organisations are coming into the market and similarly many customers may now be ready to make repeat purchases. Consequently serious consideration needs to be given to any changes which may be felt necessary to maintain the competitive edge and not lose market share at this early stage.

Rather than compete just on price, new product features or enhancements can be introduced to ensure customers stay loyal to an organisation. After all, the investment in developing the new product may not have been recovered and threat of intermediaries stocking and distributing competitor products, along with retailers giving additional space to the competitor product, will threaten the financial investment made.

> Mobile phone companies seem to be continually enhancing their product range in order to keep customers loyal. While lengthy contracts of 12 or 18 months keep customers locked in, there is intense competition between the phone companies to add additional features and benefits.

Many commentators argue that making enhancements to the product at maturity stage is of little value as the product has run out of power and argue that new products should be introduced with the current one left to move into decline.

THE PLC AND THE MARKETING MIX

For those organisations operating across countries it should be remembered that a product can occupy different positions on the PLC in different countries and that the PLC will be different for each country that the product is offered. Table 2.4 shows the role of the marketing mix throughout the PLC.

A Critique of the PLC

The PLC is a useful tool to deepen understanding of the product portfolio but it is not a forecast of future sales, and for many organisations the PLC extends well beyond the planning timeframe which could be from 1 year to 5 years.

We have seen how 'fads' can change the PLC and different patterns will develop depending on the nature of the product, the management or modifications made to it and environmental conditions, so it is difficult to know how long each stage will last. The PLC will vary according to the industry in which the product operates and the nature of the competition.

Table 2.4	The role of the marketing mix throughout the PLC			
Marketing mix	**Introduction**	**Growth**	**Maturity**	**Decline**
Product	Basic product, but quality assured and any legal protection needed is in place	Additional product features maybe added or existing features enhanced	More variety	Maintain, harvest or discontinue
Price	Skim or penetrate the market	Maintain	Maybe lowered to match or beat the competition	Maintain
Place	Selective or limited	Increasing in line with demand	Now reaching critical mass	Now declining
Promotion	Build awareness or tell people how to use the product. Often high impact/ awareness	Broader audience which maybe for building image or encouraging repeat purchase	Now about reminding and encouraging purchase	Reminding may also be confirming discontinuation

THE BOSTON (BCG) MATRIX

Developed by the Boston Consulting Group in the 1970s, this is generally regarded as an important model of marketing and strategic planning (Brassington and Pettitt, 2006) The model helps organisations to identify potential opportunities and problems associated with a product. It does this by categorising the organisations products into four categories (see Figure 2.3).

The purpose of the BCG Matrix is to help marketers develop their forward planning by suggesting strategy for the future development of the range; selectively invest in Problem Children; invest in and grow stars; maintain Cash Cows; and evaluate dogs removing them as necessary (McDonald, 2007). Many organisations, particularly those with large numbers of products may find they have a large number of Dogs.

The BCG matrix can operate at a number of levels including:

- Corporate

- Product

- SBU (Strategic Business Unit)

It is based on the principle that cash, not profits, drive a product from one box to another within the matrix (McDonald, 2007) and helps an organisation to develop its growth strategies. It is based on two dimensional variables:

- relative market share

- market growth rate

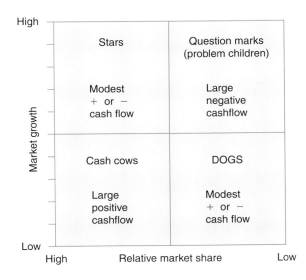

FIGURE 2.3

BCG matrix.

Market share is measured against the product's nearest competitor, i.e. the degree of dominance the competitor enjoys, while market growth reflects the potential market opportunities and also indicates the organisation's likely cash needs.

The need which prompted this idea was, indeed, that of managing cash-flow. It was reasoned that one of the main indicators of cash generation was relative market share, and one which pointed to cash usage was that of market growth rate.

For each product, a circle can be plotted on the matrix to pictorially represent the value of sales in the category as well as likely cash flows.

However, when each product is plotted on the matrix, the organisation can see how balanced the portfolio is. Too many dogs and the business will be losing cash rapidly. The importance of having cash cows became only too real for many organisations when UK banks were reluctant to lend money in early 2009. The cash generated from cash cows was used to give organisations liquidity rather than fund other products. Those organisations without cash cows found it difficult to continue in business and many ceased trading.

An analysis of the portfolio will help with the planning process as it would certainly appear to be unrealistic for an organisation (say) to want to increase sales by 10% in the coming year when the portfolio consists of mainly dogs.

> Nestle, one of the world's largest food companies, generates 70% of its sales from six of its brands and the Nestle brand itself generates 40% of sales. Brassington and Pettitt (2006)

Equally products can be in different quadrants if they are made available by the organisation in different countries and this must be considered when reviewing the portfolio as must the direction of travel of the products between the quadrants.

The Quadrants of the BCG Matrix

Dog

A dog maintains a low market share in a low growth market and is likely to be cash neutral or consuming a modest amount of cash flow and resources. A dog may have been a solid performer, but has subsequently declined in terms of performance. Given its low market share and lack of growth potential the organisation will generally want to remove the product from the portfolio i.e. divestment, unless the cash flow is strong in which case the product could be harvested.

Stars

A star occupies a high growth share in a high growth market. It generally requires a substantial investment to support expansion, but it is cash neutral and generally regarded as a potential investment for the future. Existing market share should be protected, or a larger share of new consumers should be sought.

Cash Cows

A cash cow maintains a high market share in a low growth market. It generates cash which can be used to support other products. Market position or pricing should be maintained, or the profits used to invest in new processes.

Problem Child

Some times referred to as Question Marks, problem children can occupy a low market share of a high growth market. It consumes cash just to maintain its market share and requires cash to support product development. Strategies for Problem Child include divesting, harvesting, or removing from the portfolio. Looking externally another strategy is to buy a competitor in order to build a large market share.

An Example of a UK Bank Portfolio

This is illustrative only and will in reality depend on many variables and of course will change over time.

Category	Examples
Dog (low market share/low growth)	Mortgage products
Star (high share/high growth)	ATMs
Cash cow (high share/low growth)	Personal current accounts
Problem child (low share/high growth)	Corporate Accounts

A Critique of the BCG Matrix

Like the PLC, the BCG matrix is not without its critics. It is generally accepted that any analysis undertaken on the matrix will result in an over simplification of the position because it is based on just two dimensions.

Organisations do not just launch products with the intention of being a market leader, often products are launched for strategic reasons, i.e. to position against the competition.

The BCG matrix should not be seen as a single tool; it has individual merits which can be utilised most effectively as part of a tool of techniques to deepen the understanding of the customers needs in the context of the business.

GENERAL ELECTRIC (GE) MATRIX

Another tool available to marketers is the GE matrix that, like the BCG matrix, uses a two dimensional approach. Both models can be used as an aid to future planning or to evaluate an existing portfolio or the current level of investment in a SBU.

The GE matrix uses two dimensions; industry attractiveness and business strength. In contrast to the BCG matrix these dimensions are broken down into other factors which are rated and combined into an index of industry attractiveness. Business strength also uses an index which is then ranked into strong, average or weak.

To use the GE matrix an organisation would need to identify key factors which would make the market attractive to it. These factors would include:
Industry attractiveness:

- How large is the market now and in the future?

- What is the expected annual growth of the market?

- What are the expected profit margins?

- How easy is it to enter the market?

- What is the competition?

Business strengths:

- Current market share

- Organisation's current rate of growth

- Ability to influence the market

- Available resources

- Current profit margins

Having compiled its strengths and ranked them strong, weak or medium, the organisation can then map them across industry attractiveness. This will then produce a position on the matrix (see Figure 2.4).

The positioning on the matrix then offers three potential strategic options.

Where the organisation has identifies strong or medium business strengths and the industry has been medium to high attractiveness (indicated x on the matrix) it should invest for growth.

Having identified a market with low to medium attractiveness, linked with medium to weak business strengths (indicated xx on the matrix) then the consensus would be to withdraw from the market or harvest.

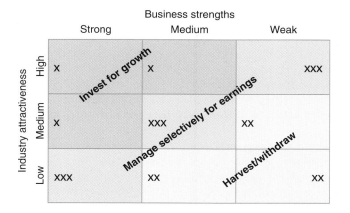

The remaining positions i.e. weak strengths linked with medium to low industry attractiveness (xxx) on the matrix should be managed selectively. Careful consideration is needed here to establish the most appropriate strategy.

EXAMPLE

An overseas business school may identify a growing market for the provision of MBA programmes in the UK and has ranked the industry as highly attractive. However, it has also recognised that at the current time its 'Business strength' is weak as it does not have sufficient lecturers (along with other limitations) to deliver the programme. Therefore the overall attractiveness is regarded as medium and the business school would need to improve its strengths in order to move into that market and for the time being should concentrate on its existing markets

Where an organisation has strong business strengths and identifies a highly attractive industry the decisions are much more straightforward.

Kotler *et al.* (1999) sums up the aim of portfolio analysis as being 'to direct firms away from investing in markets that look attractive, but where they have no strength'.

INNOVATION IN THE PUBLIC SECTOR

If we want to embed innovation in our organisations we must recognise the vital link with our people and the way we work, look for ways to empower staff to accept innovation as part of the way they work and recognise the rewards for getting it right.

Colchester Borough Council is the fourth largest district authority in the country, rated as excellent by the Audit Commission and progressing a very ambitious regeneration agenda in East Anglia. Our targets for housing, jobs and inward investment are challenging and our level of ambition substantial. The key to our achievement lies in the success we will have in empowering all of our people to innovate to deliver our vision for Colchester as a prestigious regional centre.

Over recent years we have invested heavily in developing a vision for Colchester as a prestigious regional centre and have some notable successes with partners in bringing cutting edge architecture and investment in urban growth to Colchester. We have a clear vision of what we are here for and recognise the importance of our roles in offering strong community leadership, shaping the behaviour of our residents, delivering customer excellence for all of our customers and of course delivering efficient services. But we have to make sense of that vision internally for our staff if we are to fully engage them on our journey.

We have done that though a major internal change programme which focuses on empowering all of our colleagues to deliver innovation in bringing our purpose as a district council to life. We have achieved this through making fundamental changes to the way we work focusing on changes to our working practices and in particular flexible working, investment in enabling information technology, influencing the shape of the place in which we live, focusing on the changing needs of our customers and importantly investing in our people. We recognise that anything we achieve will be driven by our people and through them we will achieve the level of innovation in the organisation which we need, to continue to be judged as an excellent organisation in meeting the ever changing needs of our customers. Our learning and development strategy is an important part of that process and is closely aligned to the needs of the business to ensure that all of our people have the opportunity to engage with learning in ways which equip them to deliver our ambition. We are empowering our people through learning and not in an esoteric way but grounded in the needs of our business to deliver excellent services. So we are providing an environment where our staff can improve their management skills, coaching and mentoring competences, participate in cultural change, improve performance and in ways and at times that meet their particular learning styles and situations. We are placing a particular emphasis on providing the right customer skills so that our people are empowered in a meaningful and practical way to deliver our ambition for customer excellence. This will be delivered through service-based customer excellence training, work with our elected members to ensure our people have the right level of political awareness to support them effectively and through awareness of how customer excellence is delivered in the very best organisations.

Through our staff we have learnt so much about how we engage with customers, how we can share best practice and how through doing things differently we can significantly improve the experience our customers have when they do business with us. The feedback we have received points to the power of the awards in driving cultural change and moving the organisation closer to the goal of customer excellence. Staff feel they are being provided with the skills, environment and time (although there is never enough) to do the job to the best of their abilities and feel supported corporately through the coaching network established to guide each colleague through the process. This has been truly inspiring, with staff, many of them frontline, uncovering attributes and skills which they will develop in the future for the benefit of the customer experience in developing innovative solutions to the challenges they bring to us.

Corporately our challenge is to capture the learning, maximise the potential in our people and harness it in a way which promotes and embeds innovation in the organisation as a whole, becomes a responsibility for all of us and an integral part of the way we work. We will do this by taking the challenge to innovate very seriously and recognise that the innovation challenge is all around us. It comes from the drive for efficiencies, the challenge to deliver more, the need to influence the behaviours of our citizens and the requirements of the customer to find increasingly personalised and tailored solutions for the problems they experience, not the ones we define for them.

Understanding Our Customers

Our work to understand our customers will drive this agenda as we invest more resources in sensing and defining the ever-changing needs of our customers. This drives innovation in a way which customers will recognise and which staff will engage with as they make the critical connection between understanding our customers and delivering improvement through service delivery. This can only ever be achieved if we recognise that sustainable innovation, although keenly influenced through technology and streamlined business processes can only ever be achieved if we make the vital connection with people; in Colchester we are recognising that through the engagement of all our people in driving and leading cultural change to make a difference to the way we all work to create a better, brighter future for the people of Colchester.

Source: This article has been adapted from the original which was written by Dr. Pamela Donnelly, Executive Director, Colchester Borough Council
http://www.sfi.uk.com/publications.htm

ACTIVITY 2.2

For your own organisation (or one you are familiar with) identify its product portfolio and place each product in the appropriate category in the BCG matrix.

SUMMARY

This Chapter has outlined the role of product management and how it contributes to adding value to the customer proposition. New products cannot be added in a random manner but need to expand the portfolio in line with the organisation's objectives and customer needs. A range of strategic planning tools have been introduced that help an organisation evaluate how effective the product range is and enables it to make informed decisions on when to develop new products as well as removing older and less profitable products.

The Chapter also introduced the PLC that developed the concept of a product from Chapter 1. An organisation will want the PLC to be as long as possible in order to ensure an adequate return on the original investment. This will require careful identification of the different stages and taking the appropriate action to move the product along the PLC or extend certain stages.

QUESTIONS

1. What is the marketing mix?
2. Blythe identified a range of six customer needs. What are they?
3. What are the key components of the PLC?
4. What is the purpose of the BCG matrix?
5. Why do you think that so many organisations have so many 'dogs' in their portfolio?

FURTHER STUDY

www.Colchester.gov.uk.

BIBLIOGRAPHY

Blythe, J. (2006) *Principles and Practice of Marketing*. Thomson.

Brassington, F. and Pettitt, S. (2006) *Principles of Marketing*. FT Prentice Hall.

Kotler, P., Armstrong, G., Saunders, J. and Wong, V. (1999) *Principles of Marketing*, 2nd European edition. Prentice Hall.

McDonald, M. (2007) *Marketing Plans: How To Prepare Them, How To Use Them*, 6th edition. Butterworth-Heinemann.

CHAPTER 3

The Role of Branding and Branding Strategies

LEARNING OBJECTIVES

By the end of this chapter you will be able to:

- Evaluate the role and importance of branding
- Analyse and apply various branding strategies in different organisational contexts
- Assess the issues and challenges faced by organisations in building and maintaining a global brand

BRANDING – A DEFINITION

Kotler *et al.* (1999) suggests a brand is 'a name, term, sign, symbol or design, or a combination of these that identifies the goods or services of one seller or group of sellers and differentiates them from the competition'.

Blythe (2006) defines branding as 'the culmination of a range of activities across the whole marketing mix leading to a brand image that conveys a whole set of messages to the consumer about quality, price, expected performance and status'.

The role of the brand is to create a position of differentiation in the mind of the consumer, so that the brand is understood (see brand values) and clearly differentiated from the competition to encourage purchase.

Such is the power of branding that most products are branded. Branding has a number of advantages for the consumer, the manufacturer and retailer:

- Customers will be attracted to a product because of its branding, sometimes totally to the exclusion of other brands

- It creates an image in the customer's mind that can be hard to replicate in other brands

- The risk associated with the purchase is reduced because of the known qualities associated with the brand
- Pricing can be higher because of the positioning
- Loyalty towards the brand will generate additional sales
- Customers will be attracted to a store which stocks a particular brand, it also gives an indication of the service that can be expected
- Can help with market segmentation i.e. developing new products for different segments

> Motorway service areas now show the logos of the brands available on signs outside the service area to show motorists the choices available and indicate the quality you can expect if you pull in.

Successful brands create strong, long term and lasting impressions with consumers. However, it should be noted that an individual can have an impression about a brand without actually experiencing it.

BRANDING CATEGORIES

Dibb *et al.* (2005) suggests three types of brand:

- Manufacturer (corporate brand)
- Own-label
- Generic

Manufacturer

This is a brand type where the manufacturer sells the goods under their own name. The product is clearly associated with the manufacturer although may be sold in a range of different outlets, for example, Cadbury's, Samsung, or Kodak.

Own-label

The manufacturer's name does not appear on the product. The manufacturer has sold the product to an intermediary who has given it its own name, known as an own-label brand. An example is Sainsbury's Own brand.

Generic

The number of generic brands i.e. brands that do not have a brand name, or any other identifying terms, has been falling dramatically because of the growing importance of brands to the consumer.

BUILDING A BRAND

A successful brand is an identifiable product, service, person or place, augmented in such a way that the buyer or user perceives relevant unique, sustainable added values, which match their needs most closely (De Chernatony and McDonald, 1998).

Building a brand (De Pelsmacker *et al.*, 2004) means that an organisation will invest significant sums of money building a brand's favourable image and position in the marketplace, such that long term benefits will be achieved both in brand awareness (recognition) and brand value (financial).

To become successful a brand must meet a number of criteria. Figure 3.1 shows the key factors in developing a successful brand.

The success criteria is:

1. Differentiation
It needs to be clear to the consumer what the unique benefits of the product are. Brand values play an important role here.

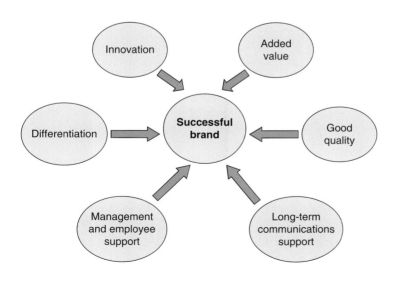

FIGURE 3.1
Successful brands.
(De Pelsmacker et al., 2004).

2. Added value

What additional value does the consumer receive from buying the product? This can encompass a range of attributes from service, status, confidence or making things simple.

3. Quality

'Top' brands are usually considered being of high quality within their category and the quality will need to extend to any intangible aspects of the product. Service dimensions are usually much harder to replicate by competitors.

4. Integrated communications

Consistent, regular and targeted communications need to be developed. Consumers can easily forget about the brand, or be exposed to competitor brand messages and therefore constant communication is needed to ensure 'front of mind' with the consumers.

5. Management and employee support

Internal marketing is crucial to success. It is a waste of resources to communicate with external customers if the internal dimension is overlooked. Staff must be clear on the importance of the brand and act as 'brand ambassadors', but this requires motivation and training.

6. Innovation

Brands must constantly respond to the changing needs of its customers or they will become irrelevant to the consumer. This is equally true of new and established brands.

Brand Values

Dibb *et al.* (2005) say that brand values are 'the emotional benefits and less tangible identifiers attached to the brand providing reassurance and creditability for targeted consumers, supplementing the specific brand attributes in making the brand attractive'. Brand values support the more visible attributes that organisations demonstrate in their brands, and can be important when the consumer is thinking of making a purchase, i.e. are the organisation's values understood and in keeping with the purchaser's own values?

Brand Equity

This chapter has made the case for the importance of brands. In the 1980s it became increasingly important to agree on some measure of a brand's worth from a consumer or financial perspective, or both, and that is what brand equity seeks to measure. We need to be clear on what is being measured and brand equity is generally referred to as *the value of possessing a specific brand name compared to a generic brand of the same type in the same category.*

Some organisations view the concept of brand equity from an economic perspective which is considered to be *the sum of the future profit associated with the brand discounted over time*. The actual value is not 'set' but can and will vary over time depending on how well the brand is managed.

In a take-over or merger situation the value of the brand becomes important. BMW in the UK sold off the Rover Group for a nominal £1, but kept the 'Mini' brand which has been an outstanding success and not just in the UK, but as far afield as the USA. Huge sums of money are paid for brand portfolios (De Pelsmacker *et al.*, 2004).

A brand can now have more financial worth than the organisation's tangible assets such as property and equipment. As we saw at the start of the unit a brand can be a powerful thing and therefore it needs to be managed with care and attention if it is to survive in the long term.

We can look back at brands such as Midland Bank, British Leyland and Marks & Spencer to see the consequences of brand management.

BRAND STRATEGIES

Any strategy must start from the point 'do we want to put our brand name on the product?' It can be argued that for some product categories, there is little point in branding. This is often true for undifferentiated or homogeneous products such as aluminium foil. However, this trend is reducing with organisations opting to name the brand as branded goods are generally easier to sell. When an organisation looks to develop its brand range it can adopt the following strategies:

1. Brand stretching
Stretch the brand (brand extension) typically into a new or modified product in a similar category. All brands will carry the same name, so for example Caterpillar moving into clothes from its traditional association with earth moving equipment.

2. Line extension
Here the organisation develops a new product closely related to an existing product by developing a new form. This is quite common as it is a low-cost and generally low-risk approach to increasing sales within the same market. There is always the fear that the consumer can become confused with the choices available. A classic example is Kit Kat, a chocolate bar produced by Nestle which for many years remained unchanged. Then in no particular order, orange and dark chocolate versions appeared, chunky milk chocolate and peanut chunky versions followed along with Kit Kat minis and Kit Kat ice cream. NatWest bank launched its mortgage subsidiary NatWest Home

Loans which initially offered two mortgage products, some years later the two products had effectively been extended to thirteen.

3. Multi branding

Organisations often introduce additional brands within the same category. Royal Bank of Scotland (RBS) offered car insurance under the Churchill, Direct Line and Privilege brands, with each appealing to a different target audience. In the FMCG market, a range of brands will often secure important space on the supermarket shelf. As well as offering the benefits of segmentation, it also means the competition has to compete across a number of brands. Equally, multi-branding allows an organisation to remove a brand which is underperforming quickly and without a serious impact on the existing owned brands.

4. New brands

Sometimes an existing brand will not fit in a new product category. Toyota introduced Lexus to position the new luxury brand away from the existing and very successful mass market range of cars. NatWest offered a new range of (cheaper) credit cards branded Lombard to maintain the premier pricing on its other range of credit card products.

The choice of branding strategy depends on what the organisation is trying to achieve.

ACTIVITY 3.1

What are the key characteristics of a successful brand? Describe in detail at least two of the characteristics.

REBRANDING

Rebranding can take place at both the organisational and product level.

Rebranding is the process by which an organisation changes the way a product is marketed or distributed using a different brand. This usually involves changes to the brand's logo, name, image, marketing strategy or advertising, but this is not always the case. The changes are generally aimed at the repositioning the product in the market.

Kaikati and Kaikati (2004) have identified proactive and reactive reasons for wanting to carry out a rebranding exercise. In practice any rebranding undertaken can encompass aspects of both elements.

An organisation may over the years have developed or acquired a number of regional brands and may want to bring them together as one global brand.

JIF, a cleaning product, became CIF in the UK; similarly Opal Fruits (confectionary) became Star Burst. Marathon a chocolate bar, became known as Snickers. The rationale in each case was to enable the organisation to introduce economies of scale when marketing the one brand across the different markets.

Sometimes it is necessary to reposition a product in the mind of the consumer and this can be for a variety of reasons ranging from price differentiation to expanding into overseas markets. It can be done to overcome perceived service problems, or position the product more correctly in the consumers' mind.

> National Savings, one of the UK's largest savings institutions, changed its name to National Savings and Investments (NS&I) to reflect the fact that much of is business is investments rather than just savings. A new logo and image was also introduced to have more general appeal.

New products, mature products, or even products still in development phase can be rebranded. Mergers and company take overs can often involve the need to rebrand a product, especially if more than one of the companies involved offers the same or similar products.

> London Metropolitan University was established in 2002 following the merger of the University of North London and London Guildhall University. A new brand was created to umbrella the two previous universities.

Organisations can also rebrand themselves in an attempt to change their image or move into different markets, but care needs to be exercised.

> Anglia Polytechnic, based in Essex, when granted university status changed its name to Anglia Polytechnic University (APU) to reflect its heritage. But 'University and Polytechnic' in the title was considered to be confusing and ultimately rebranded to Anglia Ruskin University.

'GO' was launched in 1998 as a subsidiary of British Airways in an attempt to compete in the growing budget airline market. Four years later it was bought out by easyjet, another budget airline. On completion of the deal, all GO planes were rebranded in easyjet orange.

Sometimes change needs to evolve slowly; British Midland, a successful UK airline gradually changed its name to BMI by showing both names in publicity material before phasing out the name British Midland.

> British Airways was originally called BOAC. (British Overseas Aircraft Corporation)

ACTIVITY 3.2

For an organisation you know well, identify its key brand values. Do you think they accurately reflect the image the organisation is trying to portray in the market?

CASE STUDY

In 2003, Morrisons, the UK supermarket, bought Safeway, another supermarket that was underperforming. The acquisition offered a golden opportunity for expansion. However, bringing the two supermarkets together proved a major task.

Morrisons' unique brand identity suffered and the retailer's relationship with customers was weakened and after 36 years of unbroken sales and profit growth, its market share began to fall.

At the heart of this dramatic fall from grace was a perception of poor food quality. Even in its northern heartland, Morrisons was regarded as having the worst food of any of the big four supermarkets and in the South of England it became a by-word for 'pies'.

Frustrated by this inaccurate perception Morrisons appointed an agency to relaunch and reposition the super-market and boost its food quality credentials. The objective was to create a competitive brand identity which would bridge the gap between perception and reality and halt the decline in market share.

The agency quickly picked up on the 'Market Street' element of Morrisons; the retailer ties to its market stall origins. Morrisons also prepared more food in-store than any other supermarket. This was built upon and a dynamic repositioning: 'Morrisons: the food specialists for everyone'.

Morrison's new identity was launched in March 2007 and the result has been a reversal of the sales decline and an increase in revenue of over £350m.

Crucially, the supermarket's food credentials have also received a significant boost, along with a much-sought-after change in perception of quality.

GLOBAL BRANDS

Standardisation of products generally produces economies of scale, which, given the high costs involved in product development, encourages expansion beyond the home market into initially a few, then an ever-increasing number of overseas markets. However, organisations take different approaches to brandings; some believe the benefits of a single global brand outweigh the benefits of country-specific brands with their own brand identities.

Arguments in favour of global brands (Yeshin, 2006) are:

- Economies of scale as the products are standardised across each market

- Developing technology ensures similar product use

- Rapid and readily available communication channels such as the Internet and Satellite TV

- Increasing similarity between segments across countries

- Global brands can be seen as better quality than local brands

However, it should be noted that that the product (as opposed to the brand) does not need to be exactly the same. For example KFC in the UK serves its meals with French Fries, in Hong Kong the meal would be served with mashed potato.

Aaker and Joachimsthaler (1999) suggest that global brands are 'brands whose positioning, advertising strategy and personality, look and feel are in most respects the same from one country to another'.

Byfield and Caller (1996) suggest 3 categories for a global brand:

- Long term international brands which are exploiting a universal heritage

- New products developed with the global market in mind

- Brands which have been exported to other markets

Table 3.1 indicates the differences between adaptation and standardisation of branding.

Table 3.2 shows the top 20 global brands for 2008. It is based on the annual survey carried out by Interbrand on the world's biggest brands.

Coca-Cola has once again retained its status as the world's most valuable brand. The advent of healthier drinks has forced Coca-Cola to develop 'better-for-you drinks' such as the vitamin- and mineral-enriched Diet Coke Plus and the continued push behind Coke Zero, which is now available in more than 80 countries.

Coke has also worked hard to engage consumers, with innovative online campaigns such as 'Design Your Own' that invited people to design their own Coke containers and share them with the world (Interbrand).

ACTIVITY 3.3

Visit the Interbrand website www.interbrand.com and look at the list of top global brands for 2008. Make suggestions as to why the ranking may have changed over the previous year.

QUESTION 3.4

Do you believe brands should be standardised or adapted according to the market they operate in?

Table 3.1	Adaptation versus standardisation
Adaptation	**Standardisation**
Different customer needs	Large number of buyer similarities
Infrastructure variation	Easier to control campaigns from a central source
Varying levels of education	Technology advances allow consistent brand image to be maintained
Economic, cultural and political conditions vary	Economies of scale
Inconsistent local management experience, abilities and skills	

Table 3.2	2008 Top global brands					
Rank 2008	**Rank 2007**	**Company**	**Industry**	**Country**	**2008 Brand Value $**	**Change %**
1.	1.	Coca-Cola	Beverages	USA	66.667	2
2.	3.	IBM	Computer Services	USA	59.031	3
3	2	Microsoft	Computers Software	USA	59.007	1
4.	4.	GE	Diversified	USA	53.086	3
5	5.	Nokia	Consumer Electronics	Finland	35.942	7
6.	6.	Toyota	Automotive	Japan	34.05	6
7.	7.	Intel	Computer Hardware	USA	31.261	1
8.		McDonalds	Restaurants	USA	31.049	6
9.	9.	Disney	Media	USA	29.251	0
10.	20	Google	Internet	USA	25.59	43

Source: Interbrand

SUMMARY

Brands are a valuable resource for an organisation. They convey a series of messages to the customer which collectively differentiate it from the competition and this is the value which the customers perceive.

Branding also conveys a range of emotions which contribute to the overall brand appeal through conveying, for example, confidence, security, statutes, or success.

Retailers and supermarkets will want to stock successful brands because of the appeal to customers. Brands which are successful in their home country are often taken overseas and the implications of this decision need to be carefully considered if the brand identity is to be protected.

FURTHER STUDY

http://www.interbrand.com/images/BGB_reports/BGB_2008_EURO_Format.pdf.

BIBLIOGRAPHY

Aaker, D.A. and Joachimsthaler, E. (1999) The lure of global branding. *Harvard Business Review*, 77(6).

Blythe, J. (2006) *Principles and Practice of Marketing*. Thomson.

Dibb, S., Simkin, L., Pride, W. and Ferrell, O. (2005) *Marketing: Concepts and Strategies*, 5th European edition. Houghton Mifflin.

Byfield, S. and Caller, L. (1996) Building brands across borders. *Admap*, June.

De Chernatony, L. and McDonald, M. (1998) *Creating Powerful Brands*. Butterworth-Heinemann.

De Pelsmacker, P., Geuens, M. and Van den Bergh, J. (2004) *Marketing Communications: A European Perspective*, 2nd edition. FT Prentice Hall.

Kaikati, J.G. and Kaikati, A.B. (2004) Identity crisis: the dos and don'ts of brand rechristening. *Marketing Management*, January/February.

Kotler, P., Armstrong, G., Saunders, J. and Wong, V. (1999) *Principles of Marketing*. FT Prentice Hall.

Yeshin, T. (2006) *Advertising*. Thomson.

CHAPTER 4

Pricing, Pricing Concepts and Price Setting

By the end of this chapter you will be able to:

- Analyse the role of pricing in influencing customers
- Evaluate and apply a range of pricing approaches and strategies
- Examine the factors that influence the pricing of goods and services, in both domestic and international markets

INTRODUCTION

Pricing will now be considered with a view to deepening the understanding of the impact that a variety of pricing strategies can have on the product position in the market. We will explore the ways in which pricing can be used to manage the product at various stages in its lifecycle in order to maximise the appeal of the product and profitability.

Readers will be appraised of the importance of setting pricing objectives as a benchmark and to guide strategic product development. The role of the customers' view of different strategies will also be considered particularly in terms of the perception of value for money over which pricing strategies have significant influence. The role of pricing in building market share will also be considered as a key element ion the marketing mix.

THE ROLE OF PRICING IN PRODUCT MANAGEMENT

Price is 'the amount of money charged for a product or service' (Armstrong and Kotler, 2006). It is the value that someone is prepared to pay for the product. It is also the one element of the marketing mix that generates revenue, income and profit for the organisation, i.e. it has a direct impact on the bottom line and needs careful management.

51

While organisations do not compete with each other on price alone, it can be an important consideration for the consumer when choosing to make a purchase. Different organisations selling a (very) similar product can charge different prices, which are often brought about by internal calculations of 'cost'. Different costing approaches will make a difference to the price which can be charged to the consumer if an acceptable profit is to be made by an organisation.

Setting prices is a strategic decision that must be reflected in the other elements of the marketing mix. Potential consumers will have a perception about price in relation to the organisation's promotion style, including the brand, the product itself and where it can be purchased.

PRODUCT MANAGEMENT CONSIDERATIONS

While pricing decisions must reflect the organisation's business objectives, they must also take into consideration value for money, customer satisfaction, and the level of competition in the market. In other words pricing must be coordinated with indirect and non-price competitive strategies.

While organisations view price as a revenue generator, customers view it in a different way; for example they will ask how the quality compares with a similar brand, or simply regard the product as too expensive and leave the organisation with lower than expected sales.

PRICING DECISIONS

There are six key factors summarised in the table below to consider when making pricing decisions:

1. *Pricing objectives*: What are the pricing objectives which will support the business objectives?

2. *Buyers' perception*: What does the price mean to the customer?

3. *Perceived value for money*: What benefit will the customer receive as a result of buying the product?

4. *The competition*: How are competitors pricing their products?

5. *Marketing mix*: Does our pricing reflect the other elements of the marketing mix? Does the marketing mix reflect the price?

6. *Channel members*: What are the implications of price for the members of the distribution channel?

Taking each consideration in turn:

Pricing Objectives

Pricing objectives represent the measurable goals a company wants to achieve through its pricing policy. Dibb *et al*. (2005) sets out different objectives which are summarised in Table 4.1.

Buyer Perceptions

Organisations must interpret what the customer response to the price will be. Dibb *et al*. (2005) suggests that an organisation needs to understand:

- What messages that price communicates to the customer and how they respond to it.

- The degree to which the price will improve their satisfaction with the product

Often a low (relative) price will convey low levels of satisfaction which maybe unfounded. Bringing the price more into line with the competition

Table 4.1	Pricing objectives according to Dibb *et al*. (2005)
Pricing objective	**Summary**
Survival	Here the organisation simply wants to ensure it remains in business.
Profit	Organisations generally like to increase profits on a year-on-year basis. Therefore taking into account potential sales a specific profit level will be anticipated.
Market share	Here it is the share of market that is important (i.e. market leader) and therefore an organisation will be willing to reduce price(s) to maintain its market position.
Cash flow	Cash generation is very important in some organisations and the price is set to bring cash into the organisation quickly.
Status quo	An organisation may simply want to retain its position in the market compared with the competition, i.e. be content to be the 'number 2' in a particular category and therefore while it may match the price offered by the competition it has no intention of beating them on price.
Product quality	Here the organisation wants to offer the 'best product' in terms of quality. In terms of the price paid it could be considerably be more expensive than similar products. However, if reliability is more important to the purchaser because breakdowns mean lost income which potentially would be well in excess of any quality premium, then a high price can be justified.

may generate more sales. Similarly higher prices would suggest higher levels of satisfaction. Organisations need to recognise the price vs quality decision as determined through regular marketing research and respond accordingly.

Customers will refer to an internal reference price based on their previous experience, i.e. this should cost around £x. For example, a customer is considering the purchase of a can of beer before embarking on a train journey. They could have planned ahead and bought it at the supermarket for £1. Failing that the purchase could have been made at the railway station prior to boarding the train for £2. Having done none of this, the purchase can now be made on the train for £3. While each price point could be considered expensive, experience may suggest the price is reasonable for the circumstances and pleasure derived for the customer at different points.

Where there has been little previous purchasing experience reference in the category the consumer may refer to external information such as that provided by a retailer, manufacturer, service provider or adviser, friend or colleague.

Perceived Value for Money

This is the benefit the customer derives from the purchase of the product. The organisation needs to understand the value that the customer places on the benefits received and then price the product accordingly. Effectively, customers assess the price and measure the benefits received. The benefits can be measurable and real or associated with confidence, or status. An example is the cost of 'Black credit card' which is offered to customers by invitation only. The price may be £500 per year which the customer justifies on the status the card confers alone.

Other factors which affect the perceived value of the product include:

- Service and after-sales service quality
- Level of differentiation from competitor products
- Quality of any packaging
- Product functionality
- Any substitute products which maybe available

Ultimately it is the customer and not the organisation who decides on the value received.

The Competition

Organisations do not operate in a vacuum and must be alert to any competition in the market. That does not mean that the prices need to be the same. Understanding competitors' objectives such as market leader, follower, or profit maximisation will enable an organisation to establish its own pricing position. Competition should not simply be based on price alone. For example, if organisation A reduces its price to below competitor B (which has more financial resources), then it may well be able to retaliate by offering deeper discounts. This ultimately has a cost to both organisations, which will be difficult to sustain beyond the short term.

Sometimes the published price is not the price actually paid as discounts can be offered for:

- *volume purchases*: when a purchase over a specific quantity will trigger a price reduction.

- *trade discount*: a discount is offered to an intermediary such as a wholesaler because of the role they play in the market.

- *'one off' discounts*: because of seasonality, or the state of the market.

- *loyalty discounts*: given because of the length of time seller and buyer have had a relationship.

Marketing Mix Variables

While the price charged affects the other elements of the marketing mix, the other mix elements also affect price. It would generally be considered that a Rolex watch will attract a premium price reflecting its positioning in the market place. Rolex is generally distributed through a highly select range of retailers. Imagine therefore if Rolex were to take advertisements out in the national press offering a 70% discount! This would cause confusion with the consumer who may question if the offer was genuine having regard to Rolex's overall image. However, if Next, a UK clothes retailer, were to advertise a similar discount, shoppers would have no hesitation to rush into the shops to take advantage of the offer.

Channel Members

Organisations (or individuals) involved in the distribution channel will have profit expectations, such as volume discounts, or income for performing value-added activity.

BUILDING MARKET SHARE

An essential element of pricing is its relationship with the PLC.

An organisation will seek to maximise revenue through a carefully managed pricing strategy that may change at each stage of the PLC in order to build market share in line with its stated objectives.

When a new product is introduced into the market, the most difficult task is to set a price. There are two options at this stage; price high to attract a specific segment, or price low to appeal to a wider market.

As the product continues its journey into the growth stage, competitors enter the market and consequently one of the considerations is how to price the product. While the focus may be on product improvements, often it is necessary to price aggressively which may involve price cuts.

At product maturity when sales growth is slowing, organisations now start to consider price reductions as some competitors start to leave the market.

When the product moves into the decline stage, the organisation has a number of pricing options. It can increase the price in order to 'milk' the product. Alternatively, a price reduction could be initiated to slow the rate of decline.

PRICING STRATEGIES

Organisations can adopt two generic pricing strategies: skimming and penetration. A comparison is shown in Table 4.2.

Skimming

Skimming is where a high initial price is set to 'skim' income from those buyers who are prepared to purchase at this price. Buyers will be from small and profitable market segments. Apple launched its iPhone in this way, a high price was set and product availability was through a specific telephone network (rather than being available on all networks).

Penetration

Instead of charging a high price, the price is set below the price of any competing brands that may be in the market or about to enter the market. The intention here is to attract a large number of buyers in order to achieve a substantial share of the market quickly, or take share aware from competitors, or a combination of both.

Table 4.2 Product pricing strategies

Market skimming	Market penetration
■ High price charged	■ Low initial price charged
■ 'Just' worthwhile for some segments to adopt product	■ Attracts large sales volumes quickly
■ Increased competition keeps price low	■ High sales volumes reduce costs
	■ Economies of scale achieved

PRICING FRAMEWORKS

There are three broad pricing frameworks strategies for pricing frameworks, summarised in Table 4.3. These strategies help an organisation decide on the most appropriate way to price its existing products.

Cost Based

Here a specific sum of money or percentage is added to the cost of the product. This can be cost-plus, or mark up.

Cost Plus

No account is taken of market needs. Costs are established and an amount of money (£) or percentage (%) is added.

> **EXAMPLE**
>
> Goods are manufactured for £100 (i.e. cost) per unit and £50 is added to determine the selling price of £150. Alternatively 50% could be added to the cost price of £100 to bring the selling price to £150

Cost plus pricing is a simple and common method of pricing particularly in the commercial environment where costs can be difficult to identify with certainty. It also has the advantage that any changes in the cost of materials can quickly be reflected in the price.

Mark-up

Here the price is calculated by adding a fixed percentage (the mark-up) to the price. It is a method often used in the High street, or when purchasing wine in a restaurant and can be displayed as a percentage of cost or sales.

Table 4.3   Pricing frameworks

Pricing framework	Summary
1. Cost based	There are two approaches: Cost plus and mark-up pricing
2. Customer based	This includes: Psychological pricing, promotional pricing, differential, product-line and promotional pricing
3. Competitor based	Pricing near or away from the competition
4. Professional pricing	The price does not relate to the time taken providing the service

---

EXAMPLE

A bottle of wine is purchased by a wine merchant for £3 and adds £2 mark-up bringing the cost to £5.
  Mark-up as a percentage of costs= mark- up/cost which is 2/3 × 100 = 66%
  Or expressed a percentage of the selling price =mark-up/selling price × 100 = 40%

Mark- ups vary according to the industry sector, but it is not unusual to see a 100% mark-up on a bottle of wine purchased in a restaurant.

This method also has the advantage of simplicity as the mark-up can easily be calculated. However, it does not take into account any competitive pricing aspects nor how much the customer may be willing to pay.

With cost plus pricing no changes are made for volume or volume changes. To overcome this we need to understand the relationship between cost, price and volume; a concept known as breakeven analysis.

Breakeven Analysis

Breakeven analysis identifies the level of output where total revenue equals total cost, i.e. no profit or loss is sustained at this point. This is the breakeven point. Sales or output beyond this level starts to generate profit.

EXAMPLE

A small manufacturer sells a product for £200. Its fixed costs are £200,000 per year while its variable costs are £100 per unit.
  Its breakeven point is 2000 units per year.
  This is calculated by total fixed costs/unit price-variable costs, or £200,000/£200-£100.

Customer Based

This is based on the perceived value as seen by the customer.

There are a number of pricing methods, as seen below.

Psychological Pricing

The price says something about the product that makes the purchase an emotional rather than a rational purchase. The prime purpose of psychological pricing is 'to influence a customer's perception of price to make the product more attractive' (Dibb *et al.*, 2005). Everyday low prices or a price point of £9.99, or £19.99 can achieve this. Alternatively pricing high can have the same effect, e.g. a £100 bottle of wine becomes attractive to some segments because it reflects status, or makes the purchaser feel confident.

Promotional Pricing

Products are sold at below their usual price for a specific period of time to raise the level of sales. This is usually temporary and can take a number of forms from the special event approach, e.g. a discount is offered for all purchases made on the night, to the supermarket selling a product below cost, in order to encourage sales on other (higher margin) products.

Differential Pricing

A different price is charged to different purchasers of the same product, i.e. the price can vary.

A standard price for the product is clearly easier for the purchaser to understand. However, differentiated pricing is commonly used. Consider the purchase of a holiday overseas, this will typically be much more expensive during the period of school holidays. Leisure facilities may charge less for those aged over 60.

Product-line Pricing

Here the price is set in relation to the total number of products contained within the product line.

Competition

Organisations need to consider the structure of the market, i.e. number of competitors and the customer's perceived value of the product.

The more the product is seen to be unique by consumers, the greater the opportunity to raise the price.

Some organisations want to be price leaders and set the prices in the market, others prefer to be followers and have others set the prices which they look to as benchmark or point of reference. Organisations can then choose to price near or away from the competition.

EXAMPLE

A new business start-up has opened a car hire business on the outskirts of a UK provincial airport. All the cars were purchased secondhand and have high mileage.

The market leader (Hertz) charges an average of £100 per day for car hire. The new business charges £70 per day to attract a more price-conscious customer.

Professional Pricing

Professional pricing is used in situations where the provider of the service has a particular skill and maybe regarded as an expert in their field. Professional pricing covers a wide range of situations and can be applied in a number of ways.

Doctors' and consultants (of all types) operating outside the NHS, i.e. in the private sector, may charge a standard fee for a consultation irrespective of the time taken. Typically an initial consultation may take 10 minutes but the 'standard' fee is £200.

The legal profession operates in a similar way, buying or selling a house commands a standard fee irrespective of the work which needs to be carried out.

Auctioneers and estate agents tend to work on a percentage basis, i.e. do not set a fixed fee but charge 2.5% of the price of the property or goods sold.

In some situations professionals will charge on a daily rate which reflects the nature of the particular contract, or if the work will take an extended period to complete they may charge a fixed price for completion. Consequently with a fixed price if the work takes longer than expected the profit margin will be smaller and may turn into a loss. Conversely if the job is finished earlier the profit margin will be increased.

Builders like to charge on a day rate so that if unexpected problems arise during the course of the work, they simply keep charging for the work undertaken. In this case the clients' final bill may be much more than they were expecting or had budgeted for.

PRICE ELASTICITY OF DEMAND

Price elasticity of demand is a measure of consumer sensitivity to changes made to the price of a product, and organisations need to understand the relationship in order to manage demand.

There are three forms of elasticity of demand:

- Products are said to have *elastic demand* where a small increase in price produces a large percentage decrease in demand.

- *Inelastic demand* is where a small percentage increase in price produces a very small percentage change in demand.

- *Unitary demand* is where the percentage change in price results in an identical change in the demand.

CALCULATION

Price elasticity of demand = % change in quantity demanded/ % change in price

The higher the level of price elasticity, the more sensitive the market. However, different situations affect price elasticity in different ways.

Products which represent a small proportion of a consumer's overall spending are likely to be inelastic as the price increase is likely to appear insignificant. Where the product enjoys high brand awareness, inelasticity may well be higher because of the loyalty that may be attached to the brand.

The importance of price sensitivity needs to be fully understood if price is to be used effectively (i.e. optimised) and in relation to the rest of the marketing mix.

The UK government uses price to encourage motorists to consider more fuel-efficient cars by levying a higher duty on cars that emit high levels of pollution.

INTERNATIONAL MARKETS

Pricing for international markets offers the same options as the domestic market, but there are other factors that need to be taken into consideration.

The international distribution channel is going to be more complex than an entirely domestic one and this must be recognised when considering pricing and a whole channel perspective needs to be evaluated.

It is recognised that distribution channels vary in length and complexity and between countries. However, in some markets, not only do marketers have to set the prices, but they may also have to arrange the finance for some of the intermediaries.

A European company marketing in China must operate through a maze of state-controlled wholesalers and retailers.

An organisation can choose to offer a product at different prices in each of the markets it operates, or set a uniform price worldwide in relative currency terms.

Setting a uniform price may have some benefits, but it could also mean that the product is simply too expensive for some markets and will not be able to compete with the local competition. However, if there is no local competition a uniform price can be set. Airbus sells aeroplanes at the same price across all markets.

Most organisations will price the product in accordance with the needs and conditions of the local market, taking into account cost considerations.

Factors which need to be taken into consideration when setting different prices for each market include:

External

- Economic conditions, which may allow a greater (or less) price to be charged

- Level and strength /of competition in each market

- Currency exchange rates operating between markets

- Legal implications, i.e. selling below cost price on the overseas market

Internal

- Marketing objectives for each market

- Customer perceptions of your brand

- Products position within the PLC

Doole and Lowe (2008) suggest the following additional factors that need to be considered as part of the international pricing decision:

- Economies of scale should reduce the product costs

- Markets can be cross-subsidised

- Different segments require the marketing mix to be adjusted

- Global trading requires a continuous need to source products at the lowest cost from around the world

Pricing Strategy

Hollensen (2004) suggests the following pricing strategies:

- Pricing across products (product-line pricing)

- Pricing across countries (standardisation v differentiation)

Pricing Across Products (Product-Line Pricing)

Products can be broken down into basic, standard and deluxe, offering the consumer a choice of different price points which offers the organisation the opportunity to take business away from the competition at one or more of the levels.

Pricing can be set such that the price of one product offers a subsidiary to another. Finally an organisation can initially offer the product at a low price and then charge relative higher prices for subsequent purchases. A classic example of this is Gillette where the initial purchase of a man's razor and a couple of blades costs about the same as the subsequent purchase of blades alone.

In Chapter 13 the example of Rolls Royce shows a situation where Airlines were happy to buy its engines, but bought replacement parts from other suppliers because they were cheaper and perceived to be of the same quality.

Once again we can use the example of mobile phones where the manufacturers will offer the consumer a free or subsidised as the income is generated from the calls or data downloads.

Pricing Across Countries (Standardisation vs Differentiation)

As an organisation has to make choices about the product offered, and the way it is marketed, choices have to be made about the way the product is priced across markets, i.e. one price or different prices according to the market.

Standard pricing is based on the price of the product as it leaves the 'factory gate' and a selling price is set and applied in all the markets that the product is sold. The organisation does not take into account local conditions.

Differentiated pricing allows the price to be adapted to meet local conditions and therefore the price can change from country to country.

Some organisations also have to consider 'transfer pricing' which is the internal price set between different divisions (or companies) within a group when goods move between these different divisions or companies. The transfer price will need to be factored into the other costs that can impact on the price levied in the overseas market.

Having considered the additional factors of pricing overseas markets, the same pricing framework available to domestic markets can be applied.

SERVICES PRICING

The pricing of services can be difficult; not only has customer perception to be taken into consideration, but there is also value, costs and regulations to be considered.

We have already seen how different professionals set prices, but if we now look at services a little wider we can understand the problems. Chapter 8 will outline the difficulties of services i.e. the fact that they cannot be owned, stored or touched, and are often produced in advance of the purchase.

Sometimes prices are set by external organisations such as the NHS or regulated by consumer bodies. Prices can also be set in accordance with supply and demand, e.g. consider a marketing consultant who had a full client list in 2008, may find business has slowed down and would reduce his fees to secure business.

Prices can reflect seasonality; a family holiday will cost more during the school holidays.

The price of a hotel room would typically be offered at the standard or 'rack' rate for bookings made in advance, and reduced nearer to the date if available, as the hotel would not want to be left with an empty room. Flights were similarly priced until the advent of Ryanair and easyjet when the model changed; flights booked in advance were cheaper and got more expensive as the date nearer. This helps manage availability and rewards people for forward planning. The same principles now apply to many railway companies.

MANAGING PRICE CHANGES

The price charged for a product does not remain constant over time. Inflation often causes minor price changes which can immediately be passed on to the customer, or absorbed within the organisation. This decision can be made in order to protect the level of sales and offer a potential advantage against competitors. However, the effect could be to reduce profitability.

Sometimes it is necessary to increase the price of a product because consumers (wrongly) assume that the low price reflects low quality rather than value for money.

The timing of the price change also sends an important message to the market; the first organisation to reduce prices may be perceived as the most customer orientated, similarly with the last to increase prices.

EXAMPLE

Aldi, a supermarket operating in the UK has the slogan, 'spend a little, live a lot'. It has always been associated with 'cheap' products, mainly food. In the difficult economic conditions in 2008, customers started to recognise that the quality was much better than the price suggested.

In fact Aldi won the Retail Industry Award 2008: 'Outstanding Achievement of the Year'.

Aldi responded by reaffirming its commitment to offering consumers something extra special at exceptionally low prices.

The Aldi philosophy of offering an outstanding combination of incredible quality and unbeatable value has meant that an increasing number of people are switching to Aldi for their weekly shopping.

The other large UK supermarkets looked at own 'value' range and made a number of changes to counter Aldi.

Apart from the financial impact, price changes can signal important messages to the market. A small price reduction could be seen as the organisation simply passing on to consumers the price changes taking place through the supply chain. For example, the garage that reduces the price of petrol, because of the price change in the wholesale market, or the bank that reduces the price of borrowing as a result of a change in the Bank of England base rate.

Tesco, a UK leading supermarket, will often reduce the price of products by a small amount in support of its slogan of 'every little helps'.

There are three main reasons for cutting prices (Brassington and Pettitt, 2006): capacity utilisation, market dominance and market defence.

Capacity Utilisation

Where there is excess capacity in the market, an organisation may lower prices to encourage consumer take-up. The price reduction may be sufficient to enable the production lines to be maintained (although at a smaller capacity), rather than close them down completely.

Market Dominance

If an organisation already enjoys a strong position in the market for price and cost, for example Ryanair or easyjet, it may want to further strengthen its position by offering 'deep' price cuts. However, it will need to consider whether its strengthened position would contravene current legislation in the UK or overseas.

Market Defence

Where demand becomes weak, compared to alternative products which could be purchased, then a price reduction could be initiated to reduce the impact. It is important to avoid a 'price war' as this generally has a negative impact on the players in the market as they make price reductions which impact on profitability.

PERCEIVED PRODUCT VALUE

Beamish and Ashford (2008) suggest the perceived value of a product has a major impact upon the customer's decision to buy. Key factors that affect perceived value include:

- *Life cycle of the product*: customers will generally be happy to pay extra for 'new' products but will expect to pay less as the product moves through the PLC. Consider mobile phones and Laptops computers as they become more mainstream.

- *Service and technical support*: should a product break-down, then the availability of 'experts' will be an important consideration. Consider after-sales for computers.

- *Prestige and status*: are key factors. The purchase of a prestigious brand does not always offer better quality, but it will confer confidence and status to the user or wearer of the product which maybe of much greater importance. Consider the fashion brand Hackett.

- *Packaging which reflects the status of the product*: e.g. consider the difference in packaging between Sainsbury's 'taste the difference' range and Sainsbury's 'basics' range.

- *Ease of use*: the more straightforward a product is to use, then the less time that has to be spend getting accustomed to the product. Consider the purchase of a new mobile phone, or computer.

- *Availability of competitor products*: the fewer substitute products the greater the perceived value.

QUESTIONS

1. What is the role of pricing in product management?
2. Why would an organisation want to offer its products at the same price across all markets?
3. What is meant by professional pricing?
4. Why are services difficult to price?
5. What are the key factors which affect value?
6. What is meant by price elasticity of demand?

SUMMARY

Chapters 1 to 4 have provided the reader with an overview of the key elements associated with effective product management. It has appraised the reader of the importance of managing the product portfolio strategically and they key techniques available to do so. However, it recognises that each technique provides insights that are useful but at the same time acknowledges that each technique has limitations which have to be understood. The relevance of different strategies in different industry sectors has also to be appreciated. It is often necessary to use a range of techniques to produce a breadth of understanding to allow the marketer to do his/her job; this is to understand the changing needs of the customer, finding ways of responding to those needs through effective product development and at the same time deliver profits for the organisation.

The reader will have recognised the need to keep the product deployment process alive, flexible and responsive to completion and changing customer needs. The chapters of study in this section have also illustrated the need for a process in all of this which allows the marketers to explore the opportunities to adapt the portfolio of products in a logical and structured way. The process explored here are tried and tested and provide opportunities for the marketer to manage effectively.

In any competitive market, organisations seek to differentiate themselves in a sustainable way over the product life cycle and to maximise this wherever possible. Branding is illustrated in this section as a way of achieving this. Branding theory is explored and the impact on the customer and his/her perception of value is also considered. It should be clear to the reader that although in managing the overall portfolio it is necessary to consider the individual component parts, in practice a more holistic view needs to be taken.

To achieve maximum customer satisfaction and corporate profitability all the variables of the marketing mix need to be seen together, as the customer sees them and the interdependence of each on the other needs to be appreciated, with an equilibrium being maintained to sustain the relationship with the customer. The mix of variable needs to be balanced in a way that is meaningful to the customer, offers a clear product proposition and avoids confusion.

This is particularly the case in the context of pricing where decisions are made about how a product or range of products is priced; this often has an immediate impact on customer perception, the concept of value and the position of the product in relation to competitors. The impact of decision made about this variable can have a long-term and significant influence on the customer, their perception of value and the long-term sustainability of the organisation.

The theory of product management is an important starting point for the reader in developing understanding of this section of the syllabus. However, the reader should be aware of some of the practical limitations as well as the important direction which the theory provides. Although the chapters provide some useful examples of effective product management, readers should stay alert to the opportunities all around them to spot examples of how organisations continue to search for ways to differentiate their products from the completion in an ever-crowded market and with the expectations of customers continually rising.

FURTHER STUDY

Dibb, S., Simkin, L., Pride, W. and Ferrell, O. (2005) *Marketing: Concepts and Strategies*, 5th European edition. Houghton Mifflin.

BIBLIOGRAPHY

Anderson, C.H. and Vincze, J.A. (2004) *Strategic Marketing Management*, 2nd edition. Houghton Mifflin.

Armstrong, l. and Kotler, P. (2006) *Marketing: An Introduction*. Pearson.

Beamish, K. and Ashford, R. (2008) *Marketing Planning*. Butterworth-Heinemann.

Brassington, F. and Pettitt, S. (2006) *Principles of Marketing*. FT Prentice Hall.

Dibb, S., Simkin, L., Pride, W. and Ferrell, O. (2005) *Marketing: Concepts and Strategies*, 5th European edition. Houghton Mifflin.

Doole, I. and Lowe, R. (2008) *Strategic Marketing Decisions*. Butterworth-Heinemann.

Hollensen, S. (2004) *Global Marketing*. FT Prentice Hall.

Senior Examiner's Comments – Section One

By the time that students have completed Section One they should have a detailed knowledge and understanding of:

- How and why products/services and product portfolios are managed;

- How and why new products are developed;

- The different branding strategies available to organisations and the considerations when implementing branding (both domestically and in international markets)

- The meaning, role and importance of positioning in product management; and

- The importance of pricing; the pricing approaches and strategies commonly used and the factors that influence pricing decisions (domestically and in international markets).

Importantly, students must be able to apply what they have learnt to organisations in various sectors, including business-to-business, business-to-consumer, goods, services, public sector and not-for-profit. Students must also be able to apply learnings to organisations trading domestically, in overseas markets and globally.

Students are urged to find their own examples, for instance from reading their local and national media, and from case studies. Students are also urged to apply the various theoretical tools, models and concepts that have been examined in this section to gain a deeper insight into the practical application of theory.

Students should also examine how the tools, models and concepts which have been examined in Section One have been deployed successfully by organisations to achieve key marketing goals, for example income generation, customer retention and new business acquisition.

Channel Management

Channel Management, Distribution Strategies and Control

At the end of this chapter you will be able to:

- Evaluate different channel management and distribution strategies
- Apply management controls to different types of channels domestically and internationally

INTRODUCTION

This section of the syllabus introduces the concept of channel management. While touching on the concept of the physical management of the goods from manufacture to the consumer, it is more concerned with the information flows that pass between the different members of the channel. In Chapters 5, 6, 7 we will explore how effective distribution channels work, why they are chosen, what makes them effective, and how they can be monitored.

Distribution channels are an important consideration for any organisation and, as we will see, the relationship between the various parties can be complex and extend beyond the formal channel relationships into a wider network which still has to be managed.

Chapter 5 focuses on the different types of channels and how they are used domestically and overseas.

DISTRIBUTION CHANNELS

Distribution channels refer to a group of individuals or organisations (intermediaries) that move goods from the producer to the consumer or industrial user of the product. In other words a distribution channel is the way an organisation gets its product to the consumer. Sometimes distribution channels are referred as marketing channels.

Distribution channels do not just involve physical products, but can equally apply to services which tend to have a shorter channel. Channels can extend beyond geographical boundaries and have an important role to play in overseas markets.

Without an effective distribution channel, products, even the best products, are more likely to fail, so organisations are continually looking to develop cheaper and faster ways of selling their products.

Organisations use distribution channels for a variety of reasons including the need to reduce cost, maximise sales and customer satisfaction. However, in return for reaching a wider market, there are often challenges to be faced through the management of the various channels members and a particular issue for most organisations is the loss of control over elements of the channel which could include pricing and promotion.

The distribution of products to consumers has two main management components:

- Getting the tangible or physical products to the customers (the supply chain)

- Controlling the flow of communication between the various parties that make up the distribution channel

Our focus is on the distribution channel, but an example of the supply chain is shown in Figure 5.1.

In Figure 5.1 we see the flow of materials from suppliers to customers, but we need to note that information flows in the other direction and has

FIGURE 5.1

The supply chain.

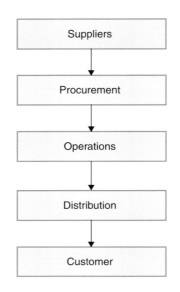

been referred to as the 'information highway', where all the partners in the chain have access to the same information.

ACTIVITY 5.1

For your own organisation, or an organisation of your choice, identify the distribution channels used.

Functions of a Distribution Channel

There are four key functions of a distribution channel which are summarised in Table 5.1.

Channel Structures

Figure 5.2 shows the typical channel structures for business–business channels. However, depending on the nature of the business being conducted, members of the channel may be called dealers, distributors, agents, outlets, or partners. It can be seen that organisations can go 'direct' to customers and this is typical in financial services.

Within the table there are four channel structures from direct to the longer channel where agents, distributors and customers are involved. Each member of the channel has a role to play in ensuring the efficient movement of the product to the end user.

Figure 5.3 shows a typical channel structure for the consumer (B2C) market.

As we will see later, an organisation will often use multiple channels to get the product to the customer, such as that shown in Figure 5.4.

ACTIVITY 5.2

For your own organisation identify the different channels used to get the product to the consumer. Do you think each channel is being used effectively? Are there additional channels which could be used?

Channel Objectives

The structure and the objectives for the channel depend on the need of the end user, and this in turn is affected by the nature of the end user, i.e. consumer or industrial products.

Channel objectives must be set which must be SMART, i.e. specific, measurable, time bound, realistic and achievable. Usually objectives are set which meet customer needs at the most effective price.

Table 5.1	Functions of distribution channels
Functions	**Summary**
Creating utility	This refers to time, place, possession and form.
	▪ Getting the product to the customer at a time when they actually want it. ▪ Making the product available where the customer wants to buy it. ▪ Giving the customer the legal right to use the product. ▪ Assembling the product to the format wanted by the customer.
Facilitating exchange efficiencies	Using intermediaries can reduce the distribution costs by eliminating (for example) many of the journeys that would take place. A manufacturer of washing machines would save costs by using an intermediary (also distributing products for other manufacturers) to get the product into the various retailers.
Alleviating discrepancies	Discrepancies break down into two: quantity and assortment.
	▪ Organisations need to produce in bulk to generate cost efficiencies. Many operate production runs turning out hundreds of thousands of the product each and every day. Consumers may only want 'one' and retailers (depending on size) will want smaller quantities. ▪ In other words, the manufacturer produces far more products the typical customer can use. This is 'discrepancy in quantity'
	A discrepancy in assortment' relates to the fact that a consumer generally want a number of products which constitute an assortment. However, a manufacture may only produce a small range of products (assortment) which produces the discrepancy.
Standardising transactions	Products, packaging, pricing, delivery is standardized through the channel.
Customer service	The intermediary will be providing service to other members of the channel or the end user.
	Wholesalers will be expected to advise the retailer on any technical issue. Retailers or distributors will be expected to deal with customer enquiries and deal with any issues that may arise.

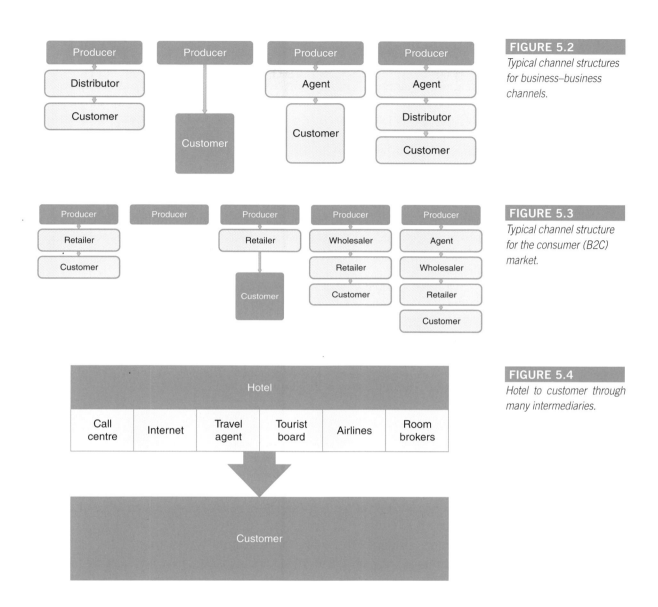

FIGURE 5.2

Typical channel structures for business–business channels.

FIGURE 5.3

Typical channel structure for the consumer (B2C) market.

FIGURE 5.4

Hotel to customer through many intermediaries.

The structure of the channel will depend the capabilities of the organisation, i.e. how large is it? What resources does it have available? What are its key skills?

Kotler *et al.* (1999) suggests that objectives should be set in terms of the levels of services to be provided.

However, this does not mean the same levels of service have to be provided to all customers. Different customer segments can have different service levels attached to them and should reflect the value of the customer.

Consumer Channels

Where goods are moved directly between the producer and the consumer there are advantages for both parties as the intermediary is eliminated. The producer has control and the consumer can be in direct contact with the manufacturer so that customer service, queries and complaints can be dealt with.

There are various forms of 'direct', but the increasing popularity of the internet and sophisticated databases make this channel more popular and another way for customers to access the product.

Amazon, the books-to-music retailer has made a great success of this channel, but others have been less than successful as they need to rely on others to actually get the product to the customer and this part of the distribution channel has not worked as well as could have been expected.

Interestingly we are now seeing the internet disintermediate other channels.

Another short distribution channel is the producer to retailer to consumer. This channel is the most common one where the manufacturer produces the product in bulk which is sold to the large retailers in typically large numbers, who then sell to the end consumer who purchase in much smaller numbers. This channel only works where the retailer has a large turnover and can sell the product to the consumer quickly and in small quantities. A good example is a supermarket.

Producer > Wholesaler > Retailer > Consumer

A longer channel is the *producer, wholesaler, retailer and consumer channel*. The manufacturer still produces in bulk and sells in smaller quantities to the wholesaler. This channel is also appropriate for smaller manufacturers who cannot sell direct to retailers. The wholesaler also brings together a wide range or deep range of products for the benefit of the end user or retailer.

Producer > Agent Wholesaler > Retailer > Consumer

The *producer, agent wholesaler, retailer and consumer channel* is used when overseas business is involved. The manufacturer, when seeking to enter a market he is not familiar with, will appoint an agent who will have local knowledge of the market and will be able to advise on channel strategies. However, in return for local knowledge the manufacturer loses control over aspects of delivery.

B2B

B2B channels tend to be much shorter than consumer channels, as the users prefer the dialogue with the manufacturer in view of the (often) complex nature of the products involved. Consider the building of the Olympic village in the UK and the importance of having key components at exactly the right moment. Similarly with Airbus Industries and the building of their aeroplanes; components are built across Europe to be assembled in France. Each component, wings, fuselage, etc. must arrive at the factory for assembly at just the right time, otherwise the knock-on effect is considerable.

Direct

A short channel categorised by direct contact between the manufacturer and the user. *Direct channels* are generally used for complex or expensive products. The method is preferred as there is direct access to the manufacturer's technical help team, which is particularly important for non-standard products. However, there is often a need for the manufacturer to maintain a direct sales team along with some representative offices.

Manufacturer > Distributor > User

This channel can be likened to the wholesaler approach for the consumer market. Large quantities of the product are sold to distributors who sell them in smaller quantities.

Manufacturer > Agent > User

An agent is used where it would not be economic for a manufacturer to deal directly with the user. The agent will have expertise in the products, and knowledge of the local market, but equally depending on the agreement between the parties may also act as agent for a competitor product.

There are attractive cost advantages to be achieved as the agent will usually be paid on a commission basis so there will be no fixed costs.

Manufacturer > Agent > Distributor > User

The longest channel, but again one used when selling to overseas markets. The agent is used for his market knowledge which is used to supplement the role of the distributor who will be responsible for ensuring product availability at a point where the customer wants it.

DISTRIBUTION STRATEGY

The standard channel structures have been outlined above and the actual choice will depend on the product and the nature of the market.

A key consideration in establishing the 'right' channels is the concept of market coverage. Brassington and Pettitt (2006) suggest market coverage is 'about reaching the end customer as cost effectively and efficiently as possible, while maximising customer satisfaction. Having decided on the types of distributor, the manufacturer now has to select the type of distribution to be undertaken'.

To achieve market cover there are three strategies that need to be considered:

■ *Selective*, where carefully chosen distributors are chosen

■ *Intensive*, where as many as possible distributors are chosen

■ *Exclusive*, where distribution is highly restricted.

Let's look at these in closer detail.

Selective Channel

A small number of carefully chosen distributors selected usually within a defined geographic area. Typically this involves consumer goods, but can include industrial goods.

An organisation will use this channel where only a small number of outlets can be handled by the organisation effectively, or the nature of the product only requires customer access in specific areas.

Intensive Channel

Blanket coverage as the manufacturer wants as many outlets as possible to take the product i.e. mass distribution. Generally used for convenience goods, with the rationale being to make the goods available at a place which is convenient for the customer.

Exclusive Channel

Typically an outlet will cover a large geographical area. Consumers tend to purchase on an infrequent basis and the product price is often expensive. Often distributors can be franchisees.

INFLUENCES ON CHANNEL STRATEGY

We have seen the various ways a channel can be constructed: direct, indirect, business to consumer, business to business and the roles that each intermediary can undertake. Organisations then select the most appropriate channel, or channels, as they are not restricted to one channel as they can use multi channels, i.e. many different routes to market, which can include direct and indirect channels.

The actual choice of channel or channels can be influenced by five factors (Brassington and Pettitt, 2006): the product, organisational objectives, market size and location, consumer behaviour and changing environment (Figure 5.5).

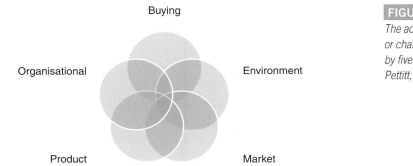

FIGURE 5.5

The actual choice of channel or channels can be influenced by five factors (Brassington and Pettitt, 2006).

The Product

We have seen that where complex or expensive products are involved, the end user will often prefer to be in direct contact with the manufacturer so that any technical or design issues can be discussed or resolved without the need to go through an intermediary. Similarly once the product has been installed any after-sales issues can be dealt with direct.

Objectives

Organisational objectives determine the overall channel approach. If the brand has an 'exclusive' image then it may want to open a new channel rather than use an existing one.

> Lexus is the 'upmarket' brand from Toyota. When the brand first launched it chose not to offer the brand through the existing Toyota network, but open up a new network of dealers who sold only Lexus vehicles. In this way Toyota sought to develop an exclusive dealership which keeps the brands separate in the minds of the consumer.

> The Post Office is looking to make its distribution network more efficient and closing post office branches that are not profitable. At the same time it is opening or relocating post offices into major stores like WH Smith which are more accessible to the public.

Sometimes an organisation will reduce the number of distributors in order to reposition the brand in the mind of the consumer. This was one of the strategies used by the Rover Group as it sought (unsuccessfully) to change customer perception of the brand.

One of the key concerns for organisations at the moment is consideration for the environment and how distribution channels can become 'greener'.

> Boots, the high street chain, has a fleet of vehicles delivering to branches across the UK. It constantly reviews its distribution strategy and has polices in place to reduce the miles vehicles travel and improve its 'green credentials' by using empty delivery vehicles to return to Head Office with waste for recycling.

While channels need to be designed with the consumer in mind, the channels also need to be aligned with the organisation's stated objectives.

An organisation that was initially established to service a small niche market, finds it now wants to expand and consequently its distribution strategy would move from exclusive to select.

Objectives change over time and need to be reflected in the distribution channel. More effective distribution channels may require new or different intermediaries e.g. Tesco Home delivery. Customers no longer need to visit the store to purchase; they can have the groceries and more delivered direct to their home within a two hour time period.

Market Size and Location

Where there is a substantial market for the product, an organisation may choose a direct channel and, in the case of an overseas operation, may open an office or presence and this will cut out the need for intermediaries. The organisation retains complete control over all activities.

If the market is small, the use of intermediaries may be necessary as the organisation can rely on intermediaries to get the product to market without the need to invest heavily in a new infrastructure, as the intermediary will already have it in place.

Similarly, the market for the product may be located some distance from the where it is produced and the cost of a physical presence would be too expensive to justify. An intermediary could be used to manage the distribution and represent the organisation through its own network.

Where the size of the market is small and does not warrant a large distribution chain, for example expensive designer label clothing, the channel will be short, with few outlets (exclusive).

Newspapers on the other hand will require a highly complex channel if the reader is to be able to purchase at convenient location and time.

Consumer Behaviour

For some general 'low involvement' purchases a consumer maybe happy to make the purchase from a general retailer such as Argos. However, when considering the purchase of, say, a TV which incorporates the latest design and technical features, it may be more appropriate to visit a specialist

TV retailer. The retailer will be able to add value to the purchase through detailed product knowledge as well as being able to offer a wide product range to choose from.

Many consumers like to purchase from out-of-town stores with the convenience of easy parking and a small range of stores, but large range of products. Equally some consumers prefer to travel into town, wander around the shops and enjoy a coffee before making a purchase.

Changing Environment

The changing business environment needs to be reflected in new and evolving distribution strategies.

Organisations need to recognise the importance of being 'green' and making the distribution of goods as effective as possible across a new of dimensions which increasing needs to include environmental considerations.

Working with intermediaries can lead to reduced fuel and pollution costs through more efficient vehicles and distribution methods. Sharing of best practices will also contribute to efficiencies.

While there are usually a number of channel strategies to consider, it can be the case that external environmental considerations affect the availability of channels.

We are seeing Local Authorities refuse planning permission for supermarkets to open out of town stores, encouraging them back on to the high street. The closure of Woolworths was an opportunity for the supermarkets to buy their single floor high street locations.

Technology has fundamentally changed the nature of distribution channels, allowing more direct channels, more self service options and the intermediation of many channel intermediaries.

SETTING CHANNEL OBJECTIVES

Channel Structure

We have suggested that a distribution channel is a group of individuals that move goods to the consumer. This ignores the relationships that exist between the channel members. Often the members will be independent of each other, or they may be some connection such as ownership. Equally the channel member can also be a member of another channel which may be a competitor to you. Relationships and potential conflicts can easily occur within the channel. Therefore it is necessary to define the structure of the channel so that all members are clear on their roles and responsibilities, are willing to cooperate with each other and will maximise the benefits of being a member of the channel.

Vertical Marketing System (VMS)

In a conventional channel, as identified above, role and responsibilities can be confused, or blurred (Figure 5.6). To overcome this, the VMS was introduced and is broken down into three types:

- *Corporate VMS:* Here an organisation can own and operate intermediaries within the channel and the dominant member of the channel may in fact not be the manufacturer. For example, TNT Post, a competitor to Royal Mail, collects mail from clients and distributes them into Royal Mail's central depots who is then responsible for delivery to offices and offices in the UK. Another example is Sainsbury's petrol; it is Sainsbury's who owns the petrol tankers and the filling stations, but no other part of the channel.

- *Contractual VMS:* Where members of the channel retain their independence, written agreements are put in place to specify the exact role and responsibility of each member. It will be clear, for example, as to who is responsible for pricing, promotion, stock levels, finance packages, delivery dates, manufacturer, etc. Franchising comes under this category and is commonly perceived as an example of best practice as the key details of the relationship between franchisor and franchisee are clearly detailed.

- *Administered VMS:* There is not usually a legal agreement between the channel members; rather there is a dominant member who assumes responsibility for the coordination of the other channel members. This domination could come about because of their position in the channel or the nature of their business.

> "At TNT, we aim to exceed our customers' expectations in the way we transfer their goods and documents around the world. We deliver value, by providing the most reliable and efficient solutions through our global delivery networks."
>
> *Source*: TNT Website http://www.tntpost.co.uk

OVERSEAS CONSIDERATIONS

Many organisations are content to operate in their home market. However, for a variety of reasons and circumstances, an organisation will look to operate or sell their product overseas.

Working with an organisation's home market is less risky than venturing overseas. Within the UK laws are generally the same, language is known and distribution channels understood. No need to worry about currency

Marketing Channel

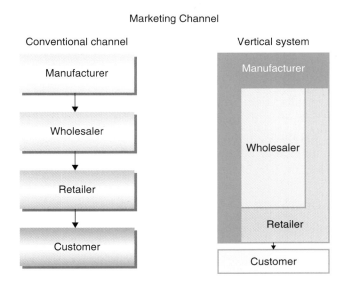

FIGURE 5.6
Conventional channels vs vertical system.

fluctuations and PESTEL factors are generally very well appreciated and changes can be anticipated. Nevertheless there are often good reasons to consider entering into an overseas market.

An organisation that wants to enter an overseas market must consider the most appropriate entry method. They include:

- A saturated domestic market, where sales are slowing down and the competition is becoming stronger.

- Efficiencies of scale, where the opening of an overseas market reduces the unit cost of production

- Existing customers may be expanding overseas and there is an opportunity to support them

Paliwoda (2003) suggests six factors to be taken into account:

- *Speed:* How quickly does the organisation want to enter the market and what share will it obtain in the timescale?

- *Cost:* What are the costs of the entry methods and which represent better value?

- *Flexibility:* How much flexibility is needed? i.e. what are the alternatives if things do not proceed to plan?

- *Risk:* What is the organisation's view on risk, including financial, reputation, economic and social?

■ *Payback:* How quickly does the investment need to generate a profit, or what level of profit is needed by a certain date in time?

■ *Long term profit objectives:* What are the long term plans for the market?

Having considered the key factors, the organisation can select from a variety of distribution channels:

Although the international channels of distribution are broadly similar to domestic channels they are more complex in their management and culture forms an important part of the relationship.

In-country Operation

An organisation can choose to produce goods in the home country and export them to the overseas country. It can achieve this through 'indirect exporting' where an agent is appointed in the home country with specialist knowledge of the overseas market(s). Alternatively the producer can export the goods direct to the overseas country (direct exporting).

Direct exporting brings options. An organisation can manage its exporting operation from within the domestic market by establishing an exports division or department. Alternatively it could set up an overseas office to handle sales, distribution and potentially marketing (see Figure 5.7).

UK universities are keen to recruit student from overseas, particularly Asia and the Far East. As the market has developed, a number of the universities have set up representative offices in the overseas country where multi-lingual staff can manage the recruitment process and deal with any issues that may arise in the overseas part of the channel.

Previously members of staff from the Universities would have visited the country at regular intervals, but customer satisfaction and recruitment numbers have generally increased for those universities with an in-country presence.

Strategic Alliances

A strategic alliance is a commitment between a numbers of organisations (minimum of two) that agree to work together for a specific purpose(s). It is a collaborative agreement where organisations work with each other to develop, or improve a product, or exploit a specific market. There is similarity with joint ventures (see below), but while the number of strategic alliances in increasing, they are not without their problems or risks.

The strategic partner(s) must be carefully selected and have similar aims or objectives. The technology industry has seen many strategic alliances that have successfully developed new products or opened up new markets

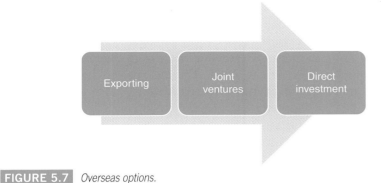

FIGURE 5.7 *Overseas options.*

through new distribution channels which individually the partners would not have been able to do. However, as we have seen already, trust and commitment are essential requirements for members of a channel and in a very challenging environment, members of a strategic alliance could quickly find that they are competitors for the same market, leading to the breakdown of the alliance. Finally, strategic alliances are often formed for a short period of time; there is no sense of long term commitment necessarily.

Joint Venture

A joint venture shares many similarities with a strategic alliance, but differs in the sense that it is more formal; a joint venture will usually involve establishing a jointly owned business with an overseas partner. The overseas partner(s) will help the domestic organisation in a number of ways:

- Share distribution channels
- Expert knowledge of the market
- Builds synergy

The relationship can also hasten the time needed to get into a new market as the organisations will be working jointly together for a common purpose, rather than possibly competing with each other.

Digital/Virtual Channels

Electronic channels open up new markets and opportunities for organisations of all sizes; smaller organisations can now access markets that previously could not have been reached and it gives larger organisations an alternative channel for supplementing existing channels. In many instances the need for a physical presence has been reduced along with the associated costs.

While the presence of a website supports the buying process, e-commerce is necessary to facilitate a truly integrated channel. E-commerce provides the capability to accept and make payments across the internet.

Cost reduction is a key motivator for the use of digital channels and the electronic and instant nature of the channel means that transactions are processed quicker and payment received faster leading to improved efficiency.

Even before an organisation looks to an overseas market, the internet is a rich source of information, saving time and cost, in areas such as:

- Key financial statistics

- Exporting terms and conditions

- Media availability

No longer do brochures need to be sent out by mail to potential customers, they are made available on-line. Customers visiting a website are also a valuable source of information that can be used to improve existing channels.

A two-way dialogue can be established where any queries can be dealt with immediately. Errors are reduced as it is often the purchaser who keys in their requirements.

Larger organisations develop extranets, where suppliers, distributors, joint venture partners, any channel intermediary or end user can have access to a specific area of the organisation's website.

In the extranet each user would see a website customised to their needs and the key purpose includes:

- Raising awareness for new products or procedures

- Facilitating purchase and payment

- Sharing in advance sensitive information

- Rapid response to changing market conditions, so price changes can be communicated

The internet has benefits for most organisations, but like all other channel choices should be used appropriately in line with organisational objectives and customer needs. Complex and expensive products will rely on traditional channels, but technical information can be made available on the web or extranet to support other channels.

For the smaller business, the web will remove barriers, give access to a wider range of overseas suppliers and may become the sole distribution channel.

Agent

An agent can be used where it is not viable or practical for an organisation to have a physical presence. An agent will not own the goods but may stock them and buy and sell on behalf of the principal. The agent will have been carefully selected for their knowledge of the market or for their network of contacts in the overseas market and will often sell through distributors.

An agent is generally paid on a commission only basis and does not contribute to the fixed costs, but can be a substantial variable cost depending on the commission terms agreed between the parties.

MANAGING CHANNEL RELATIONSHIPS

In selecting a new channel or evaluating an existing channel the organisation will have carefully considered the cost incurred in setting up the channel, the ability of the channel to effectively distribute the products, the characteristics of the product and of course the customer.

While organisations understand the importance of managing costs, it is only one of a range of measures that can be used to monitor the performance of channels.

Cateora (1993) offers a framework for evaluation based on 5 Cs that are applicable to both the domestic and international markets.

- *Coverage*: How well the channel performs in achieving sales, or market share, or penetration of the market.

- *Character*: Compatibility of the channel with the organisation's desired positioning for the product.

- *Continuity*: How loyal the various channel members are and the length of time they have been a part of the channel.

- *Control*: How well the organisation is able to control the marketing programmes within the channel; this can be of particular concern where long international channels are involved.

- *Cost*: This will cover the cost of investment, variable costs, and expenditure.

MARKETING TOOLS

To be effective, an organisation must design the marketing mix to offer synergy and consistency with its channel members.

Where the organisation also has overseas markets, there is the additional dimension of whether to standardise, i.e. use the same strategy across all the markets it operates in, or adapt the strategy, i.e. have a different marketing strategy for each country.

The effective use of the marketing mix will:

- Build profitable and different relationships with intermediaries
- Establish one-to-one communications and dialogue

Marketing mix considerations include:

- *Product:* can be a physical product, idea or service.
- *Price:* usually negotiated for channel member, but may be set for end user.
- *Place:* range of channels depending on B2B or B2C. Internet can be used to cross both channels. Length of channel will depend on the nature of the product.
- *Promotion:* Branding and heavy advertising is necessary in the FMCG (Fast Moving Consumer Goods) sector, along with push and pull strategies. More complex products would require trade advertising and extranet support.
- *People:* high degree of training with carefully selected and accountable staff.
- *Process:* clear processes which are well documented and have clear timescales for completion.
- *Physical evidence:* internal and external appearances of any buildings need to reflect the product qualities, similarly through brochures and the web.

When considering the international dimension the following should be noted:

- *Product:* may need to be adapted to the needs of the local market and the product positioning may be different. KFC offers mashed potatoes with its fried chicken in Hong Kong. Coca Cola alters its recipes for different countries.
- *Price:* other currencies make pricing more complex, but should reflect the positioning in the overseas country.
- *Place:* reflects the different entry strategy, e.g. joint venture, in-country operation, etc. E- commerce is worthy of specific consideration reflecting the immediacy of the channel in ordering goods.

- *Promotion:* may need to be adapted for cultural, ethical and taste reasons.

- *People:* high degree of training with carefully selected and accountable staff, but recognising some of the difficulties this may cause depending on the market.

- *Process:* clear processes that are well documented and have clear timescales for completion.

- *Physical evidence:* internal and external appearances of any buildings need to reflect the product qualities, similarly through brochures and the web.

We have already seen the importance of channel members and the importance of the role they play. The roles, activities and function they perform are integral to the success of the channel. However, even though distribution channels are generally portrayed as a linear process, they are far more complex than this and stakeholders can form complex relationship networks through collaboration, joint ventures and alliances. This is known as the 'extended enterprise'.

ROLE OF COMMUNICATIONS

While it sounds like a cliché, poor communication often lies at the heart of channel conflict; mixed or confused messages are communicated through the channel or only communicated to certain members and then often in reaction to an event which has occurred. Proactive and clear communication should be the norm in distribution channels.

Fill (2006) offers a succinct definition of communications which is: 'marketing communication is an audience-centred activity designed to encourage engagement between participants'.

In other words the needs and motivations of each channel member needs to be understood as well as the environment in which the message is being delivered and received. The nature of the relationship between the channel members also needs to be recognised and appreciated.

Consequently, marketing communications will need to convey not just product information, but convey relationship building through trust and commitment. This is best done using the DRIP model:

- *Differentiation:* messages explaining how the organisation is different from other others in the industry and the competitive advantages it confers.

■ *Reminding:* reminding, or reinforcing the importance of the relationship and benefits that the parties accrue from each other as a result of being part of the channel.

■ *Informing:* sharing with others exactly what the capabilities of the organisation. Common or potential areas for misunderstanding can be dealt within a proactive manner.

■ *Persuading:* messages to encourage potential channel members, or encouraging existing members to continue with the relationship.

The DRIP model is a useful framework from which communication tools and media can be deployed effectively. This can range from regular e-mail updates, to monthly sales meetings to an annual meeting.

For any communication strategy to be effective there must be a basis of trust between the parties, otherwise any messages conveyed will be ignored or dismissed. Trust is formed by the parties in the channel agreeing to a culture of mutual commitment, cooperation, understanding, openness and a willingness to put rectify mistakes rather than adopt a 'blame culture'. A lack of trust inhibits the development of the channel and can lead to conflict becoming a constant feature of the channel.

EVALUATING CHANNEL CRITERIA

An organisation will evaluate a number of channels and select one or multiple channels that will best meet its business objectives.

When selecting the 'best' channel the organisation must use the following three criteria (Kotler *et al.*, 1999).

Economic

An estimate of the potential sales, investment and channel costs will be made for each channel. Different scenarios will be modelled to understand the effects of variations from any central estimates to see the potential affect on income.

Identifying the most effective channel now and in the future can be difficult. The measure of profit must be established; this could vary from ROI (Return on Investment) to shareholder value and will need to consider:

■ Any assets which may need to be shared

■ Replacement of existing assets to meet the needs of the channel

■ Redundant assets, no longer needed in the channel

■ Exit costs of leaving the channel

Control

In order to widen distribution of the product and made it more accessible to customers, intermediaries are used which dilute the overall control over product marketing. Procedures should be put in place to clearly define responsibility of the intermediary to avoid a lack of overall control.

Adaptive

Establishing a channel usually involves a long-term commitment which goes beyond financial dimensions and the channel needs to be able to respond to changes in the market. This could involve changes to purchasing behaviour, the introduction of new technology, environmental issues and economic conditions. A channel that readily adapts will be often able to secure a competitive advantage.

CHANNEL PROFITABILITY

We have outlined the key selection criteria for channel members and channel selection ensures the right product is available to the right customer at the right time and we should add at the right price.

An organisation will want to maximise its ROI. This determines the price that needs to be charged to produce a specific return on the organisation's investment. To calculate ROI an organisation needs to clearly establish not only its costs, but potential revenue streams which will flow through.

Channel members are an important contributor to overall profit as they:

- Generate long term relationships which produce 'repeat' business.
- Reduce inefficiencies by combing activities or undertaking activities they are uniquely skilled to carry out.
- Reduce cost, by having highly structured processes and systems which means the time from when the product is manufactured to the time its sold is much faster.
- Add value at stages of the process.

Clearly the value added by channel members has to be more then the cost of carrying out that activity and this must be continually monitored.

COMPETITOR STRATEGIES

It is usually expected that competition for an organisation's products would come from outside of its own distribution channel. However, the often complex nature of distribution channels and the interconnectivity between channel members, who may also have relationships with customers and suppliers through other distribution channels, can bring about competition from within the channel as well as beyond it.

Palamountain (1955) suggests four types of competition shown in Figure 5.8.

Horizontal Competition

This is where competition occurs between intermediaries of the same type, e.g. wholesalers where each may seek to develop marketing or product strategies to gain a competitive advantage over the other. Some may chose a broad range of products, with little choice within the category; others may choose a small but deep product range.

Intertype Competition

Here competition takes place at the same level in the channel, e.g. a bicycle manufacturer wants to make its bicycles available to a broad range of customers. It has a choice of selling through high street retailers, small local shops, or national chains who operate out of town.

The manufacturer would need to develop different strategies for each outlet, but overall it must be seen to be fair and even-handed. Unnecessarily favouring one outlet leads to frustration in the channel, and also customer dissatisfaction if they find they cannot make the purchase from their chosen

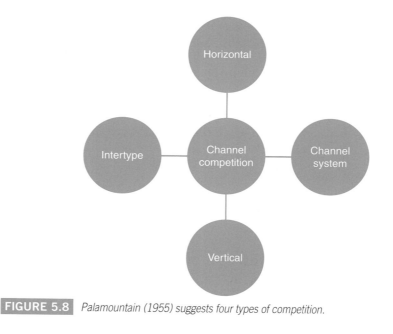

FIGURE 5.8 *Palamountain (1955) suggests four types of competition.*

outlet, possibly because the manufacturer makes stock available to the larger retailer in preference to the small independent retailer.

Vertical Competition

Competition takes place at different levels in the channel, e.g. between wholesaler and retailer.

Channel System Competition

In channel system competition a channel of distribution is in competition with another but parallel distribution channel.

This is now common in the motor industry. Tyre manufacturers compete with each other so that each wants to be the first choice for the consumer (or retailer). They will want to ensure adequate stock is always in place and that the marketing messages encourage purchase and replacements are readily available. The competition will be looking at the other channels and will similarly want to make sure their channel is performing better.

BENCHMARKING

Benchmarking is the process of comparing the cost, time or quality of company products against that of another organisation which is usually best in class or a competitor. Knowing how you compare is a useful way for an organisation to identify ways to improve product quality or performance in order to gain more business.

There are various types of benchmarking including:

- *Process benchmarking*: which involves looking at a competitor's processes and identifying best practice. It is also necessary to apply some estimated costings to the processes being observed.

- *Financial benchmarking*: undertaking a financial in order to establish and assess your overall competitiveness.

- *Performance benchmarking*: to establish the competitive position by evaluating competitor products with similar and different distribution channels.

- *Product benchmarking*: identifying competitor products to secure ideas for new products of your own.

- *Functional benchmarking*: focusing on the channel or a single aspect of it such as finance or logistics.

When looking at the industry sector or overseas markets, then strategic benchmarking could be employed.

Often an organisation will look within its on industry to identify 'best in class'. However, it is often unwise just to look within the industry. Looking outside will identify world class organisations and improve procedures.

> A local authority that previously benchmarked itself against other local authorities found it was performing well. When it looked to benchmark itself against 'best in class' retailers it found areas when it could improve upon.

An organisation can choose to benchmark any aspect of its process in order to improve its performance. Table 5.2 provides some examples.

Camp (1989) suggests that an organisation that benchmarks itself derived the following benefits:

- Best practice from other industries can be adapted and implemented the organisation's own systems and procedures

- Benchmarking provides motivation to improve organisational processes

- Reluctance to change can often be overcome. People are often more receptive to change when it originates outside their own organisation or industry

- A technological break can occasionally be achieved.

INSIGHT: MEDICATION DISTRIBUTION

Exclusive drug distribution deals that cut out wholesaler suppliers could cost taxpayers hundreds of millions of pounds.

A report published by the Office of Fair Trading (OFT) in December 2007 also raised concerns that exclusive 'direct to pharmacy' schemes could result in patients having to wait longer for life-saving medicines. The watchdog found that such deals raised a 'significant risk' of extra costs to the NHS because they allowed manufactures to set prices paid by pharmacies.

The OFT has urged the Government to change its pricing policy – the Pharmaceutical Price Regulation Scheme – but says pharmaceutical firms should be allowed to choose their methods of distribution.

In March 2007 Pfizer, the world's largest drugmaker and the supplier of 15% of Britain's prescription medicines, announced a deal with UniChem, the wholesaling arm of Alliance Boots, to bypass its traditional wholesale suppliers and sell directly to pharmacies.

Since then Novartis and AstraZeneca have decided to restructure their distribution channels. The Pfizer scheme has been attacked by independent pharmacists, MPs and wholesalers who argue that restricting the distribution of all the company's products to one British supplier poses a threat to competition, drug pricing, patient welfare and the NHS.

Pfizer denies the scheme increases the cost of medicines to the NHS and says it needs the new system to stamp out the sales of counterfeit medicines.

The new deals are fiercely opposed by independent wholesalers who want to ensure fair competition, security of supply and best value for the taxpayer.

Source: based on an article in *The Times* by Lilly Peel and Robin Pagnamenta, December 12, 2007.

Table 5.2	An organisation can choose to benchmark any aspect of its process in order to improve its performance

Marketing mix

- Product; sales by segment, warranty claims, market share
- Price; price by segment, discount levels
- Place; channel costs, channel volumes, stock levels, delivery time
- Promotion; cost per contact, media coverage, sales per telephone call

The organisational structure

- Number of employees
- DMU constitution
- Staffing structure
- Roles and responsibilities

Resources

- Utilisation of plan and equipment

Financials

- ROI
- Profitability

ETHICAL CONSIDERATIONS

Marketing ethics are the principles and standards that define acceptable marketing conduct as determined by the various stakeholders, including government regulators, private interest groups, consumers, industry as well as the organisation itself. They go on to define an ethical issue as 'an identifiable problem, situation, or opportunity requiring a choice between several actions that must be evaluated as right or wrong'.

Increasingly organisations are being viewed not just on the products sold, but their ethical credentials. Many organisations publish a code of ethics, so stakeholders are aware of the standards that they can expect to be adhered to. There is generally an understanding that being ethical is the norm and in line with customer expectations.

Given the nature of distribution channels the following outlines a range of ethical considerations:

- Does the channel result in higher prices for the end user?

- Are prices open and transparent?

- Is product fit for purpose?

- Are staff sufficiently trained to ensure staff provide reliable and informed information?

- Changes to terms and conditions?

For e-channels the American Marketing Association (AMA) has developed a code of ethics. This inter alia refers to:

- Ethical practices being applied to stakeholders

- The rights and privacy and access to information

- Risks and polices relating to internet marketing

Marketing is concerned with delivering value through longer term relationships. Organisations therefore need to behave in such as way that stakeholders will want to continue working or buying from each other.

The examples below from Marks & Spencer and B&Q illustrate the importance that ethics play in society today.

Organisations need to be aware of the ramifications of their actions and a formal process of CSR needs to be established.

Figure 5.9 (Carroll, 1991) recognises the different stages an organisation goes through or remains at and is used to recognise and measure the dimensions of its CSR policy.

The pyramid suggests that there are four levels against which an organisation can measure itself.

Economic

At the very least an organisation has a responsibility to it stakeholders to be profitable so employees can continue to be employed and benefits can accrue to the local community. However, size can give an organisation undue influence over a sector.

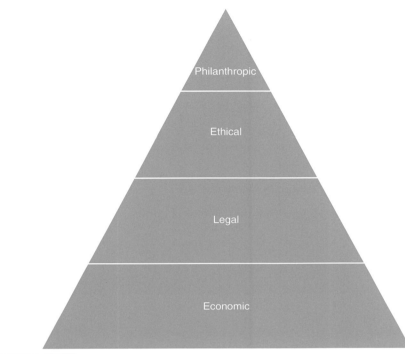

FIGURE 5.9 *The different stages an organisation goes through or remains at.*

Legal

It is expected that all organisations operate within the law, but where there are long distribution channels covering different countries this can prove problematical. Competition law and fair trade practices need to be considered. Often organisations will introduce their own polices on what is acceptable the law.

Ethical

Ethics define what is right and wrong by establishing a set of guiding principles for people or organisations to work to.

For many organisations the concept of ethics has been successfully use to gain new business. Marks & Spencer launched a high profile campaign in 2008 setting out a highly detailed ethical code.

Philanthropic

The ultimate 'corporate citizen' where it works in partnership with the local community for mutual gain.

Some ethical concerns include:

- Misleading or false advertising where the product or price is misleading

- Shocking, tasteless or indecent material

- High pressure sales techniques to encourage purchase when it may not be in the consumers' best interests

- Payment of bribes to secure business or keep competitors out of the distribution channel

- Reward systems should be open and fair

- Privacy and respect for members of the channel

B&Q'S SOCIAL RESPONSIBILITY

Ethical Trading

Our business has a direct impact on the lives of people all over the world and we are committed to doing business in a way which ensures that everyone in our supply chains benefits from trading with us. We believe that high workplace standards, good health and safety, and fair pay and employment conditions are all elements of a successful, professionally run business and contribute to its efficiency and productivity. Our approach is one of engagement with suppliers and workers and recognises and respects the cultural diversity within our supply chains.

Our customers want great products at great prices, but not at the expense of the people who make them. We are committed to sourcing products responsibly:

- **It is our policy to...**
- Only work with suppliers who share our aims and values
- Know which supplier is making every product we sell and where these products are being made
- Set and assess workplace standards for our suppliers' factories, including minimum standards which must be met as a condition of supply and higher standards which suppliers are required to meet within agreed timescales
- Work in partnership with our suppliers, governments and non-governmental organisations to address challenging issues within our supply chains
- Provide guidance and help to those factories making our products to help them achieve the required standards

Source: www.homeretailgroup.com

MARKS AND SPENCER STATEMENT OF ETHICS

Shareholders

Marks & Spencer is owned by the individuals and organisations that hold our shares. We are focused on building a sustainable business for the long term, generating shareholder value through consistent, profitable growth. We keep honest and accurate records of our performance, and are committed to transparent reporting. As an integral part of planning and review we have an ongoing process in place for identifying, evaluating and managing the significant risks to achieving business goals.

Suppliers

Marks & Spencer sources products from around the world, respecting third party rights and design integrity in order to provide customers with the best quality products at competitive prices. We work in partnership to ensure that all our suppliers comply with the requirements of our Global Sourcing Principles and over time adopt the recognised international standards contained in the Ethical Trading Initiative Base Code. We never give or accept improper payments or gifts in order to conduct business anywhere in the world.

Environment

The natural environment provides all the raw materials we need to operate our business. Marks & Spencer is committed to the principle of sustainable development which underpins our 'eco plan', Plan A. We have a responsibility to current and future generations to use natural resources in a responsible manner and to prevent unnecessary pollution. We include environmental considerations in all our decisions and specifications. We publicly report on our environmental (as well as social and governance) performance every year.

Source: http://corporate.marksandspencer.com/documents/specific/investors/governance/code_of_ethics.pdf

In the UK there has been an increasing trend for larger supermarket chains to purchase 'corner shops', or convenience stores. These shops would typically serve the needs of the local community by having long opening hours, but would charge a premium on the price for the goods sold.

Restrictions on opening out-of-town stores has meant that supermarkets have been looking for alternative locations and have been buying small local chains to increase their market share.

Local towns have been campaigning to retain their local stores and prevent the large supermarkets opening, because the residents claim the supermarkets are putting local shops out of business and people out of work.

CHANNEL INNOVATION

There are various definitions of what innovation is and innovation has already discussed in the broad sense of product development. Here the focus is on innovation in the distribution channel.

Innovation is concerned with the introduction of new aspects or procedures in the channel so that costs, efficiencies and customer satisfaction is improved.

In particular, intermediaries can offer new products as a result of their position in the channel and their relationship with other members. This could lead to improved customer delivery times through the introduction of more effective ordering systems.

EXAMPLE

Consider the following. A financial services organisation has 10 products in its portfolio and distributes its products through a network of 5000 outlets. Each outlet needs to maintain 5 weeks stock, because they only receive a distribution of marketing material on a monthly (four weekly basis). If each outlet sells 10 of each product, consider the cost savings to the organisation if distribution could be conducted on a weekly basis.

Through customer feedback, organisations may find that unacceptable level of goods are damaged upon receipt. New forms of packaging, or better procedures (training or the physical act of packaging) could reduce the complaints to a more acceptable (industry standard) level.

Increasingly the concept of just-in-time supply is being utilised. This often involves the introduction of sophisticated computerised ordering and product systems. Car manufacturers utilise this approach, e.g. as a completed car leaves the factory exit, new replacement components are being delivered to the entrance to be incorporated in to the next car. This requires the components manufacturer and the car manufacturer to work closely together to achieve these synergies.

Generating cost efficiencies is important. Competition in the market is usually intense and any additional margin that can be achieved can make a difference to sales.

While mass production techniques are important, technology now allows for customisation within the process. BMW effectively allows customers to design their own car in the showroom, while Mercedes-Benz has a similar offer, but will also allow the customer to collect the car off the production line.

Innovation can be linked to performance and growth through improvements in efficiency, productivity, quality, positioning, and market share and customer satisfaction. While it is evident that all organisations are capable of innovation, not all do, either because they choose not to, or do not have the processes in place to facilitate innovation.

It is important to recognise and reward innovation which brings about improvements However, innovation comes about through research and competitor analysis and a balance needs to be struck between the costs of research and development and the potential benefits to be derived.

Increasingly we are seeing trends in the market where organisations are actively seeking to reduce the number of intermediaries (not levels, but the physical number) to develop collaborative relationships to support innovation and added value; just-in-time supply is a good example of this concept. Organisations will work together towards joint targets and effect solutions to problems that individually would have been difficult to solve.

All organisations, whatever their shape or size, face the constant challenge of innovation. To be effective the process needs to be managed cross functionally and typically inter-disciplinary teams are formed to bring together a broad range of skills and knowledge.

NEW AND EMERGING CHANNELS

The cost of setting up a new distribution channel is costly and time consuming. A manufacturer who opens a new channel to market risks upsetting existing channel members if it is not handled sensitively and in line with any agreements in place.

The concept of emerging channels is fundamentally different and can radically change the way in which products are distributed and sold.

The 'corner shop' once operated by individuals who served the needs of the local economy is being replaced by the main UK supermarkets.

Supermarkets also have petrol stations located near the store and we are seeing supermarkets move into house sales, car retailing and, with the change in legislation, into legal services. All of which change the nature of the distribution channel and the way we purchase.

Banks in the early 1990s generally believed that the internet would speed up the rate at which bank branches would close. The feeling was that customers would prefer to bank via the internet as it offered convenience and flexibility. In fact branches did not close down and the internet became only another channel for customers to access their money.

E-marketing has brought about disintermediation, i.e. eliminating channel members who no longer have a role to play. The internet had a major impact on the travel industry. It spawned the arrival of no-frills airlines that embraced technology and allowed customers to design their own travel itinerary which was a serious concern to travel agents. While this goes against the role of intermediaries, i.e. they are there to bring a range of products to the end user when they need it, the internet has brought a new type of intermediary who 'aggregates' products in one place and this in turn has brought about reintermediation i.e. the addition of a new channel member.

The role of the internet is to challenge conventional channels, which will need to adapt if they are to remain successful. Tesco, Asda and Sainsbury's are integrating the on-line shopping channel with the more conventional trip to the supermarket.

Consider the impact of Amazon and I-Tunes on the purchase and distribution of books and music.

While the extranet is a useful way for organisations to communicate with each other, it also a useful tool to manage distribution channels. Selected stakeholders will be given access to a specific area of the website where a range of key information can be accessed. Key management information can be located on the extranet allowing stakeholder's access to a pool of data covering (for example) supply dates, volume discounts, and transaction levels.

Where there is no market sensitivity to data, catalogues known as e-catalogues can be posted on the website. Other uses of the web include:

- CMS-contract management systems that replace many of the paper-based systems previously used in distribution channels. Legal agreements can be issued through CMS along with performance management, i.e. how well the intermediary performs against targets.

- E-commerce, payment to and from intermediaries. This can cover automated invoicing or the movement of funds between the various intermediaries.

- EDI (Electronic Data Interchange) where standard documents used between the parties can be accessed.

While new channels do not have to be technology based, increasingly this is the case. The following offers a summary of the impact of emerging channels:

- *Quality of service:* the Royal Mail and other courier companies offer services which allow the customer to track exactly where the item is located.

- *Greater product ranges:* different channels can stock different product ranges.

- *Low costs*: through the elimination of intermediaries (see Chapter 6) that can be replaced by cheaper electronic channels.

- *Virtual channels* can be established through a 'virtual' group of intermediaries located around the globe.

- *Team working and partnerships* are improved. Electronic channels can allow existing members to access information that would have been difficult to obtain in a timely fashion.

QUESTIONS

1. What are the four key functions of a distribution channel?

2. In what circumstances would an organisation go 'direct' to customers rather than using a longer distribution channel?

3. What are the difficulties involved in long distribution channels?

4. Outline the three types of VMS channel.

5. What are the three advantages of a joint venture approach when selling to an overseas market?

SUMMARY

This chapter has outlined the different distribution channels and strategies available to an organisation in order to get its product(s) to the customer. Selecting the 'right' channel is essential if an organisation wants to secure wide distribution for its products in a fast and efficient way.

Competitors who may also be part of the distribution channel will be similarly concerned with the same factors. The cost of establishing a channel is expensive and should be selected on the basis of a long lasting relationship. However, markets change and the channels should be continually monitored against an agreed set of criteria to ensure they are constantly effectively and offer the right balance between control of the product and access to a wider market.

Longer channels are more complex to manage and any internal dimension makes the process management of control critical.

BIBLIOGRAPHY

Brassington, F. and Pettitt, S. (2006) *Principles of Marketing*, 4th edition. FT Prentice Hall.

Camp, P.E. (1989) *Benchmarking: The search for industry best practices that lead to superior performance*, New York: ASQC Quality Press.

Caroll, A. (1991) The pyramid of corporate social responsibility: toward the moral management of organisational stakeholders. *Business horizons*, July–August, 42.

Cateora, P.R. (1993) *International Marketing*, 8th edition. Irwin.

Fill, C. (2006) *Marketing Communications: Engagement, strategies and practice*, 4th edition. FT Prentice Hall.

Kotler, P., Armstrong, G., Saunders, J. and Wong, V. (1999) *Principles of Marketing*, 2nd European edition. Prentice Hall.

Paliwoda, S. (1993) *International Marketing*. Butterworth-Heinemann.

Palamountain, J. (1955) *The Politics of Distribution*. Harvard Business Press.

Intermediaries

At the end of this chapter you will be able to :
- Examine the various types of intermediaries in the distribution channel
- Assess the role and responsibilities of intermediaries

INTRODUCTION

Having examined the different types of channel strategies, we will now assess the nature and scope of intermediaries and assess the criteria for selecting partners and the impact that different intermediaries can have on an organisation.

The selection criteria must be robust, as each intermediary will bring a selection of strengths and weaknesses which need to be exploited, or overcome in the case of weaknesses. Their roles must be clearly defined and the financial benefit an intermediary can add must be clearly determined.

TYPE OF INTERMEDIARIES

An intermediary is an organisation or individual through which goods pass on their way from the manufacturing organisation to the consumer.

There are different types of intermediary. Each intermediary has a different role to fulfill which may also include taking legal ownership of the goods, adding some form of value (e.g. customer service), volume (i.e. storing goods) and/or then selling smaller quantities to other intermediaries or the end user. The types of intermediary and descriptions of their roles is shown in Table 6.1.

Table 6.1	Intermediaries and descriptions of their roles
Type of intermediary	**Description**
Wholesalers	Not usually consumer facing, but will typically deal with other intermediaries in the channel. Ownership of the product is a feature along with physical possession.
	Will usually take in bulk and distribute to other intermediaries in smaller quantities. Wholesalers can be categorised into:
	■ *Merchant wholesalers*: independently owned businesses that take title to the goods and includes full-service and limited service wholesalers (see below)
	■ *Full service wholesalers*: These wholesalers offer services such as maintaining stock levels. They will have a sales team and offer credit facilities. Additionally they will provide a delivery service. There are two types of full-service wholesaler: wholesale merchants and industrial distributors.
	■ Wholesale merchants: Sell primarily to retailers and offer full range of services
	■ Industrial distributors: Sell to manufacturers rather than retailers and similarly offer credit and delivery services
	■ *Limited service wholesalers*: As the name implies they offer a reduced level of services and include: cash-and-carry and mail order wholesalers.
	■ Cash-and carry: this group carries a small to medium range of goods typically fast moving consumer goods which are sold to small retailers mainly for cash
	■ Mail order: responsible for distributing catalogues through the post or courier
Retailers	Consumer-facing and will have purchased the products from the wholesaler (above) or direct from the manufacturer.
	Takes ownership and physical possession and sells direct to the consumer.
	Retailers vary in size, product and location. Examples of retailers include: supermarkets, department stores, convenience stores, speciality stores and factory outlets.
Distributors/Dealer	Distributors have the right to sell the products in a defined geographical area and can add value to the product by making it available locally to the consumer. Dealers add value by offering their expertise as well as representing the manufacturer. They don't always take ownership of the product and typically represent the manufacturer, e.g. a car dealership
Franchisees	The most common franchise allows the franchisee (the person or business who has the contract) to sell a specific product or service in accordance with the terms agreed with the franchisor. In return for a payment (fixed fee, percentage of turnover or both) the franchisor shares much of the intellectual property rights of running the business.

(Continued)

Table 6.1	(Continued)
Type of intermediary	**Description**
Licensee	Similar to a franchise, but the not as comprehensive. Typically the licensee is given the right to operate a business for a particular organisation within a given area.

Agents/brokers	This group of intermediaries will act on behalf of the organisation, but will not take ownership or legal title to the product. Their role is to generate wider distribution and make the product more accessible to the customer.
	
	■ *Brokers*: Their role is primarily to bring the buyer together with the seller. They do not hold any stock and get paid by the manufacturer when the sale has been completed. A typical example would be an insurance broker.
	■ Agents: There are four types of agent: manufacturers, selling, purchasing and commission merchants.
	  ■ Manufacturer's agent: sell similar lines from more than one manufacturer. A formal contract is agreed between the parties and are often used when a manufacturer cannot afford its own sales force.
	  ■ Selling agent: A selling agent has the ability to sell a manufacturer's entire range.
	  ■ Purchasing agent: These agents will buy goods, receive them and inspect them for quality.
	  ■ Commission merchants: Here possession of the goods is obtained and takes a range of goods to a central point to be sold. Payment is by way of commission.

THE ROLE OF THE INTERMEDIARY

The role of the intermediary is to simplify the distribution process add value and reduce costs.

Consider one manufacturer that has 10 buyers. If another buyer enters the market and has the same 10 buyers, then 20 separate journeys are being made to the buyers. What would be the effect of both manufacturers of using one intermediary to make the deliveries? Multiply the effect hundreds of times and the benefits will readily be seen.

Webster (1979) suggests there are three groups of value-added service provided by intermediaries as seen in Figure 6.1:

- facilitating
- transactional
- logistics

FIGURE 6.1

Three groups of value-added service provided by intermediaries (Webster, 1979).

Facilitating	Transactional	Logistics
Finance training information after sales	Risk marketing administration	Stock storage transport bulk breaking

Table 6.2	Intermediary tasks
Element	**Description**
Information	Collection and distribution of market research and intelligence data, such as sales data to help the planning process.
Management	Setting objectives and channel plans along with any risk that needs to be taken or managed.
Matching	Adjusting the offer to fit a buyer's needs, including grading, assembling and packaging.
Promotion	Setting promotional objectives and communicating through the different tools.
Price	Setting pricing policies and financing policies.
Distribution	Managing the transport, storing and stock control of goods.
Customer service	Providing channels for advice support and after sales service.
Relationships	Facilitating communication and maintaining relationships in the channel.

Intermediaries may perform one of more of these tasks. Beamish and Ashford (2008) have broken these elements down and Table 6.2 is based on their assessment.

SELECTING CHANNEL INTERMEDIARIES

The final stage of developing a new channel is to select those organisations that are going to undertake the various roles within the channel.

Channel members are appointed as part of a channel strategy, when a number of intermediaries may be appointed, or when circumstances require a new appointment. There are various reasons to appoint a new channel member including:

- Unsatisfactory performance of an existing member

- Intermediary ceases trading or declines to renew contact

- Conflicts of interest

- Expansion of the network requiring new intermediaries and skills

- Market expansion

Selection is important and is usually undertaken against set criteria. Brassington and Pettitt (2006) offer a range of criteria which is broken down into strategic and operational criteria.

An organisation will have its own selection criteria based on it specific needs.

> The notion of reverse selection should be noted. Intermediaries are often looking for different manufacturers to meet customer needs. Also it is not always feasible for an intermediary to stock an ideal range of manufacturers' products, so some selectivity or prioritisation has to be made.

IMPACT OF INTERMEDIARIES ON PROFITABILITY

It has already been stated that the role of the intermediary is to add value and reduce costs and an important consequence of this is to increase the manufacturer's overall profitability.

Intermediaries provide a range of services that the manufacturer may not have the skills or resources to undertake. A manufacturer may be skilled in manufacturing widgets but will not have the capability to ship the goods overseas.

Intermediaries can impact on profitability in the following ways:

- *Increased sales*: the intermediary will can have its own sales team with an expert knowledge of the domestic and overseas markets

- As the intermediary will often take ownership of the goods, it will also *take responsibility for taking stock away from the manufacturer*, so if goods do not sell this will not impact on the manufacturer's profits

- *Packaging together* of groups of products to widen customer choice and appeal

- *Efficiency*: rather than dealing with possibly hundreds of retailer, distribution and hence control can be managed through a few (for example) wholesalers

- *Warehousing and transport costs can be shared* with other organisations, which may also eliminate the need for purpose-built facilities

- The value added by the intermediary may allow the price of the product to be *premium priced*.

QUESTIONS

1. What are the main advantages of using a wholesaler as an intermediary?

2. Why is innovation important in a distribution channel?

3. What are the main impacts that new electronic channels will have on current ones?

4. What are the key criteria for selecting intermediaries?

SUMMARY

This chapter has identified the different types of intermediaries involved in distribution channels. Each intermediary has a set of strengths and weakness associated with it and of course the channel can have a number of intermediaries either vertically or horizontally.

The choice of intermediary is crucial and the selection process must take into consideration not only its innovative capabilities, but the potential roles and responsibilities it will be required to take and the impact it will have on overall profitability.

Markets are not static and channels will need to change or adapt in line with market conditions. However, this should be a proactive, rather than reactive, process if competitive advantage is to be maintained.

BIBLIOGRAPHY

Beamish, K. and Ashford, R. (2008) *Marketing Planning*. Butterworth-Heinemann.
Brassington, F. and Pettitt, S. (2006) *Principles of Marketing*. FT Prentice Hall.
Webster, F. (1979) *Industrial Marketing Strategy*. John Wiley & Sons.

Stakeholders

At the end of this chapter you will be able to:

- **Analyse the role of stakeholders within the distribution channel**
- **Examine the factors which cause conflict in both domestic and international channels**

INTRODUCTION

Channel members are also stakeholders (Johnson and Scholes, 2005).

We have seen that the distribution channel is a complex web of relationships and this chapter explores the concept of stakeholders in more detail, outlines the 'six' markets model and examines the concept of stakeholder analysis.

Organisations use intermediaries or distributors to get their products to the consumer and the various intermediaries will themselves have relationships with other suppliers' distributors, i.e. multiple stakeholders, and the importance of building relationships with these groups needs to be understood.

Such a diverse stakeholder group often presents organisational difficulties, i.e. how do you manage the relationships effectively as so many different divisions are involved in the process, so that there is coordinated effort and communication?

WHAT ARE STAKEHOLDERS?

Stakeholders are those individuals or groups who depend on the organisation to fulfil their own goals and on whom, in turn, the organisation depends.

113

Stakeholders can be categorised into three groups:

- Internal
- Connected
- External

Channel members are connected stakeholders, i.e. have an economic or contractual relationship with the organisation.

Fill (2006) suggests that there are two main concerns when moving a product through the distribution channel:

- Management of the product (supply chain)
- Management of the intangible aspects of ownership and the communication between the different stakeholders

Our focus has been on the latter aspect and we will continue to examine this in more detail by determining the needs of the individual stakeholders within the channel.

We will see later in the chapter that stakeholders build up a complex set of relationships and that the various members of the channel can in fact be customers of each other and a series of networks can be established.

Organisations enter into partnerships because they see mutual benefit and an important element of maintaining these mutually beneficial relationships is the communication that takes place between the stakeholders.

It is necessary to understand the needs of stakeholders and this can be achieved through a stakeholder audit.

Having identified who the key stakeholders are through the process of mapping they are grouped together to identify the interdependencies between the stakeholders and establish any networks that may have been established.

The strength of the relationships can then be assessed along with the 'fit' of stakeholder with the organisation's objectives. This will then determine the nature of the communications that will need to take place.

The analysis will include:

- What are the needs, concerns and interests of the stakeholders?
- What power and influence do the stakeholders have on each other and the channel as a whole?
- Are there are any conflicts or potential conflicts in the channel?

STAKEHOLDER NEEDS

The exact needs of stakeholders will vary between organisations. Table 7.1 sets out the generic needs of stakeholders.

Table 7.1	Supplier and intermediary needs

Suppliers

- Will want to build long term relationships, so that any costs invested in the channel will be recovered with an acceptable financial margin
- Participative relationship which allows for innovation and efficiency in the systems and processes used
- Clarity of information through well documented processes and SLAs so that errors are minimised
- Clear process for tending or applying for new business
- Terms of payment clearly stated and payments made within the agreed time agreed
- Clear CSR policy

Intermediaries

- Clear CSR policy, particularly relating to sourcing of materials
- Continuity of supply, e.g. components and parts
- Transparent remuneration policy, especially with other members of the channel
- Clear rules on competition
- Clarity on roles and responsibilities within the channel

Other stakeholders include:

- Shareholders

- Customers

- Financial providers

The needs of these stakeholders are also considered in Table 7.2.

MANAGING STAKEHOLDERS

The six markets framework (Figure 7.1) highlights the key stakeholder markets (sometimes referred to as 'market domains') enabling an organisation to manage relationships more effectively. The model reflects the fact that not all stakeholders are equally as important and distinct must be made.

Christopher *et al.* (2002) suggests that markets should be defined more broadly as being 'one in which the competing interests are made visible and therefore more likely to be managed'.

Customer Markets

Relationship marketing has at its heart that an organisation must build lasting relationships with customers and the customer market is central to the six markets model.

Table 7.2	Stakeholder needs

Financial providers

- On-going relationship to capture new business opportunities
- Capable management team
- Regular financial and monthly accounts to ensure that any finance extended can be repaid in accordance with the loan agreement

Shareholders

- Acceptable financial return recognising the level of risk associated with the investment
- Market for the buying and selling of shares (deepening on the legal status of the organisation)
- Top class management team so that opportunities for business growth can be identified and implemented leading to improved financial returns

Customers

The saying 'The customer is King' is still important today. If the customers do not like the product, or the way it is sold they will look elsewhere to satisfy their needs.

- Acceptable product at an acceptable price (will be a range of options in terms of acceptable price depending on product and segment)
- Ease of purchase through a range of channels
- Enjoyable purchasing experience.

FIGURE 7.1   *The six markets framework highlights the key stakeholder markets.*

The customer market reflects the distribution channel and its exact composition was discussed in Chapter 5.

But as a reminder; channels can be short, i.e. direct to the consumer. This is often used in financial services where a customer will make a purchase direct from a high street branch. B2B organisations include more complex examples, when wholesalers, distributors and retailers are included.

Organisations often develop informal referral groups, which as well as generating additional income also adds value to the customer proposition.

Referral Markets

Organisations work with their customers to move them through the ladder of loyalty so that they act as advocates actively marketing the organisation. However, non-customers such as third party introducers will also refer customers.

Customer recommendations are an important source of new business across all sectors and here business is directed to the supplier through sales leads.

Christopher *et al.* (2002) breaks this category down into:

- Customer referrals
  - Advocacy referrals
  - Company initiates customer referrals
- Non-customer referrals
  - General
  - Reciprocal
  - Incentive-based
  - Staff

Internal Markets

Internal markets are linked to two things: first, how staff within the company interact with each other to meet the goals and expectations of the company. The second involves the idea that every staff member is a potential customer – every person is both a supplier and a customer.

Influence Markets

The B2B market has a more formal purchasing process known as the DMU (Decision Making Unit), also referred to as the buying centre. The individual members of the DMU can exert influences on the buying process and therefore each member needs to be carefully managed.

There are many external influences that impact on an organisation and these include:

- Government (local and central)
- Pressure groups
- Shareholders
- Press and media generally
- Trade Unions

It can be a long list and it is generally recognised that the influence market includes the most diverse group of stakeholders.

Supplier and Alliance Markets

The supplier and alliance market refers to the partnerships an organisation builds with the supply chain in order to build efficient, cost effective value-adding activities.

Christopher *et al.* (2002) suggest that supplier and alliance markets are viewed separately:

- *Supplier markets:* are suppliers who provide the organisation with the physical resources such as components, or the raw materials that go into the product. It is recognised the physical product can be augmented by services.

- *Alliance markets:* also suppliers but supply competencies and knowledge-based capabilities. Often this market develops because the organisation needed to outsource any activity previously undertaken in-house as part of the value chain. Collaboration, joint promotions, and strategic alliances are examples of alliance markets.

Recruitment Markets

Increasingly people are becoming scarce resources and therefore organisations need to recruit, train and maintain the 'best' staff.

Organisations are not bound by geographical boundaries and will look to recruit staff from across the globe if necessary in order to ensure the continuity of the resource.

The recruitment can be categorised into:

- The *external labour market:* i.e. those people who have the skills to work for the organisation wherever they are located. Potential employees can interface directly with the organisation or through third parties (see below).

■ *Third parties:* this group of people or organisations can facilitate access to the organisation or act as an access channel. This group includes:

❏ Recruitment agencies

❏ Executive search consultancies

❏ Universities

❏ Colleges

❏ Staff

STRENGTHS IN NUMBERS

Charities are discovering that it pays to work together, but this doesn't mean they need to sacrifice their own identities.

The old mantra that two heads are better than one is increasingly ringing true for UK charities. Partnerships and collaborative working is increasing as the voluntary sectors role in public service, delivery and campaigning grows.

The special unit set up at the national Council for Voluntary Organisations (NCVO) to provide a central source of information and advice on all forms of joint working has seen a fivefold increase in hits on its website.

To many voluntary organisations, working in partnership means the chance to split costs and share ideas. At the same time service users stand to gain a double dose of experience and expertise.

Coalitions, formed by various groups joining forces for lobbying and policy work, are also on the rise.

Partnerships of service delivery charities are similarly increasing. In 2005, the NSPCC and The Children's Society set up a special IT company, Charityshare, that merged the organisations' helpdesk, training and technical support. Technical staff were housed at the NSPCC's head office while service staff remained at the Children's Society. The partnership saved an estimated £800,000 per year through sharing back office functions.

'Working in partnership is increasingly offering us more opportunities to access wider groups of service users,' says Liz Woods, operations director at disabled education charity LearnLinks. It joined with local group the Hampshire Deaf Association (HDA) to run the SeneAbility project which received funding from the LSC (Learning Skills Council). By then end of the first year the two charities had combined their expertise with visually and orally impaired service users, trained more than 50 learning advisers and helped more than 200 people to access educational opportunities. But not all the benefits are without problems. In Hampshire for example, under the terms of the two charities' relationships, LearningLinks worked as the lead partner and was directly accountable to the funder, which on occasions caused tensions.

But because the parameters of the relationship and protocols were set and managed through steering committees, problems were easy resolved.

Clashing cultures and different management styles can also create problems with smaller charities feeling robbed of recognition and accreditation by a large household name partner.

The Association of Charity Chief Executives of Voluntary Organisations (Acevo) warns that charities must be aware of all potential pitfalls before rushing headlong into a relationship. 'It's really important to work out whether there really are shared goals or whether the differences between the organisations might lead to conflict over outcomes or working practices,' says Nick Aldridge, Avecos's director of strategy and communication.

Yet in the last few years the number of charities working together has been increasing with the realisation that information and skills can be shared while retaining their own identity.

Source: Adapted from an article written by Annie Kelly in *The Guardian* 13 June 2007.

THE NATURE OF THE STAKE

The nature of the relationship with individual stakeholders helps an organisation to:

- Recognise the role played by the stakeholder, its contribution to the channel, the implications of it not being there, and identify any potential conflicts which may arise through its relationship with other channel members or the extended enterprise.

- Keep the stakeholder motivated to ensure customer needs are met.

Channel members may have contractual, i.e. legal agreements to provide a specific role; failure to comply brings a range of penalties in law if the members have failed to carry out their responsibilities in the agreed manner, typically this would be seen in an Administered VMS.

However, there may be no legal agreement and through informal arrangements the member provided added-value services such as expertise, knowledge, resources or facilities.

Developing a distribution channel requires careful planning. The costs involved can be significant especially if a new facility, e.g. warehousing, is needed, or overseas selling becomes a feature. Consequently organisations will look to build long-term and lasting relationships with channel members as it is not in anyone's interests to start deconstructing the channel because of the additional (and unnecessary) costs and the additional work, which detracts from the main purpose of sales and customer service.

Stakeholder Power

Having built a distribution channel we will see later that problems can arise and it is helpful to examine the 'power' that the various stakeholders can exert in the management of the channel.

Channels can take different forms and the stakeholders will need to agree roles and responsibilities. Stakeholders get their power from a range of sources.

Legitimate Power

Legitimate power arises from any legal agreement which may have been written to formalise the relationship between the parties.

An intermediary may have been appointed to undertake specific roles and therefore it can challenge anyone or any organisation that does not comply with the roles given to it.

Legitimate also arises through a process of delegation where an organisation (or individual) allows their own power to be given to another party.

Expert Power

An expert power intermediary may be appointed because of the skills or knowledge they possess. An international shipping company may be used to post products to customers, or because of the value added by the organisation.

Resource Power

This refers to the management of resources by the organisation. The intermediary may have been appointed because of the availability of talent resources (people) in bringing the product more effectively to the customer.

Referent Power

Here power arises from the quality of the organisation because of its reputation in the market or the strength of its brand.

Coercive Power

A dominant supplier in the distribution channel may withhold supply or work.

Brassington and Pettitt (2006) also cite 'dependency' as another source of power. Here intermediaries actually cannot survive with each other and there is mutual dependency on each other.

Channels perform effectively when all the stakeholders are working together; otherwise the objectives initially set may be compromised and conflict between the members develops.

It must be clear where the balance of power lies. It does not necessarily need to rest with the manufacturer. However, having identified the channel leader, it must clearly guide the other channel members.

The different forms of power dependency raise another interesting area and that is 'atmosphere'.

ACTIVITY 7.1

For your own organisation, or one you are familiar with, identify who the key stakeholders are.

CONFLICT MANAGEMENT

We have seen that cooperation between channel members delivers the best results.

No matter how good the planning process has been, conflict within the channel is likely to occur at some point and some form of conflict resolution mechanisms must be in place to deal with them. Shipley and Egan (1992) define conflict as 'the breakdown or deterioration in the levels of cooperation between the partners'.

Conflict is a disagreement between two or more intermediaries with different or parties with different views or principles. It can arise from a huge variety of specific issues, or more general areas.

Brassington and Pettitt (2006) suggest examples that include exclusivity, payment terms, profit margins, appointment of new channel members, lack of information or cooperation.

National Savings and Investments (NS&I) for many years had exclusive rights to sell its range of savings and investment products through the Post Office. To broaden its product range Post Office now offers products through another provider – Bank of Ireland (BOI). NS&I and BOI products compete for business at the Post Office.

In 2008 numerous organisations reduced the payments made to channel members, citing the economic downturn. Members had to accept the reduced payment terms, or seek alternative business opportunities. It subsequently transpired many members had no contracts and therefore legally there was no redress, but the ethical dimensions must be questioned.

Brassington and Pettitt (2006) suggest there are two different types of conflict; manifest and underlying conflict, which can then be grouped into five areas.

- *Manifest:* open conflict between the channel members which may potentially prevent achievement of the channel objectives/goals. Clear procedures need to be in place to address the problem.

- *Underlying:* while not overt, underlying conflict can easily develop into manifest conflict. It is important to identify the conflict at an early opportunity and take action in order to prevent the cessation of cooperation between channel members

Table 7.3, based on Brassington and Pettitt (2006), outlines the five areas for underlying conflicts.

Conflict in the channel, whether it is manifest or underlying, causes tension within the channel. It must be addressed if the organisations involved are to achieve their stated objectives. Some channels, as we have seen, are a simply a group of organisations that come together without any form of legal agreement and will exert a range of influences on channel members.

Some members will have significant influence over members; this can be termed power dependency.

Table 7.3	Underlying conflict areas
Areas of conflict	**Summary**
Incompatible goals	Members of the channel disagree on a range of issues, including strategy, new ways of doing things, or financial returns.
	■ A manufacturer may want to widen the channel to open new markets, by opening up new markets. Existing members my object because additional investment maybe necessary or it conflicts with their other business.
	■ A retailer who is failing to achieve target margins, may want to reduce the amount of stock held to reduce costs and improve margins
Role conflict	Members of the channel cannot agree on the role each should take.
	■ The manufacturer believes the retailer should take responsibility for managing the promotional aspects at point of sale. However, the retailer may not agree, believing the manufacturer has more experience.
Domain differences	This concerns who should make the marketing decisions
Perceptions of reality	Different channel members may interpret issues in different ways
	■ In the Post Office example above, NS&I could see BOI as a threat, whereas the Post Office saw it as an opportunity to expand the business.
Expectations	Changed circumstances may bring about a change in the way channel members may want to do things differently should be done in the future.
	■ A downturn in the British economy causes a manufacturer to consider its options. It decides to reduce production by 50% for six months and maintain margins. Channel members may prefer to see price and margin reductions, but try to expand the market.

Power dependency can manifest itself in a number of ways;

■ *Reward power:* where one channel member has the ability to reward another member

■ *Coercive power:* rather than rewarding a channel member, so a form of penalty could be imposed

■ *Expert power:* where the member is seen as having some specialist knowledge not easily replaceable

While conflict is generally not to be encouraged, if managed correctly it can improve a distribution channel. A member who runs a distribution depot may express concern at the length of time goods have to remain in storage before being transported to the retail stores. Rather than demand extra money, a better solution would be to re-engineer the process to make it more effective which is to the benefit of the entire channel.

At the heart of any relationship is the concept of trust.

Trust is the 'belief that another company will perform actions that will result in positive outcomes fro the firm, as well as not take any unexpected actions that would result in negative outcomes for the firm' (Anderson and Naurus, 1986).

When trust is lost within the channel it is much harder to build back relationships as the stakeholders are less likely to share information that limits the depth of the relationship.

Communication and information exchange between channel members builds trust, promotes supportive relationships and minimises conflict.

It has been suggested by Leuthesser and Kohli (1995) that information can be exchanged between channel members in three different ways:

- Initiating behaviour

- Signalling behaviour

- Disclosing

Initiating behaviour involves a better understanding the needs of the stakeholders so that they can add greater value to the process, and also ensures that cooperation improves the position of the parties with the channel.

Signalling behaviour involves the giving of additional information to the stakeholders in advance about future changes that may be about to take place

Finally signalling behaviour occurs where one stakeholder gives information that may affect the other position.

Trust offers the opportunity to engage in mutually beneficial behaviour and encourage openness.

Regaining trust reduces the effects of any damage caused by previous conflict and helps to build back relationships quickly.

Transparency also helps address conflict by developing a mutual understanding of the various parties needs possibly through the exchange of information which supports the concepts of trust and commitment.

Building commitment, which is the desire of one or more stakeholders to continue in a relationship, also contributes to overcoming conflict.

Conflict is clearly best avoided but once identified needs to be managed effectively and some guiding principles have been given above.

In practice, organisations will need to have in place a comprehensive set of procedures, e.g. service level agreements, regular meetings, key account management or research to identify potential issues that can then be addressed through cross organisational visits and training. In addition supporting communication through internet or extranet access, emails and briefings will help to reduce the conflict.

COMMUNICATION IN THE CHANNEL

The responsibility for communication must rest with the channel leader or a nominated party. The role of communication is to improve the overall performance of the channel network.

The communication consists of two components:

- *Data flows:* the operational, i.e. day-to-day, information that flows across the channel.

- *Marketing communications:* the use of the promotional mix designed to influence the channel to take a particular course of action. Other purposes include motivation, goodwill and understanding.

The data flows between organisations can extend beyond operational and cover market and strategic data flows.

Communication needs to be consistent and coordinated to ensure the shared values and attitudes of the various stakeholders are maintained.

SUMMARY

Stakeholders offer an organisation a number of potential advantages if managed correctly. As has been noted, no matter how strong the relationship is, conflict can arise. Processes should be put in place when the relationship commences so that when the inevitable arises, it will have been anticipated and can be dealt with through existing systems and structures. At the heart of any relationship is the notion of trust, which should be nurtured and managed.

Effective communication is an important part of channel management and needs to be clearly coordinated and managed ideally by the channel leader.

Finally the important contribution by stakeholders in getting products to market quickly through efficient transport or distribution systems, or their expert knowledge of the market should not be ignored.

QUESTIONS

1. What do you understand by the term 'stakeholder'?

2. How does conflict arise?

3. How can conflict be managed?

4. What is the role of communication in channels?

BIBLIOGRAPHY

Anderson, J. and Naurus, J. (1986) Towards a better understanding of distribution channels working relationships. In: Bachaus, K. and Wilson, D. (eds) *Industrial Marketing: A German-American Perspective*. Springer-Verlag.

Brassington, F. and Pettitt, S. (2006) *Principles of Marketing*, 4th edition. FT Prentice Hall.

Christopher, M., Payne, A. and Ballantyne, D. (2002) *Relationship Marketing: Creating Stakeholder Value*. Butterworth-Heinemann.

Fill, C. (2006) *Marketing Communications: Engagement, Strategies and Practice*, 4th edition. FT Prentice Hall.

Johnson, G. and Scholes, K. (2005) *Exploring Corporate Strategy*. FT Prentice Hall.

Shipley, D. and Egan, C. (1992) Brewer-tenant distribution channels. *International Journal of Service Industry Management*, 3, 44–62.

CHAPTER 8

Contractual Requirements and Service Level Agreements (SLAs)

LEARNING OBJECTIVES

At the end of this chapter you will be able to:

- Analyse the role of service level agreements within the distribution channel
- Evaluate and apply performance monitoring of Key Performance Indicators

INTRODUCTION

This final chapter on channel management looks at two specific issues: contractual requirements and service level agreements (SLAs).

Organisations need to be reassured that the investments made in developing customer-focused channels will be rewarded through satisfied customers and the prospect of an acceptable return on their money.

While many organisations may have worked together for many years and 'trust' has been the foundation of the relationship, increasingly organisations are formalising their relationships through contracts and service level agreements. This ensures that when things do go wrong each of the parties to the agreement can adopt a specific course of action to correct the situation. Of course if the contracts are well written the consequences will have been anticipated and action taken proactively to address.

THE LEGAL FRAMEWORK

When organisations come together to do business they do so for mutual benefit. The guiding principles and rational for the mutual exchange should have been enshrined in the organisations' strategic planning process. However, organisations that trade overseas are also subject to national and local government influences in the countries in which they operate and will have to adhere to the legislative and competitive framework that applies. This will cover aspects such as contract law, protection for consumers, finance, competition and trading practice.

In the UK, parliament is responsible for passing legislation, but increasingly implementation is the responsibility of other bodies such as the Office of Fair Trading (OFT). Within Europe we are seeing an approach to standardise legalisation across member states and for some organisations this will be welcome news.

Legislation is most profound in the area of competition and the affect of legislations can still favour local rather than international suppliers and this is still particularly true in Germany and Denmark.

In the international economy there is no one legal system and the organisation that uses different channels in different countries will in effect be responsible for adhering to the laws of each of the countries in which it operates.

Within Europe, there is legislation that prevents distributors selling outlside their allocated territory in response to unsolicited enquiries.

Another consideration to note is the concept of product quality standards. Globalisation is pushing standards higher and often smaller players in the market find they cannot meet the minimum standards and therefore have no choice other than to leave the market, which is then left to the bigger players to dominate.

Common law which has guided legal systems in most countries of the world, requires disputes to be solved on the basis of tradition, common practice and the interpretation of existing statutes.

Civil law on the other hand, has at its basis that all foreseeable circumstances are identified and codes of law are then written for the various legal sectors such as commercial, civil or common applications. This includes issues such as copying, the use of brand names, impact on the nature and profitability of international trade.

Different industry standards may require that a product is modified for the local market, which in reality can mean a different product for each market in extreme circumstances. Products must also be sold in the unit of measurement applicable to the market, so a pint, or litre. But different countries have different sized pints!

CONTRACTUAL REQUIREMENTS

A range of contractual issues are identified below.

Restricted Sales Area

A producer will often grant a specific geographical area (postcode area, town, or region) to an intermediary such as an agent or distributor. This is favoured by the parties as it is clear who has responsibility for sales, or business development. The intermediary can identify the sale potential within the designated area and confirm its viability. The legality of granting such a territory has been challenged in court and apparently conflicting judgements made. While clarity is sought, organisations must continue to be cautious in the approach.

Tying Contract

In return for the rights to sell a particular product, producers may insist that intermediaries must purchase other items as well. Often this is done to encourage sales of weaker items, however, in some situations a manufacturer will insist on arrange of products being supplied. A good example of this is in a franchise, where the franchisee is required to purchase a range of ancillary products from the franchisor generally for reasons of consistency.

Exclusive Deal

A producer may insist that an intermediary does not stock competitor products, i.e. offers an exclusive deal only. This affords the producer significant protection, but it will generally be permissible if similar products are available.

Refusal to Deal

Producers, as we have seen earlier, go to considerable trouble to select the right distributor for their products. Equally they may choose not to allow certain intermediaries to distribute their products for a variety of reasons such as image or cost.

Levi, the jeans manufacturer, became involved in a high profile court case because it refused to supply Tesco with its jeans. Tesco was sourcing the jeans through an alternative channel and wanted to sell the jeans for around £10, which was considerably less than other retailers. Tesco argued that value for money offers made Tesco a success and Levi argued that selling the jeans so cheaply devalued the quality of the Levy brand. Tesco lost the case.

SERVICE LEVEL AGREEMENTS (SLAs)

The concept of product guarantees or warranties is nothing new, the idea of offering customers some form of guaranteed level of service is a lot less established, but growing steadily.

It is also worth making the point that a guaranteed level of service does not just apply to service organisations. It has been demonstrated tangible products can also have an intangible dimension to them and therefore the concept of service guarantees can apply across a wide range of organisations.

A service level agreement (SLA) sets outs the minimum level of service a third party can expect to receive measured against set dimensions.

The SLA has three main objectives, which are to:

- Act as a point of differentiation
- Improve quality
- Improve customer service

Organisations, particularly those offering some form of service, are generally considered to be similar (e.g. financial service providers), so establishing some form of differentiation can be seen as a competitive advantage.

> Some examples:
> ' Our calls centres are open 24 hours, 365 days of the year'
> ' All our call centres are in the UK'
> ' We aim to have an engineer with you within 24 hours'

The SLA is usually written or published on the organisation's website and should:

- Clearly establish the organisations' needs
- Simplify complex issues so that they are clearly understood by both parties
- Reduce areas of conflict by identifying them at the outset of the relationship
- Encourage dialogue in the event of disputes to work toward an acceptable solution
- Encourage realistic expectations

However, the production of an SLA is the end of the journey, not the start as we have seen earlier.

In developing an SLA an organisation needs to consider five aspects (Palmer, 2005).

Terms and Conditions

The terms and conditions by which the service is made available. This will set out a number of conditions which if happen, or are breached will determine a specific response. There is usually little reference to service.

EXAMPLES

- A scheduled flight is delayed by more than 15 hours which automatically offers the traveller a cash refund.
- A rail ticket bought in advance can only be used on a specific journey (i.e. set time and route).
- An estate agent will not levy any charge if you withdraw your property from sale

---

Trade or Professional Body Membership

Organisations often (or must) belong to trade or professional bodies which set out minimum standards of service the organisation must adhere to in providing the service.

EXAMPLE

- A solicitor agrees a set fee for the work to be undertaken and then at the conclusion of the work, produces a bill for double the amount agreed. You could refer the matter to the Law Society, the solicitors' professional body.

Service Guarantees

Organisations often offer specific guarantees for performance levels.

EXAMPLES

- Royal Mail have introduced a number of 'timed' delivery services which guarantee which offers:
  - delivery by 9.00am
  - compensation payment damage for late on non delivery.
- Homebase, the UK retailer, offers a 2 minute guarantee on certain queries. If they do not meet the standard, 10% is deducted from the price of the customer's purchase.

Customer Charters

Some organisations sign up to industry standards, with many banks and financial service organisations subscribing to 'Banking Code'. This is a voluntary agreement which sets outs the standards for good banking practice and the rights of remedy if customers feel the code has been breached.

Beyond this there are external influences.

Bench Mark Accreditations

ISO9001 is the internationally recognised Quality Standard. It defines the elements of the organisation required by a company to systematically deliver quality products, services or advice. It's an indication of reliability, consistency and commitment to quality supply verified by independent certification.

While ISO certification does not guarantee perfection, or indeed high quality, when things go wrong, it allows a systematic review of procedures and where fault is found allows for correction and improvement measures to be initiated.

TYPICAL SERVICE LEVEL AGREEMENTS

SLAs can be used internally within an organisation as well as externally. However, the remedies for breaching an internal agreement will need to be carefully considered given the relationship that is likely to exist.

Each SLA will be individual to the parties involved, however, it is important that there is some standardisation of clauses within the agreement. SLAs must be agreed prior to the commencement of the service and of course while serving the needs of all parties it is primarily provided to offer end user (customer) satisfaction.

Typical aspects that need to be included are:

Nature of Services to be Provided

The SLA should clearly and simply set out the services that the organisation (service provider) will deliver. If this is not clear, it will be difficult for the customer to later claim certain services were not delivered in accordance with the agreement.

Key Performance Measures

Both parties need to be clear on what exactly the measure of service quality will be. Benchmarks and any target metrics should be stated here, along with any improvement initiatives that may prove necessary. It is essential that the performance is capable of being measured.

Issues Management

It is not unusual for things to go wrong within a relationship, so it is critical to have a documented procedure to cover the eventuality. Generally when a 'failure' takes place a process to recover from the failure is initiated this will document any escalation procedures i.e. make senior management aware within six hours. It may also provide for key stakeholders to kept informed of the situation in specific timeframes. Where agreement cannot be reached in certain areas, independent arbitration maybe provided for.

Duties and Responsibilities

Both parties to the agreement need to define exactly what their duties and any associated responsibility are. This could include the need to ensure staff receive training every six months, or maintaining a certain number of staff at any one time.

Cost Associated with the SLA

If there are any costs involved in establishing the SLA they must be stated along with the party that will be responsible for paying them. Where a specific or new SLA is being implemented, certain new procedures, may need to be established, e.g. a database or new reporting process. It needs to be clear who is responsible for the costs. Once the SLA is established the client may ask for more detailed reporting of information, or on a more regular basis. Again, allocation of costs needs to be clear.

Termination

At some point. one or all of the parties may want to terminate the relationship, so its necessary for the methods for termination to be clearly set out.

A SLA can be terminated because a specific event occurs, e.g. the bankruptcy or death of one or more of the parties. Equally it can be terminated by mutual agreement. Usually there is a set period allowed to wind down the agreement.

Depending on the reasons for termination a compensation payment may be payable.

SLAs will have minimum and/or maximum terms specified, or alternatively the SLA will specify a specific time period with an interim review, e.g. the SLA will run for 5 years, with interim reviews at 12 month and 36 months. Then interim reviews may allow for termination if specific terms haven't been met.

SLA COSTS AND BENEFITS

An SLA has considerably more appeal to the end user if there is some financial benefits attached in the event the agreement is breached (see the Royal Mail example above).

Clearly, the cost and the level at which failure is deemed to occur can have a significant financial impact on the organisation delivering the service, but another consideration is the level of proactivity involved.

If a bank organisation states in the event of (say) an account not being opened within 5 days of all the paperwork being received from the customer, a payment of £10 will automatically made, this is a different proposition from saying 'if your account isn't opened with 10 days of the paperwork being received you can claim £10'.

However, the costs associated with organisations delivering against a SLA are complex. It is expected that an organisation that consistently meets or exceeds its SLA will benefit from increased retention levels. Therefore one line of argument suggests a distributor will stay longer with the organisation and continue generating additional income. Consequently the organisation will have less reliance on recruiting new distributors to generate revenue. This also has the added benefit of 'price sensitivity' as distributors who stay with the channel tend to be less price-sensitive and less likely to defect to the competition.

So far this is all good news and it follows that employees may become more motivated, suppliers will want to do business and any shareholders should benefit form a more favourable market position.

If SLAs are being breached on a regular basis, then this could suggest an inherent problem within the organisation that needs to be addressed, or the organisation was being too optimistic in its targets. Either way, the organisation will now have to incur cost either by improving its internal systems and/or compensating customers for the service provided.

Organisations will need to invest in internal systems and staff if it is going to meet (or exceed) customer expectations and depending on the scale of the work involved, may have a significant cost impact, which will need to be recovered through the income to be derived through enhanced customer satisfaction. Figure 8.1 shows an example draft SLA.

MEASURING THE EFFECTIVENESS OF INTERMEDIARIES

Channel members will have been carefully selected for the value they bring to the overall channel and in accordance with specific criteria.

At regular and pre agreed dates, the performance of channel members must be evaluated against the standards or targets set to ensure the continued efficiency.

The performance criteria to be applied will have been mutually agreed and can form part of the SLA.

Typical criteria for measuring the effectiveness of intermediaries include:

- *Sales:* target levels of sales to be achieved in a given period

- *Stock levels:* minimum levels of stock which must be maintained

Draft Service Level Agreement

This Service Level Agreement forms the basis of joint venture between organisation X and organisation Y relating to the provision of a telephone service to organisation Y and its customers. The agreement sets out the roles and responsibilities of the parties in relation to the provision of the service.

1. Aims

The SLA sets out the service to be provided by X and the minimum service standards.

2. Duration

This agreement will commence on 4th September 2009 and will last for five years. Annual reviews will be undertaken and unsatisfactory performance can initiate termination procedures.

3. Service specification

The telephone service will be operated between the hours of 9am-5pm on weekdays and 9am-12pm on a Saturday.

There will be no service available on public holidays. Outside of the service hours an answer phone messaging service is available. Calls will be returned within 24 hours.

All calls received to be answered within a maximum of 30 seconds.

Organisation X will provide the technical infrastructure, premises and staff.

A back up IT system is in place which will be activated within 15 minutes if necessary.

4. Monitoring and review

Monthly performance reports will be produced in the format agreed. Additional reporting can be provided at the standard rate of £x per day.

Any failings will be noted and an Action Plan for remedy initiated.

5. Disagreements

Any disagreement must be recorded in the prescribed manner and dealt initially by the Key Account Manager (KAM) or a nominated member of the team.

If the issue cannot be resolved to the satisfaction of both parties, the matter must be referred to the Group Service Manager, who will escalate within the organisation to a nominated Director.

FIGURE 8.1 *Draft Service Level Agreement.*

- *Delivery times:* maximum time between order and delivery
- *Returns policy:* maximum period in which faulty goods can be returned
- *Training programmes:* minimum number of staff to be trained on in a set period

- *Customer service:* maximum time a telephone call can go answered, complaint handling times

- *Customer retention rates.*

A well known telephone company in the USA was experiencing high levels of customer complaints with one particular range of telephones. Customers were returning the telephones to the store for a refund, but it was company policy that all refunds had to be agreed by Head Office. Customers felt this was unfair, or at least inconvenient, and the policy was subsequently changed to allow the staff in the stores to authorise the refund in appropriate circumstances. While this proved good news for customers, it made the staff unhappy; because the decision to refund was theirs alone and they felt inadequately trained to make that decision.

QUESTIONS

1. What are the advantages of a SLA?

2. What are the key components of a SLA?

3. What criteria could be used to measure the effectiveness of intermediaries within a channel?

4. How can legislation affect the nature of the product or channel used in overseas markets?

SUMMARY

This final chapter in Channel Management examines the important, but often overlooked, aspects of SLAs and their management.

SLAs state the minimum levels that can be expected from an organisation and outlines a procedure to put things right. Equally important is the monitoring process that measures performance against KPIs on a regular basis, so that any adverse trends in service levels can be identified as early as possible. Proactive actions can be taken to resolve, rather than wait until the SLA has been breached and then the process of redress commences.

FURTHER READING

http://www.iso.org/iso/iso_catalogue.htm 28.11.08

BIBLIOGRAPHY

Palmer, A. (2005) *Principles of Services Marketing*. McGraw Hill.

Senior Examiner's Comments – Section Two

By the time that students have completed Section Two they should have a thorough understanding of:

- The development of channel management strategy and objectives;

- The range of channels available to organisations operating in different markets and sectors;

- The factors that influence channel choice;

- The role and importance of stakeholders in channel management; and

- Undertaking control and performance management of channel partners and intermediaries.

For students to succeed, they must be able to apply what they have learnt to various types of organisations. In particular, students must be able to demonstrate that they can relate the application of the various theoretical aspects of channel management to both domestic businesses and to organisations which operate internationally.

Students should examine channel management in action by identifying their own examples, for instance from reading case studies. Technology has had a major impact on channel management and, in many industries, continues to change the ways in which organisations interact with their customers. Financial services are an example of this, where today a significant number of customers, both consumers and businesses, only have a 'virtual' relationship with their chosen providers.

Students should also consider the contribution of channel management strategy and its application towards the achievement of critical organisational and marketing objectives, for example improving profitability, growing market share and increasing levels of customer satisfaction.

Managing Marketing Communications

CHAPTER 9

Marketing Communications Strategy

LEARNING OUTCOMES

At the end of this chapter you will be able to :

- Examine the role of marketing communications and its strategic aims
- Assess the contribution of marketing communications in building relationships with stakeholders
- Evaluate the role of communication in securing competitive advantage
- Examine the legal aspects of marketing communications

INTRODUCTION

We now turn our attention to the third section of the syllabus; managing marketing communications and it's worth remembering the syllabus requires students to consider the topic from an international, as well as a UK, perspective.

We will examine the role of marketing communications strategies and objectives that need to be in line with the organisation's marketing strategy and plans. Internal and external marketing segments will be identified and prioritised across different sectors.

Different marketing mixes will be evaluated and communication plans developed.

The section will be concluded with an evaluation of the manner for selecting marketing communication agencies where the work is not under taken in-house and the processes necessary to monitor the output produced.

THE ROLE OF MARKETING COMMUNICATIONS

There is no one universally accepted definition of marketing communication. Engel and Kitchen (2000) offer 'it is a transactional process between two or more parties whereby meaning is exchanged through the intentional use of symbols'.

Fill (2006) says 'Marketing communications is a management process through which an organisation engages with its various audiences'. He continues, 'By understanding an audience's communication environment, organisations seek to develop and present messages for its identified stakeholder groups, before evaluating and acting upon the responses. By conveying messages that are of significant value, audiences are encouraged to offer attitudinal and behavioural responses'.

Whatever definition chosen, the role of marketing communication is to establish a dialogue with the audience to promote the organisation and the products it offers. The organisation can choose to communicate directly with its audiences or through distribution channels.

At its heart, communication is about how well an organisation differentiates, reminds, informs and persuades (DRIP factors) the audience. It must do this in a consistent manner so that messages given to target audiences are clear, irrespective of the channel of communication used.

ALIGNMENT WITH CORPORATE OBJECTIVES

As organisations do not operate in a vacuum, the communication objectives cannot be developed in isolation of the wider business and planning process conducted by the organisations. The marketing communications plan (see below) is set against the background of other planning tools and forms a hierarchy of interconnected activities which collectively link the process together.

The communications objectives are directly derived from the marketing objectives that in turn come from the corporate objectives, themselves coming from the mission and vision statements.

A typical hierarchy could look like this that shown in Figure 9.1.

FIGURE 9.1

Communications hierarchy.

Corporate mission
Corporate objectives
Marketing objectives
Marketing strategy
Marketing communication objectives

MARKETING COMMUNICATIONS AND MARKETING COMMUNICATION PLANS

In order to ensure all parts of the organisation are focused on effective communications, a clear marketing communications plan is necessary.

Generally organisations communicate with more than one audience and each audience may need a different message. The marketing communication plan will identify each audience and develop a different communications channel to develop a meaningful dialogue. The plan will also measure the effectiveness of individual campaigns as well as overall effectiveness.

A typical marketing communications planning framework is summarised below. However, the plan can be broken down into discrete sections: Context, Objectives, Strategy and Integrated plans, as shown in Figure 9.2.

While the plan is presented sequentially, in practice many of the activities can take place at the same time.

Context

The context in which the communication is to be undertaken needs to be identified and understood so that the key message(s) can be developed and communicated.

This is particularly important when a number of different audiences are involved. Research helps organisations to understand the context in which the organisation must communicate and helps it position the messages correctly in the minds of the audience, encouraging them to take action. Fill (2006) suggests the research should provide information on the needs of the audience, their perception, attitudes, and their decision making characteristics.

As the marketing plan will already have been produced, the focus here is to build on the information already available. The point 'build on' needs to

1.	Context	The research programme
2.		Assumption-qualitative/qualitative
3.		Corporate objectives
4.		Marketing objectives
5.		Budget considerations
6.	Communication objectives	Marketing communication objectives
7.	Strategy	Target market
8.		Target market justification
9.		Agency selection
10.		Creative planning and execution
11.		Above/through and below the line objectives and strategy
12.	Integrated plan	Controlling the marketing communications plan
13.		Contingency planning
14.		Budget breakdown

FIGURE 9.2

Marketing communications plan.

be emphasised as the work being undertaken here must not duplicate previous work undertaken earlier in the planning process. Key messages will be developed.

Staff will need to have a rough idea of the budget available to carry out the plan.

Marketing Communication Objectives

We have seen already the importance of linking the corporate objectives to the marketing objectives and finally to the marketing communication objectives. This allows the organisation to develop positioning strategies. Key stakeholder(s) will be identified through segmentation or stakeholder analysis and the detailed messages developed, in order to achieve the objectives which typically relate to awareness, brand attitude, perception or positioning.

Communication Strategy

The nature, location and types of customers make a significant difference to the tools that can or will be used in order to achieve the DRIP objectives.

An external agency may need to be appointed to develop and implement the marketing communication plan. Alternatively the organisation may have sufficient resources to carry out the work itself. In either case, detailed planning is needed in order to develop the objectives and strategies for the communication activities (above, through and below-the-line).

Each approach needs to be justified in terms of selected audience, campaign, message and cost efficiency. A budget will need to be set, but it needs to be clear that the budget and the choice of promotional activity being undertaken is the most effective combination.

Integrated Communications Plan

Often organisations forget that to support the marketing communications plan, additional resource is needed. Finance is an important resource which must be used effectively and produce an acceptable return on the investment. The use of SMART objectives will help this process. The choice of promotion must be in keeping with the budgets and objectives set. It would be ludicrous for a small family run business to run a TV campaign at a cost of £1 million plus, where the return could not be justified. Where additional resource is needed this must also be factored into the plan. There may be cost implications, but equally where the resource is skilled staff, or new equipment, the time delay from advertising for the new staff, or placing the purchase order to delivery of the new equipment must be factored in to the plan.

Control is often managed through the use of Gantt charts which plots activities against a timeframe. It is a useful method of control as it highlights the 'knock-on' effects of delays. For example, the appointment of a new Communications manager may be delayed by 5 days but the knock-on effect is to delay the overall activity by 15 days, but other resources are otherwise engaged.

Once the plan becomes operational then the control methods will depend on what the specific objectives were. If for example raised awareness levels for the organisation were being measured, it may be necessary to monitor them on a daily basis.

Having invested in the marketing communication process, its necessary to get feedback on the key components of the process, so that those aspects that worked well can be used in future campaigns, equally things that didn't work well can be changed.

COMMUNICATION IN BUILDING RELATIONSHIPS

Organisations are increasingly looking to build ongoing relations with customers so that their life time value is enhanced through maintaining a customer for longer than expected, or purchasing additional products.

Not all customers are equally profitable and therefore organisations need to communicate with customers and potential customers in a way that reflects their current or potential worth to the organisation.

Each interaction with the customer is an opportunity to reinforce and must reflect quality and value. Porter's Value Chain (Porter, 1985) demonstrates how organisations internally seek to take a concept or product and add value by undertaking a series of activities. For example a large diamond extracted from the earth has considerably more value when it has been cut into smaller pieces and polished. The concept relies on the fact that each activity generates more value than the cost of undertaking it. Where this is not the case the activity should be monitored for effectiveness.

The value that a brand or organisation offers is determined by the consumer and is based on a number of criteria such as price or quality, or 'softer' issues should as confidence or status. Also factors such as availability of supply, or replacements parts can determine value. However, trust is at the heart of any relationship.

Transactional marketing focuses on the current product and price and relies on mass communication to get the get the message across. Relationship marketing on the other hand relies on targeted communication to emphasis the importance of the relationship between the parties and build interaction and dialogue.

EXAMPLE

Lloyds bank
TV and press advertising for Lloyds Bank in early 2009, emphasised the importance of relationship building which was encapsulated in the slogan 'For the journey'

An important role for communications is to support the concept of building and maintaining successful exchanges and build loyalty for the relationship.

The Ladder of Loyalty seen in Figure 9.3 supports the importance of using communication to move customers from being prospects to partners.

An organisation will identify potential customers, i.e. people or organisations they would like to do business with. Potential customers may be contacted direct through telephone or email, or advertising may be used to introduce the organisation for personal follow up.

Once the customer has bought a product they become a purchaser and the organisation will want to move them up the ladder and this can be done by personal selling, or direct marketing.

When subsequent purchases are made, then the customer becomes a client and the organisation want to build the relationship further through corporate hospitality, regular meeting or regular dialogue. Messages may focus on the capabilities of the organisation and its position in the market.

Having become a supporter, the customer understands the organisation and what it can do, but it is not yet ready to proactively support the organisation so now the message and activity will be about the importance of relationships to encourage advocacy.

As an advocate the customer becomes a trusted partner who is willing to recommend the organisation to others and word of mouth communications are extremely important.

Finally the customer becomes a partner, i.e. both parties work together on arrange of initiatives.

FIGURE 9.3

Ladder of Loyalty.

Partner
Advocate
Supporter
Client
Purchaser
Prospect

COMMUNICATIONS IN DIFFERENT CONTEXTS

Business to Business Market (B2B)

B2B markets consist of commercial organisations not-for-profit, schools, churches, charities, in fact any thing which is not considered personal. The market has fewer, but larger, buyers with a more formalised buying process and more rational purchasing behaviour. The commercial side of the B2B market can be broken down into four categories:

- *Retail:* goods are sold to the consumers
- *Resale:* goods are sold in to the distribution channels where the distributor adds value through packaging, distribution, quantity or storage
- *Assembly:* raw materials or components are sold which are then combined to produce a finished product
- *Own consumption:* the goods are used within the business, i.e. are not on-sold

Organisational buying behaviour and the actual buying process differs from the B2C market and therefore there is a difference in the marketing communications mix.

Organisational buying behaviour is more formal than in the consumer market. A group of individuals known as the Decision Making Unit (DMU) will make the purchasing decision and the that decision itself contains additional risk depending on whether it is a:

- *New buy:* this is the first time such a purchase has been made
- *Modified rebuy:* a previous purchase has been made, this time a change has been made
- *Straight rebuy:* no change has been made to the previous order.

A new buy carries the highest level of risk and Fill (2006) identifies seven types of organisational risk:

- Technical
- Financial
- Delivery
- Service
- Personal

- Relationship

- Professional

Effective communication is intended to satisfy the expectations of the buyer and reduce the levels of associated risk.

The promotional mix between B2B and B2C differs between the two markets. B2B relies heavily on personal selling due to the perceived complexity high or profit margins involved. A brief summary of the different forms of communication are set out in Table 9.1 as they relate to the B2B market.

Global/International Aspects of Communication

Increased internal travel, coupled with the dramatic growth in the world wide web, could increasingly lead to the belief that all markets can be similarly treated and communicated with.

Table 9.1	A brief summary of the different forms of communication as they relate to the B2B market
Communication form	**Description**
Personal selling	Allows complex products to be explained so that the purchaser is clear on the various product options.
Trade advertising	Most industries and markets have a specific journal or newspaper that can be used to target the sector.
Direct marketing	Direct mail in the B2B sector needs to be highly targeted and targeted needing considerable research.
	Outbound telesales is often used in routine purchases and a relationship can be built through this approach. It is also used to support the sales team by making courtesy calls again to build the relationship and keep the dialogue open.
Sales promotion	Tactical way to generate increased sales by offering additional incentives on selected product lines for a short period of time.
Exhibitions	Often the focus on an organisations new product range where potential buyers come specifically to see the seasons new product range(s).
PR	We will see later that PR is outside of the control of an organisation, however, it is an important tool and needs to be managed effectively so that the organisation is always at front of mind with customers.
Internet	Increasingly important medium. The web acts as showcase for the organisation and while impersonal offers cost savings and improved efficiencies especially when linked with e commerce.

International, global and multinational organisations adopt different frameworks for their marking mix:

- *International:* countries beyond the home market receive the same marketing mix(es) as the home country and home market

- *Multinational:* individually designed marketing mix(es) for each country

- *Global:* one single marketing mix

It can be appreciated that organisations will encounter a number of variables (controllable and non controllable) when communication is being undertaken outside of the home market. Fill (2006) divides the variables into two:

- Culture

- Media

Culture

Culture consists of the values and attitude of people and organisations that determine the way they communicate to other individuals and organisations. Culture is developed through learning and it recognises that not all of the markets or the people within the market will respond or behave in a similar way. Corporate culture is often regarded as 'the way we do things here' and it is important to appreciate the different kinds of culture, such as:

- *Symbols:* in some countries symbols are important, particularly where the levels of education may not be high.

- *Religion:* in many countries a particular religion has an effect on what is purchased and how it is purchased

- *Values:* the things or beliefs that people or organisations place on particular things

Media

Different countries have different media channels available and while 98% of the UK population may have a TV, such high penetration is not universal. The range and type of media availability across the global is variable and must be established prior to a campaign being initiated. Some African countries may also have multiple languages spoken each with its own set of media channel.

The advent of satellite TV has opened up communication channels has opened communication channels, similarly with the internet. However, not all countries have access to mobile telephony. Consequently outdoor media is often important in some countries.

Standardisation or Adaptation of Marketing Communications?

The choice for organisations to standardise or adapt their communications is the subject of ongoing debate and is likely to remain so. Table 9.2 shows the various arguments both for and against.

MARKETING COMMUNICATIONS AND COMPETITIVE ADVANTAGE

We have seen earlier than the role of marketing communication is to differentiate remind inform and persuade (DRIP) but how can it secure competitive advantage for an organisation?

Table 9.2	Standardisation vs adaptation

Adaptation

- A central theme can be tailored to the needs of the local market making it more tailored and relevant. It can be also be to show greater understanding of the individual market as the message can be developed by 'local people for local people'.

- Adapting the communication recognises that local needs to do vary and a generic message may not always be appropriate. Needs, wants, purchasing habits, behaviours, and so on vary across markets.

- Educational levels vary and 'sophisticated' messages may not always be appropriate. Similarly, as we have seen with the concept of culture, messages can be interpreted differently.

- Legal issues and constraints will vary across national boundaries and sometimes within countries, so what may be acceptable in one market may not be acceptable in another and similarly different codes of practice with legally or voluntarily controlled may be in place.

Standardisation

- As highlighted earlier, satellite television has broken down many barriers including culture which separated markets. Consequently many earlier arguments for adaptation are being eroded, e.g. Disney has appeal in most countries and the message can be standardised.

- Locally-developed campaigns have historically been perceived as being of poor quality which standardisation addressed

- Standardisation allows for a consistent and strong brand to be developed across all markets.

- Organisations may prefer to control campaigns in each and every market centrally because they want to maintain control.

- Costs are reduced as a result of standardisation; few advertising agencies, greater production volumes all contribute to efficiency.

- Consistency, the message can be tightly controlled leading to greater brand consistency across the various markets.

We need to remind ourselves that customers do not buy products, it is the benefit the product offers that is bought. The classic example is the customer who wants a 1″ hole in the wall, but has to buy a 1″ drill bit to get the hole! But someone may invent a better way to obtain the hole and then the customer may then evaluate that product rather than the drill bit.

Hooley offers a useful example: the manufacturer makes potato crisps, the retailer merchandises salty snacks, and the customer buys lunch!

The role of communication is to provide the organisation with a competitive advantage by clearly labelling what the product does and positioning it relative to the competition, so the customer is able to differentiate the offering from the competition and can make a clear choice about which one best meets their needs.

This requires a compelling message to be created and maintained in the mind of the target audience so that when they are ready to purchase or repeat purchase they will consider your organisation. They understand the positioning and believe the product best meets their needs. However, many academics suggest that the frequency of communication generates competitive advantage because of the customers ongoing exposure to key messages.

MARKETING COMMUNICATION STRATEGIES

Previous sections have identified the different buying approaches and highlighted the need for different communication tools and messages. However, there are three communication strategies that can be used across all sectors:

- *Push:* pushing the product in to the distribution channels, e.g. through personal selling, exhibitions, sales promotion and trade advertising.

- *Pull:* pulling the product through by encouraging customer demand through advertising, sales promotion and in-store merchandising.

- *Profile:* responding to and receiving information from stakeholders.

The example shown in Figure 9.4 is generic and the actual strategy will be customised for each organisation and campaign. It should be noted that organisations will often adopt both a push and pull strategy.

Push Strategy

With a push strategy the manufacturer 'pushes' the product through the distribution channel to those members who will add value to the product. Information is be pushed down with the manufacturer focusing on the next level in the channel. Personal selling is a key feature of this strategy as the

FIGURE 9.4

*Example 'push' marketing
communications strategy.*

Method	Responsibility
Personal selling, trade press, mail shots, or trade promotion	Manufacturer
Personal selling, trade press, direct mail and trade promotion	Wholesaler
Point of sale promotion, advertising, sales promotions	Retailer
	Consumer

manufacturer will want to provide as much information as possible in order for the wholesaler (see example above) to stock, or purchase the product, so they in turn will generate additional sales through the channel.

Personal selling will often be supported by other forms of communication such as trade advertising, sales incentives, credit incentives such as sale or return, trade advertising and increasingly through a website presence.

Pull Strategy

In a pull strategy communication is directed to the end user rather than through the distribution channel. The intention is that the increased levels of awareness will encourage some action from the consumer so that they will visit a retailer, who in turn will enter the distribution channel (if there is one) to bring the product through and satisfy demand.

Profile

The focus moves away from the choice of pushing or pulling a product through the distribution channels to developing dialogue with stakeholders in order to better inform them about the organisation and its policies and strategies and a key component of a profile strategy is an organisations brand.

RELATIONSHIP MARKETING AND MARKETING COMMUNICATIONS

Communication is an important element in an organisation's efforts to build relations with it stakeholders.

Organisation's stakeholders can be varied in nature and consist of large numbers, they include:

- All the various publics (people and individuals) who have an interest in the organisation

- Distribution channels and the various members (see previous section)
- Customers i.e. the people or organisations who purchase the product(s) on offer

Organisations want to build long and profitable relationships and will therefore want to move beyond 'one-off' transactions in order to achieve long and mutual satisfying relationships which add value for all parties.

Communication is an important part of the 'added value' process that is achieved through:

- Effective and two way dialogue; stakeholder needs are established and a dialogue is maintained so that each stakeholder, or stakeholder group, is understood and can be effectively targeted with messages.

- Regular communication which provides timely and relevant information across a range of communication media and at different frequencies depending on identified need.

LEGAL ISSUES

Marketing professionals are expected to carry out their role in a decent, honest, truthful and legal manner and legislation is in place to ensure:

- Consumer protection
- The image of the industry is maintained at a high level
- Credibility of the messages being communicated
- Decency, i.e. no one is likely to be offended by the messages or imagery being communicated
- Vulnerable groups are protected

In the UK, marketers are regulated by a comprehensive range of legislation which is intended to protect the public and in the EU centralised or harmonised legislation is also having an impact. Organisations that operate globally need to recognise and understand the legalisation applicable in each country in which they operate.

UK Legislation

Legislation in the UK includes the following:

- *The Data Protection Act 1984:* certain organisations must be registered with the data protection registrar if they hold data on individuals and there are conditions about how the data is to be maintained.

- *The Control of Misleading Advertising Advertisements Regulations 1988:* where complaints regarding marketing communications will be considered.

- *The Sale of Goods Act 1979:* requires that goods must match their description.

- *The Trades Description Act 1968:* organisations must not make false or misleading statements about the products (including services) being marketed.

- *The Office of Fair Trading (OFT):* aims to ensure that competition and consumer protection laws are followed. However, there are a number of voluntary bodies in the UK whose members agree to comply with the various codes of practice.

- *The Advertising Standards Authority (ASA)* oversees the British Code of Advertising, sales promotion and Direct marketing which should be:
    - Legal, decent, honest and truthful
    - Responsible to consumers and society
    - In line with the principles of fair competition

The ASA can only request an advertiser to change their advertising which is found to be in breach of its guidelines.

If a compliant is made by the public it is the ASA who will investigate it and if it believes the advertiser has breached its code, it will be asked to withdraw the advertisement. If the advertiser chooses to ignore the ASA warning, then a media warning will be distributed to all members of the Committee of Advertising Practice (CAP) which deals with advertisers rather than the public). The intention is to prevent organisations such as media owners carrying the offending material. Agencies which continue to breach the guidelines will find their membership of the trade bodies terminated and find it difficult to attract new business.

Companies such as Ryanair continue to publicly challenge the authority of the ASA and this is a problem with self-regulation.

As a last resort an injunction can be taken out to prevent the advertisement being run.

However, it is often not a black or white decision. Some organisations set out to be deliberately provocative either through the use of sex, or language. Bennetton, an Italian clothes retailer, ran some graphic advertising which many members of the public found upsetting and did not appear to relate to the product. Another retailer GAP used the logo FCUK (acronym for French Connection UK), that the younger generation found amusing and current, yet displeased the older generation. The campaign ran for many years, until refreshed a short time ago.

Other organisations, including charities and the UK government, run campaigns that are intended to shock people and change behaviour. Yet this can also cause offence.

TV advertisements need to be approved by OFCOM who will vet the scripts. Similarly, RACC is the Commercial Radios Advertising Clearance body and provide a script clearance service to agencies and advertisers using radio.

However, in many instances it is simply necessary for an organisation to be clear that it is not breaking the law, i.e. its materials and communications are legal. This will require the organisation to ensure that its communications are 'signed off' by its in-house legal team, or external lawyers as appropriate. The legal team would routinely be expected to advice on:

- Brochures

- Editorials

- Annual reports

- Accounts

- Recruitment brochures

- Product literature

Outside the UK

The European Advertising Standards Alliance (EASA) is the single authoritative voice on advertising self-regulation issues for Europe and promotes high ethical standards in commercial communications by means of effective self-regulation, while being mindful of national differences of culture, legal and commercial practice.

As a non-profit organisation based in Brussels, it brings together national advertising self-regulatory organisations (SROs) and organisations representing the advertising industry in Europe. EASA has three goals:

- The promotion of self regulation

- Support for existing self-regulatory systems

- Ensure cross border complaints are dealt with effectively

The International Chamber of Commerce was the first organisation to publish its International Code of Advertising Practice and all the codes operative today are based on this code. However, across Europe there are many advertising restrictions that vary from country to country and across media and each country has its own regulatory bodies. Consequently acceptability in once country does not guarantee acceptance in another.

EXAMPLES

In the UK Religious advertising is not allowed on the TV or Radio, but it is allowed in Norway and Denmark.
In Greece toys can only be advertised from 22.00-07.00.
Italy does not allow billboards to be placed near motorways.

Some countries will not allow adverts which have been produced outside the country.

SUMMARY

This chapter has introduced the concept of marketing communications and marketing communication strategies in helping an organisation to deliver its marketing strategy and plans.

For marketing communications to be effective, and hence successful, they need to be fully aligned with the organisation's corporate and marketing strategies. Otherwise not only are resources wasted, but the customer does not have a clear perception of what the organisation and its products can offer. Confused or unsure customers will go to the competition. An organisation will seek to secure competitive advantage through innovative products, but communications need to position and clarify the products in the minds of the consumer.

Communication takes place in a regulated framework which is both voluntary and mandatory, i.e. legal. Organisations which do not meet the legal requirements, whether in the UK or overseas, will often face severe consequences and therefore must ensure they have compliance processes in place and respond quickly to any breaches.

FURTHER READING

http://www.asa.org.uk/asa/.

BIBLIOGRAPHY

Engel, J.F. and Kitchen, P.J. (2000) IMC, brand, communication and corporate cultures: client/advertising agency co-ordination and cohesion. *European Journal of Marketing*, 34, 667–86.

Fill, C. (2006) *Marketing Communications: engagement, strategies and practice*, 4th edition. FT Prentice Hall.

Porter, M.E. (1985) *Competitive Advantage*. The Free Press.

CHAPTER 10

Marketing Communications in Different Organisational Contexts

At the end of the chapter you will be able to:

■ Apply marketing communications in different organisational contexts and sectors

INTRODUCTION

This chapter focuses on internal communication – something often neglected by many organisations – where the main aim is to engage with the customer. Customers do not exist solely externally, they also exist within organisations, and while in practice they may be called staff, they are also customers and they are also stakeholders. However, all too often staff and organisations forget this and the internal structures do not mirror the external environment leading to confusion and frustration. Internal marketing seeks to achieve the same level of enthusiasm for the organisation's products as would be expected from its external customers.

When developing and implementing marketing and communication strategies, staff are an integral part of the process. For many customers, it is the staff who are the sole point of contact with the brand and in effect the staff are the brand.

Organisations, in order to be successful and have a point of differentiation in the market, need happy and motivated staff. This can require cultural changes to be made within the organisation so that staff are 'engaged' and adopt a 'can-do' attitude which supports customer service excellence.

INTERNAL MARKETING

Internal marketing refers to the promotion of a marketing orientation throughout an organisation. It aims to create awareness among all employees including those who do not have direct customer contact. For many organisations achieving marketing orientation can involve major changes in working practices and culture.

Internal marketing also includes:

- Creation of customer awareness
- Quality management programmes
- Change programmes

Peck *et al.* (1999) suggest that 'internal marketing is concerned with creating, developing and maintaining an internal service culture'. This builds on the work of Berry (1981) who developed the concept of internal marketing. Internal marketing is important, not just in service industries but across all sectors.

Research has shown a strong correlation between satisfied employees and operational performance. Customers do not just purchase a tangible product, the intangible aspects such as culture and attitude affect customer satisfaction which can be more important to consumers in many situations. Therefore to achieve the stated aims and objectives of the marketing plan, an integrated approach is necessary in order to bring together the skills of the various employee groups. Organisations are increasingly competing on the grounds of service excellence and improved service quality relies on the effectiveness of the people who are charged with delivering the service.

> 'Smile, you're on the phone' was an internal communications campaign run by NatWest to encourage staff to be enthusiastic when speaking to customers who telephoned their branch.

Employees can be regarded as discrete group of customers who need to be segmented into different audiences, so that targeted communications campaigns can be developed. Staff, because of the nature of their work, are often responsible for a very small part of an organisation's output, so it is necessary to mirror customer campaigns internally, so that they see the tone and values set out by the organisation.

Equally, for many customers the only interaction they may have with the brand is with individual members of staff and therefore their attitude may impact on the customer's view of the brand. A helpful and enthusiastic member of staff will have a positive impact on the organisation and many organisations have deployed the concept of 'brand ambassadors' as a result of their internal marketing programmes.

Marketing, in addition to being a management function and ethos which permeates the entire organisation, needs to ensure effective coordination of its activities internally. Therefore systems and processes covering resources (financial, people and equipment) need to be put in place to ensure products are delivered to customers within agreed timescales to the quality standards set by the organisation. This requires effective coordination of activities so that all staff are working towards the same goals.

Internal marketing has two main aspects:

- All employees and departments have an internal and external customer

- Staff must work together in a way that is aligned to the organisation's mission

And the overall objective of internal marketing is to improve the quality of service offered to customers.

Internal marketing is shaped by the prevailing culture of the organisation as it is this culture which provides the context within which internal marketing takes place.

An internal marketing plan (derived from the overall marketing plan) is necessary to ensure the achievement of organisation goals and the key components of an internal plan could include:

- Organisation aims and objectives

- Marketing strategy

- Segmentation, targeting and positioning (STP)

- Marketing programmes (see below)

- Implementation

- Monitoring and control

INTERNAL COMMUNICATION METHODS

Marketing communications is concerned with the way various stakeholders interact with each other and internal communications relates to the way stakeholders within an organisation communicate with each other and receive marketing attention. It draws a boundary between internal and external stakeholders.

Internal stakeholders are employees and management who are interested in different issues, however, it is generally accepted that employees should be the key focus of internal communication.

Many organisations refer to the concept of 'treating employees as customers'. Indeed in many cases this may literally be true if they are also, for example, shareholders or customers. An employee of a bank may take an annual bonus in the form of shares and also maintain a current account.

The internal marketing mix consists of:

- *Product:* usually relates to the changing nature of a job role

- *Price:* the balance of psychological costs and the benefits of adopting a new orientation

- *Place:* where the activity takes place

- *Promotion:* external promotional methods can be adopted internally to demonstrate to staff the image portrayed in the market. Internal advertising campaigns can be undertaken reflecting external advertising. This is to be tailored to the different audiences but should be throughout the organisation.

- *People:* this relates to those involved in producing and delivering communication, training media and meetings. The management of service levels reflecting customer expectations

- *Processes:* the communication and media process by which the produce is brought to the customers' attention

- *Physical evidence:* training, briefings, documentation and, to an extent, place.

Internal communication is needed to reflect the messages given to other stakeholder groups, so that not only is there consistency in the message, but the values, attitudes and the general ethos of the organisation are clearly visible to all staff, so that they know what is expected of them in certain circumstances. Fill (2006) refers to this as 'living the brand'. This is particularly important in organisations where staff deal solely with internal customers.

Fill (2006) suggests that there are three roles for internal marketing communications, as shown in Table 10.1.

Hooley *et al.* (2008) identifies other roles, which are:

- *Team building:* ensuring that barriers between different divisions are broken down so that all staff are working towards providing customers with service excellence and reducing the potential for conflict

- *Goal setting:* so that the focus is on achieving corporate goals which are clearly stated and measurable

Table 10.1	Three roles for internal marketing communications (Fill, 2006)
Role	**Explanation**
DRIP	Differentiate: To differentiate the type and nature of communication across different employees or groups of employees.
	Remind : To remind staff of key values
	Inform: To provide staff with information
	Persuade: Use persuasive language or imagery to convey consistent messages
Transactional needs	Directing new initiatives or coordinating actions or using resources effectively and effectively
Affiliation needs	Generating a sense of identity with the organisation as well as promoting and coordinating activities with external groups or individuals

- *Involvement:* a channel needs to be created so that problems and issues can be resolved in a constructive manner

- *Change management:* making changes to current structures and process and responding rapidly (internally) to external changes

It must be recognised that organisational structures are evolving and increasingly the use of project teams is being used to launch new products into the market. Project teams can incorporate:

- Staff seconded from other divisions of the organisation

- Temporary staff who are employed just for the life of the project

- External consultants

- Customers

While this has the effect of blurring the boundaries between different stakeholders, it also affects the form that communication takes. Therefore, an organisation must clearly identify the different range of internal audiences so that messages can be effectively tailored to the needs of the audience.

INTERNAL COMMUNICATION METHODS

The communication of clear and consistent messages ensures brand consistency. Large organisations will have a range of staff; young new entrants, clerical, management, experts, etc. This will require different communication methods to be employed.

Table 10.2 offers a range of communication methods available to an organisation to communicate internally.

EXTERNAL AUDIENCES

Each organisation needs to identify who its key stakeholders are through a process of stakeholder mapping. Then having identified them, it needs to decide who the target audiences are, i.e. who are the recipients of any communication originated by the organisation.

Potential audiences can be categorised into three groups:

- *Consumers:* the purchasers of the product

- *Channel members:* wholesalers and other members of the distribution channel

- *Stakeholders:* the publics who have an interest in the organisation

The role of communications with the external stakeholders is to maintain relationships through on-going dialogue and through multiple points of contact. However, it is not always immediately obvious who the key stakeholders are, and therefore like other stakeholder groups, a mapping exercise needs to be undertaken to establish the key groups.

Below is a broad list of possible external stakeholders that an organisation may want to communicate with. It is generic, so different groups may have a greater relevance than others to the organisation.

The Media

A key stakeholder for most organisations as it can support the organisation in its communication efforts, or conversely it can adopt a negative stance, thereby making the organisations communication tasks more difficult.

Trade Unions

Trade Unions can influence internal practices, which affect the organisation's competitiveness in the market. Organisations may want to introduce efficiencies that may lead to a reduction in employees, these in turn may be rejected by the union.

Equally, Unions are a strong source of lobbying different sectors and may be linked with other stakeholders.

Table 10.2	Internal communication methods
Method	**Description**
Intranet	The intranet is a system for distributing information electronically through its internal network.
	Staff can access a broad range of information that can be tailored to specific groups. For example, shop floor staff may be restricted to product information and HR facilities.
	Large organisations can have a number of intranets each serving the need of a particular division.
	Information should be kept up-to-date; otherwise reliability will be questioned by staff.
	Typically the intranet will be the first screen staff will see when they open the PC in the morning.
Email	An impersonal but quick way to communicate with all staff. Fast and cost effective, it can be used to update staff on new developments, urgent changes, be information provision or action orientated when the member of staff must take some action having received the mail. The sender of the mail can check if the message has been read.
	However, staff typically get many emails every day and instructions can be 'missed'
	Staff can clarify aspects of the message if it is not understood
Seminars	Seminars bring together small groups of people generally for recurring meetings.
	A seminar will focus on one specific area of the business or market and is run by an 'expert' in the particular field.
Briefings	A briefing can be presented in writing or orally. Typically a briefing is given when procedure change or significant organisational change is planned.
Newsletters	Historically newsletters were distributed in paper format. Increasingly, newsletters are now circulated electronically. However, in some organisations, staff do not have access to the web and paper still remains the channel of choice. However, research shows that a high proportion of staff with electronic access still print newsletters off to read at a more convenient time or location.
Mobile	Increasingly mobile phones are being used as a communication for non-voice communication. Mobile phones now have access to the internet and staff can read emails, access the intranet and generally communicate internally through electronic means. This is useful for people who do electronic access externally.

Pressure Groups

Pressure groups drive public opinion and shape organisation policy. They can support organisational change, or reject it. While it is often the larger groups (e.g. Green Peace, Amnesty International, and Liberty) who have a high media profile, pressure groups operate at all levels campaigning for change. They are often an invaluable source of knowledge to be tapped into.

> Five years ago, if you wanted to buy a cup of fair-trade coffee you would have had to make a point of asking for it in the coffee shop, now the main chains actively promote fair trade coffee.

Government (all levels) Regulatory Bodies and Membership Groups

The Government affects an organisation in many different ways, from the way the annual accounts are submitted to the amount of tax paid on profits. Often the location of an organisation can be determined by the government as a result of additional grants being made available.

Larger organisations are often regulated or monitored by industry bodies, such as ASA, FSA, or Ofwat. This can influence prices charged now and in the future, determine appropriate codes of conduct for conducting business and offer customers some protection against poor or inferior practices.

Membership groups often work together to improve the public's perception of the industry, or provide consistency of approach bodies when dealing with customers.

Society

A huge and diverse group which expects to be treated in a certain way, i.e. that any products offered by an organisation will be fit for purpose, i.e. will work in a safe manner.

It also impacts on the design of products by buying, or not buying products. For example, society generally wants to be healthier, so organisations need to respond with less sugary drinks and less fat and salt in products.

SUMMARY

This chapter has considered the role of internal marketing, recognising its importance as part of the planning process.

Staff need to be aware of their roles and recognise that not all customers are outside the organisation and that not delivering on a 'promise' internally can have external ramifications.

Similarly organisations need to recognise the pivotal role played by staff and develop internal mechanisms to build motivation and brand loyalty along with a culture of priding excellent customer service.

QUESTIONS

1. What do you understand by the term internal marketing?

2. Why are staff so important to the marketing communication process?

3. How can staff affect customer perception to a brand?

4. How can staff be motivated and better reflect the values of a brand?

BIBLIOGRAPHY

Berry, L. (1981) The employee as customer. *Journal of Retail Banking*, 3, 1.

Fill, C. (2006) *Marketing Communications: Engagement, strategies and practice*, 4th edition. FT Prentice Hall.

Hooley, G., Saunders, J., Piercy, N.F. and Nicoulaud, B. (2008) *Marketing Strategy and Competitive Positioning*, 3rd edition. FT Prentice Hall.

Peck, H., Payne, A., Christopher, M. and Clark, M. (1999) *Relationship Marketing*. Butterworth-Heinemann.

CHAPTER 11

Marketing Communications and Marketing Communications Plans

INTRODUCTION

In this chapter a range of promotional tools will be introduced and evaluated. While each will be considered in turn, it is important to recognise that it is the 'mixing' of the promotional tools which will generate competitive advantage for an organisation both internally and externally. However, any marketing spend must be measured to ensure that not only is value for money being received, but the objectives set are being met.

The structure and contents of a communications plan are explored and the importance of communications in securing new customers is highlighted.

Communication plans, as we will see, are derived from the marketing plan and therefore, the more robust the marketing plan, the more effective the communications plan is likely to be.

This chapter considers the role of planning and execution in different organisational contexts and sectors, for example, B2B, B2C, Third Tier and Not-for-Profit. Similarly the importance of communication internationally and globally is addressed.

MARKETING COMMUNICATION TOOLS

There are many communication tools available to marketers and Figure 11.1 offers a broad range of examples. However, marketing communication tools

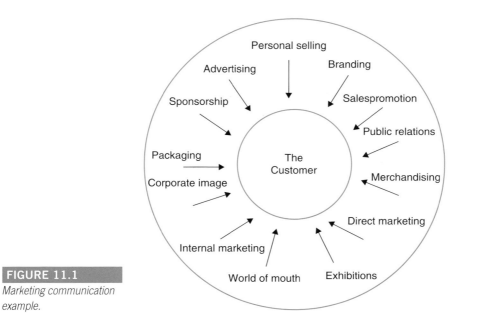

FIGURE 11.1

Marketing communication example.

are generally grouped into five categories and within each of the categories there are different media that could be use. For example, if advertising is a marketing communication tool (part of the promotional mix) then bus advertising, bill boards, newspapers, etc. are the media that could be used.

Promotional activities can also be referred to above, below or through the line.

Above-the-Line

Above-the-line activity relates to promotional activities carried out through mass media such as press, magazines, radio, outdoor, cinemas, banners and search engines. Historically the term related to the payment of agency commission.

Through-the-Line

This refers to activity that involves above- and below-the-line communications where one form of advertising points the consumer to another form of advertising, thereby crossing the line. This can include direct marketing, direct mail catalogs, telemarketing and interactive communications including the internet.

The focus has moved from mass to more personalised communications and relationships can start to be built.

Below-the-Line

Below-the-line includes sales promotion, public relations and personal selling.

There has been a shift from an intervention-based approach (aimed at getting the attention of a customer who initially may not be interested in the product on offer) towards a permission-based approach (communicating mainly with the audience who may already have expressed an interest in the product on offer). As Fill (2006) suggests permission marketing sows the seeds for a relationship which emanates from the audience and not the owner of the brand.

Advertising is better for creating awareness and personal selling is more effective at promoting action and purchase behaviour.

The increasing use of public relations and in particular publicity, is a refection of the high levels of credibility that this medium holds.

In summary the five communication tools are:

- *Advertising:* mass media is often used to create awareness or encourage trialing of a product.

- *Personal selling:* common in retail or business-to-business market. Expensive, but often needed when complex products are involved.

- *Sales promotion:* used to encourage trial or increase usage – tactical and flexible.

- *Public relations (including sponsorship):* PR is not paid for, but often requires agency involvement, which can be expensive.

- *Direct marketing:* Increasingly popular tool that can deliver personalised messages.

Let's look at these in turn.

ADVERTISING

Yeshin (2006) defines advertising as 'paid-for, non-personal communication from an identified organisation, body, or individual designed to communicate information and to influence customer behaviour'.

The range of advertising channels is huge and if an organisation operates internationally the choice is daunting. However, some potential channels may be restricted because of the nature of the product and the country of operation (or advertising).

The role of advertising is:

- Awareness building

- Engagement with the purchaser or potential purchaser.

- Positioning or repositioning brands

Table 11.1	Major advertising media
Cinema	
Internet	
Magazines	
Newspapers	
Outdoor media	
Radio	
TV	

| Table 11.2 | Advantages and disadvantages of cinema advertising |

Advantages	Disadvantages
▪ High audio and visual impact	▪ High cost
▪ Captive audience, so high degree of control, audience not able to 'skim' or 'flick over'	▪ Can be low exposure, i.e. low capacity in some screens
	▪ Measurement hard to evaluate
▪ Segmentation possible by area or region	▪ Timings depend on local cinema
▪ Good medium for the 'younger' market	

Advertising has the ability to reach a large target audience quickly, but this comes at a high cost.

Each day individuals are exposed to hundreds of advertising message and only a very small percentage of those adverts will make an impact, as we tend to 'filter out' those that that do not have any significance.

Marketers need to make decisions not only about which tool(s) to use, but to select the 'right' media in order to achieve organisational objectives effectively. Table 11.1 shows the major advertising media available in the UK.

In 2005 the UK was ranked the 4th largest country for advertising expenditure, behind the USA, China and Japan (Stokes and Lomax, 2008). The economy will impact on overall spending, therefore it becomes even more important that any spend can be clearly justified with specific objectives set.

Cinema

Despite predictions to the contrary, the number of people going to the cinema has steadily increased. It is estimated that are now approximately 170m cinema admissions per year, with just over 50% being in the 15-34 age group. Table 11.2 evaluates the advantages and disadvantages of cinema advertising.

INSIGHT: TV ADVERTISING DECLINES FURTHER

Prices for television advertisements will fall to their lowest level since 1987 according to Zenith Optimedia.

Zenith say that in real terms slots for UK TV slots cost 40 per cent less than in 1987 when it began collecting pricing data. The figures came as Thinkbox, a body promoting TV advertising, released PwC research showing the damage to advertisers of cuts in TV advertising.

PwC found that in 67% of cases, a company reducing advertising investment more than its competitors would shrink its 'brand value', defined as the willingness of consumers to pay a relative premium over similar but unbranded products. On the other hand increasing advertising spending boosts consumers 'willingness to pay' in 66% of cases.

Source: Adapted from an article in the Financial Times by Tim Bradshaw dated 11th November 2008.

INSIGHT: TV AND ONLINE ADVERTISING

New research from Thinkbox and the Internet Advertising Bureau (IAB) has shown that using TV and online together in advertising campaigns is significantly more effective for advertisers than using either in isolation. Their combined use produces major benefits for advertisers, including dramatically increased positive brand perception amongst consumers – some 50% higher – as well as significantly greater likelihood of purchase.

Conducted by Q Media Research, this is the first time the effectiveness of using TV and online in tandem has been examined in depth. The sample focused specifically on 'digital consumers'; people who own a digital TV and use broadband internet, and are medium to heavy users of each. Because the study focuses on the most 'tech-savvy' of the UK population – around 25% of its total – these results provide an indication of how future media consumption and consumer behaviour may develop. In terms of their precise media usage, 64% of the sample stated that they sometimes watch TV while using the internet, whilst 48% stated that they did this most days.

Key findings from the study include:

- Using TV and online together results in 47% more positivity about a brand than using either in isolation
- The likelihood of buying or using a product increases by more than 50% when TV and online are used together
- 48% of the sample group watched broadcast TV while online, most days
- Two thirds of this group have watched TV via online providers, primarily as a way to catch-up with broadcast TV and mainly from TV broadcasters' websites
- Both TV and the internet are used for entertainment (TV, 80%; online 56%) and both have a significant influence on driving purchase (75% and 52%)
- The findings reinforce the need to ensure creative synergy between TV and online advertising and identify best practice for better effectiveness, which requires more than simply putting together TV ads

Source: Adapted from http://www.thinkbox.tv/server/show/nav.1019

Internet

The internet is growing in popularity as a form of advertising. Customers are increasingly happy to make a purchase on the internet, having evolved from using it as an information source, with the purchase being made through a more established channel.

For marketers the internet offers a choice of web advertising through the presence of an organisations own site, the use of portals, pop-ups or banner advertising.

However, technology is developing rapidly and already we see terms such as social networks, blogs and on-line increasingly in everyday use.

Web 2.0 is another term which marketers need to understand. While there many definitions, Web 2.0 is concerned with the rapidly changing ways that web technology can be used in order to improve communications, share information and expand the concept of social networks, blogs and on-line forums.

Concepts that were initially confined to discrete market segments are now being extended. Currently blogs, online forums and social networks share information between different parties on the web. It is still unusual for an organisation to set its own social network site, typically it is customers who are happy, or not so happy, with the product who start the site and share experiences with each other, the organisation simply looking on.

In the future organisations will be able to use the new internet technology and set up their own Facebook site to build relationships with customers and potential customers. Material which would normally be posted on the organisation's website can now be put on a You Tube site.

Table 11.3 evaluates the advantages and disadvantages of internet advertising.

Table 11.3	Advantages and disadvantages of internet advertising
Advantages	**Disadvantages**
■ Relatively inexpensive to set up	■ Some issues about intrusion
■ Speed of setup can be fast	■ Still developing medium and not yet mainstream, but growing rapidly
■ Global reach	■ Often easy to delete the message without viewing
■ Creative and interactive options available	■ Not regulated as yet
■ Messages can be downloaded for later consumption	
■ Speed of getting message to consumer very fast	

NEWSPAPER WEBSITES

The financial crisis helped make September 2008 another record month for UK quality national newspaper websites, with several topping August's Olympics-fuelled traffic highs.

Independent.co.uk, Telegraph.co.uk, Times Online and guardian.co.uk all posted record figures for unique users in September, according to the latest results from the Audit Bureau of Circulations Electronic, published today.

However, September's financial turmoil, which began with the collapse of US investment bank Lehman Brothers in the middle of the month, provided less of a boost for UK popular newspaper web traffic.

Sun Online and Mirror.co.uk's unique user numbers were both down month on month, while Mail Online posted modest traffic growth of 3% compared with August and was still below its peak traffic month in May.

Independent.co.uk enjoyed the biggest month-on-month traffic boost, with unique user numbers up 21% from August to a record 7,995,958, from 6,629,235. This was a 97% year-on-year leap.

The site's previous highest traffic figure came in June, when it had 7,215,928 unique users.

guardian.co.uk maintained its position as the most popular UK national newspaper website for the fourth month running in September, topping 24 million unique users for the first time with a 5% uplift from August's previous record figure.

This was a 45% year-on-year increase, to 24,186,422 unique users for September.

Times Online also built on record traffic in August to push past 20 million unique users for the first time in September. The News International-owned website had 20,322,634 unique users last month, up 3% on August and 62% year on year.

However, Times Online remained in third place behind Telegraph.co.uk, which also achieved record traffic last month, with 22,945,934 unique users. Telegraph.co.uk was up 4% on August and 116% year on year.

"Telegraph.co.uk benefited from a surge in demand for stories about the US election and the financial crisis, which helped raise the number of page views and unique users to a record high," said the Telegraph Media Group digital editor, Edward Roussel.

Mail Online remained in fourth place with 17,913,660 unique users in September, up 3% on its August figure of 17,468,044 and up 53% year on year.

Sun Online's unique user figure fell slightly month on month, down 1% on August to 15,783,551. However, this was up 48% compared with September 2007.

Mirror.co.uk's traffic dipped by 6% month on month in September to 5,259,763 unique users.

A year-on-year comparison was not available as Mirror.co.uk did not make traffic data for September 2007 public.

Sun Online remained the UK national newspaper website with the most page impressions in September, with 286,941,127.

However, this was down from Sun Online's Olympics-inspired record of 328,196,404 pages viewed in August.

A post-Olympics dip may also have contributed to the slip in guardian.co.uk's page impressions from the record high in August.

In September, guardian.co.uk received 208,701,946 page impressions, down from 211,679,253 the previous month.

Telegraph.co.uk had 157,972,562 page impressions in September, also down slightly on its record high of 158,061,673 in August.

This trend was not reflected across all national newspaper websites, as for the second month running Times Online posted a record number of page impressions.

Times Online received 135,467,290 page views in September, up from the previous high of 134,114,119 in August.

Independent.co.uk also drew a record number of page impressions for the second month running, with 37,906,938 in September. This was up from 31,749,167 in August.

Mail Online also saw page impressions climb month on month, to 139,108,955 in September.

However, this was below Mail Online's record high of 146,452,603 page impressions achieved in April.

Source: http://www.guardian.co.uk/media/2008/oct/23/abcs-digitalmedia

Table 11.4	Advantages and disadvantages of magazine advertising
Advantages	**Disadvantages**
■ Wide range of specialist titles allowing for effective segmentation	■ Can be long lead in times especially with specialist and trade journals
■ Can be read frequently, i.e. more than once	■ Can be expensive compared with other media
■ Readership often greater than circulation (waiting rooms, hotels, etc.)	■ Often involves high quality (expensive) production
■ Long life cycle	

Magazines

Stokes and Lomax (2008) estimate that around 14% of the UK press advertising is accounted for by the spend in magazines. Generally magazines offer a cost-effective way of reaching the target audience. However, costs do vary depending on the title and circulation of the magazine.

Table 11.4 evaluates the advantages and disadvantages of magazine advertising.

Newspapers

The internet is having an impact on newspaper sales, readers are increasingly keen to read the news as it happens, or be part of the news making process the use of online blogs, as well as the availability of free newspapers.

The impact is less dramatic on local newspapers, where they still maintain a strong following and some titles are seeing an increase in sales.

Table 11.5 shows the sales of newspapers in the UK where a significant drop in sales is evidenced not just in the 'quality' papers such as the Independent, but also in the 'popular' press such as the Daily Star. Table 11.6 evaluates the advantages and disadvantages of newspaper advertising.

Outdoor Media

Outdoor media covers a rage of media from adverts in bus stops and washrooms through to billboards and hoardings. Increasingly technology, with the introduction of digital screens, is transforming outdoor media allowing for new campaigns and creative treatments. Table 11.7 evaluates the advantages and disadvantages of outdoor media advertising.

It must be recognised that digital technology will mean advertisers can target their messages by audience, location, or a specify time during the day, and they will be able to change the creative executions at different locations.

The growth of outdoor advertising has been supported by the huge growth in the numbers of hours we spend outside the home and a large increase in the investment and upgrading of key sites.

Table 11.5	ABCs: National daily newspapers, November 2008				
	November 2008	November 2007	% change	November 2008 (without bulks)	% change on last year
The Sun	3,045,899	3,078,388	−1.06	3,045,899	−0.72
Daily Mirror	1,400,206	1,518,881	−7.81	1,400,206	−7.56
Daily Star	714,192	753,476	−5.21	714,192	−8.32
Daily Record	361,857	393,593	−8.06	359,772	−6.29
Daily Mail	2,193,715	2,327,507	−5.75	2,062,560	−4.98
Daily Express	752,181	766,874	−1.92	752,181	−6.39
Daily Telegraph	835,497	882,873	−5.37	738,335	−3.95
The Times	621,831	636,946	−2.37	565,766	−3.04
Financial Times	448,523	444,880	0.82	409,024	−0.68
The Guardian	358,379	356,789	0.45	343,654	−4.24
The Independent	201,113	233,423	−13.84	165,222	−8.29

Source: Audit Bureau of Circulations

Table 11.6	Advantages and disadvantages of newspaper advertising
Advantages	**Disadvantages**
Regional newspapers	
■ High local readership, often multiple reads ■ Low cost production ■ Focused on the local area, so will have specialist sections	■ Generally weekly ■ Often not seen as objective
National daily newspapers	
■ High levels of readership, so mass market ■ Short lead in times for media is very responsive to timescales ■ Range of newspaper titles, so segmentation can be effective ■ Wide choice of advertising options, e.g. main newspaper (and choice of positioning and size), or specialist section	■ High number of competing adverts, so 'stand out' harder to achieve ■ Limited life span ■ Generally need a campaign rather than a 'one-off' advert ■ Production costs can be high

Radio

Advertisers have a choice of regional and national radio and there are a growing number of internet stations who allow for segmentation in a variety of

Table 11.7	Advantages and disadvantages of outdoor media
Advantages	**Disadvantages**
■ Repeat exposure, generally we go to work the same way, or shop in the same area	■ Opportunity to see poster can be quite short if passing in car, train or bus
■ Low cost, product cost can	■ Random viewing by people
■ Supportive of other media, i.e. reinforces messages	
■ Flexible duration of campaign	

Table 11.8	Advantages and disadvantages of radio advertising
Advantages	**Disadvantages**
■ Cheap (cost per listener)	■ Radio can be in the 'background' so not actively listened to.
■ Can have large coverage	■ Generally ads only last a few seconds, so need repeating
■ Can link in with sponsorship	
■ Can be targeted	■ Creativity currently restricted because of the media, but DAB radio increasing opportunities
■ Portable, i.e. variety of listening locations, e.g. car, home	

Table 11.9	Advantages and disadvantages of television advertising
Advantages	**Disadvantages**
■ High impact	■ High cost
■ Mass audiences, so wide coverage quickly	■ Can channel-hop and avoid the ads
■ High degree of creativity available	■ High risk, if ads poorly constructed in terms of message and tone
■ Strong sound and visual qualities	■ Can have long production times
■ Evaluation mechanisms well developed	

ways. Examples are specialists, young children, pensioners, young parents, through to people on their way home through the rush hour traffic.

Table 11.8 evaluates the advantages and disadvantages of radio advertising.

Television

Most of us are familiar with TV as a form of advertising, which is typically used by major brands, although smaller companies can use it regionally. It is the most expensive form of media and while it reaches a broad audience it is now competing with online advertising.

The Internet Advertising Bureau (IAB) suggest by 2010 online advertising spend will be larger than television. Table 11.9 evaluates the advantages and disadvantages of television advertising.

PERSONAL SELLING

Personal selling is generally used in the retail or business-to-business environments or where the product is complex or the profit margins are high as personal selling is expensive. However, sales teams now tend to be focused on particular products and ranges sale.

Personal selling also allows the opportunity to ask questions (i.e. dyadic communication). The message itself can be tailored to the needs of the potential purchaser, giving a more individual approach.

Individuals by their very nature are each different, and therefore it can be difficult for an organisation to ensure all staff are performing consistently and consequently there maybe variability in the quality of the approach adopted by each individual member of staff.

There doesn't need to be a face to face meeting, personal selling can be conducted on the telephone and this can reduce the cost to the organisation.

Stokes and Lomax (2008) identify six different types of selling situations:

- *Delivery selling:* the 'delivery' person also has a selling role. The intention is to penetrate the existing customer base at the point of delivering a product.

- *Retail selling:* selling to customers who come in to the premises to make a purchase. Often referred to as 'sales advisers' they provide assistance and advice to help the customer make the purchase.

- *Trade selling:* products are sold in to the distribution channel, e.g. wholesalers. The role also ensures the point-of-sale (POS) material displayed was in keeping with the brand.

- *New business selling:* selling to new customers, i.e. people or organisations who are not yet customers.

- *Experiential selling:* encouraging purchase through trial or testing

- *Technical selling:* complex products often require a high degree of interaction, so 'technical' assistance is needed, e.g. purchasing a pension policy.

Reid *et al.* (2002) identified three sales behaviours; getting, giving and using information.

- *Getting information:* face-to-face contact can be useful in collecting information about customers, the market and competitors. Often a member of the sales team will be responsible for compiling competition activity reports.

- *Giving information:* providing customers and stakeholders with key or critical information concerning the organisation's reputation in the market, new product information, or updating them on competitor products, sales or innovations.

- *Using information:* collecting information in order to solve a customer's problem.

As organisations are increasingly keen to build relationships with customers rather than simply having a transactional relationship, the role of personal selling can be important in the creation and maintenance of relationships.

Sales people undertake a variety of other roles which have variously been defined as:

- *Prospecting for new clients:* It's important to have a stream of new clients coming through, so the sales team will be continually looking to build leads and generate sales.

- *Communicating:* Keeping stakeholders informed about the organisation: development of new products, competitor comparisons, product and brand positioning.

- *Information gathering:* Collecting key information about the market, competitors and new initiatives.

- *Servicing:* Ongoing client maintenance through the provision of technical information. Problem solving, suggesting new products, so that the client knows they can rely on the organisation.

- *Allocating:* Managing resources and deploying them as appropriate.

- *Shaping:* Building and maintaining the relationship with the client.

The exact nature of the role carried out by the sales team will vary from industry to industry and will also vary with the size of the organisation. In larger organisations the sales team may simply be responsible for 'sales' in the narrowest sense of the word, i.e. closing the sale. Others, sometimes known as relationship managers, will assume responsibility for building the relationship and potentially developing it into a Key Account.

Exhibitions

Exhibitions are a popular form of field marketing, both in the UK and overseas which is increasing in popularity and the opening of new centres in London and Manchester for example reflect this. Exhibitions are used predominantly in the B2B market and give organisations the opportunity to meet new contacts, distributors and customers and see what the competition is offering.

Exhibitions are good for raising profile and image, however, having attended an exhibition, there is an implied assumption this will be on an ongoing rather than one-off basis. While exhibitions can be expensive, many are highly targeted offerings. There are also some large B2C exhibitions (e.g. Franchise exhibition, car show, motor show, flower show, ideal home show, etc.).

SALES PROMOTION

The following description of sales promotion is based on the Institute of Sales Promotion's definition:

> *Sales promotion is a range of tactical marketing techniques, designed within a strategic marketing framework, in order to add value to a product to achieve a specific marketing or sales objective(s).*

The tactical nature of sales promotion means that it can be implemented quickly as circumstances require. If sales are sufficiently below the level expected, a sales initiative can be initiated and it will be of sufficient duration that sales start to move quickly to the expected levels at which time it can be terminated. It is a flexible and fast way to respond to the business environment.

Sales promotions can also be used to increase demand at times when traditionally sales will be low; equally it can be used to support the launch of a new product into the market.

It is not just the consumer who is the target for sales promotion. Organisations will use it with the distribution channel.

A wholesaler may be encouraged to stock a new product, or increase sales of a range of exiting products in return for an increased profit margin or some other form of offer, such as 'sale or return'.

The remuneration paid to a sales team can be increased to encourage the sale of certain products; payment levels would return to normal levels when the objectives have been reached.

While sales promotion has many advantages if used correctly, organisations need to take care that any price reductions, particularly if considered large, may devalue the product in the mind of the consumer.

PUBLIC RELATIONS

According to the Chartered Institute of Public Relations (CIPR), public relations is about reputation - the result of what you do, what you say and what others say about you.

Public relations (PR) is the discipline that looks after reputation of a company and/or product, with the aim of earning understanding and support and influencing opinion and behaviour. It is the planned and sustained effort to establish and maintain goodwill and mutual understanding between an organisation and its publics.

The role of PR covers two aspects: marketing PR and corporate PR.

Marketing PR supports and manages an organisation's products by supporting the other elements of the marketing mix. It is usually planned and derived from the marketing plan with clear objectives, strategy and measurement. Messages will be tailored to the need of each audience.

Corporate PR tends to be long-term relationship building, clearly positioning the organisation and its values with the wider market. Again, usually planned, with specific measurements agreed. However, it also covers unplanned activities and crises. It ensures;

- key messages are agreed
- people taking to the media are consistent with the message
- information is given in a timely manner
- the tone is appropriate for the situation.

The range of PR activities includes:

- media relations
- marketing (of products, services and issues)
- copy-writing
- press office
- online PR
- Internal PR, journals and briefings
- sponsorship
- event & conference management
- research
- evaluation
- corporate identity
- publications

PR helps an organisation to manage its relationships with key stakeholders, raise awareness of the brand and the organisation's activities.

While it is often suggested that PR is free, this is far from the truth. It can be very expensive to employ a PR agency and attend exhibitions and events.

A criticism often levied at PR is the lack of control an organisation has over the final message that gets published or broadcast. At the other end of the spectrum is the concept of 'spin' where the message is clearly positioned with the audience.

The role of PR is growing and organisations are increasingly recognising the importance of PR and its different forms:

- *Press agency:* a form of one-way communication where the organisation informs or tells the various publics what it wants them to hear (spin?).

- *Public information:* Providing information that the publics need to know. Usually provided in an objective manner.

- *Two-way asymmetric:* Arguments based on research (independent?) are made to encourage the publics to change their attitude or beliefs.

- *Two-way symmetric:* PR serves to build mutual understanding between the organisation and its publics.

Publics are a group, people or organisations that an organisation needs to communicate with in order to convey its key messages. Public can be grouped into five categories (Brassington and Pettitt, 2006):

- *Commercial:* Where there is a trading relationship with, or in competition with other organisations between the parties, and synergy and understanding needs to be built, so that a positive and encouraging image can be portrayed for the industry group or market. This group can include, competitors, suppliers as well as customers.

- *Internal:* Often organisations are good at external PR, but they forget to keep staff informed of what is happening going on, which can be demotivating, but equally can negatively impact on external messages. This group can include staff, management and trade unions

- *Authority:* Public which have 'power' either because of their legal, statutory, or voluntary position to influence the organisation. This group can include government, pressure groups, buying or membership groups'

- *Media:* The media is a particularly influential group of publics which can be supportive, or adversarial. The public takes notice of this group and messages need to be carefully managed. This group can include TV, press, radio and increasingly the internet

- *Financial:* Organisations also need to keep this group of Publics informed. Larger organisations that may be listed on the UK Stock Exchange while having a legal duty to provide certain information need to manage expectations with the group both positively and negatively. This group can include the organisation's bankers, accountants, financial advisers and shareholders

Sponsorship

According to BDS consultancy, one of Europe's leading sponsorship consultancies, sponsorship can be defined as:

a business relationship between a provider of funds, resources or services and an individual, event or organisation which offers in return rights and association that may be used for commercial advantage in return for the sponsorship investment.

Reasons for sponsoring an organisation, event or sport include:

- Increased awareness for the brand

- Enhancing brand/corporate image

- Brand association with some popular activity

- Innovative product showcasing

- Product launches, raising the organisation's profile

- Providing clear differentiation from the competition

Sponsorship takes place in sport, television and radio and the arts. It is also used in cause-related marketing.

According to Mintel Research, the sponsorship market continues to grow, albeit year-on-year growth is slowing, highlighting the increasing scrutiny sponsorship decisions are under against a backdrop of continuing pressure on marketing budgets.

Sport continues to dominate the UK sponsorship market, attracting more than half of all investment in 2005, but the most rapid growth has been seen in the broadcast sector, whose value has increased by 23% to give it more than a quarter of the overall market.

The London Olympics are expected to add £700 million to the UK sports sponsorship market between now and the opening ceremony, but are expected to have a positive impact on almost all sponsorship sectors.

DIRECT MARKETING

The American Direct Marketing Association (DMA) defines direct marketing as

an interactive process of addressable communication that uses one or more advertising media to effect, at any location, a measurable sale, lead, retail purchase, or charitable donation, with this activity analyzed on a database for the development of ongoing mutually

beneficial relationships between marketers and customer, prospects,
or donors.

Direct marketing includes:

- *Direct mail:* Personalised mail to an identified addressee, used in both the B2C and B2B markets. Can be highly targeted based on the previous behaviour of the individual. Relies heavily on an accurate database being maintained. The UK is one of Europe's heaviest user of direct mail.

- *Direct response advertising:* This form of direct mail can include freepost or free phone response mechanisms, the internet and DRTV (direct response advertising in television).

- *Telemarketing:* Increasingly used as the cost of telephony reduces and technology becomes more sophisticated. A direct approach is made by telephone to existing or potential customers (outbound telephony), or where a customer is encouraged to telephone the organisation (inbound telephony).

- *E-communication:* Still in its infancy, but developing rapidly. Can include, web, email mobile and text messaging.

- *Mail order:* A traditional form of direct marketing to certain sections of the economy, where products were purchased by viewing a catalogue which was distributed direct to the consumer or via third parties (sales agents). While organisations still use catalogues this is usually linked with some other channel such as the internet. Organisations are increasingly moving to online catalogues

- *Teleshopping:* Includes a broad range of activities such as the internet through virtual stores, or shopping via the internet or telephone in response to television adverts, or home shopping channels which have developed with satellite and cable TV channels.

INTEGRATED COMMUNICATIONS MIX

Having looked at the different promotional tools individually, generally they will be used together (integrated) so that the key messages can be communicated in a consistent way. Each promotional tool and choice of media should be used to support each other and reinforce the key messages. If this does not happen then the customer is likely to become confused as a result of the mixed messages and less likely to make a purchase.

Table 11.10 shows tables summarising the various promotional tools assessed against the criteria of communications, cost and control.

Table 11.10	Various promotional tools assessed against the criteria of communications, cost and control. (a) Promotional cost; (b) Promotional control; (c) Promotional communications				
	Advertising	**Sales promotion**	**Public relations**	**Personal selling**	**Direct marketing**
(a)					
Ability to deliver a personal message	Low	Low	Low	High	High
Ability to reach a large audience	High	Medium	Medium	Low	Medium
Level of interaction	Low	Low	Low	High	High
Credibility given by target audience	Low	Medium	High	Medium	Medium
(b)					
Absolute costs	High	Medium	Low	High	Medium
Cost per contact	Low	Medium	Low	Low	High
Wastage	High	Medium	High	High	Low
Size of investment	High	Medium	Low	High	Medium
(c)					
Ability to target particular audiences	Medium	High	Low	Medium	High
Management's ability to adapt quickly as circumstances change	Medium	High	Low	Medium	High

COPYWRITING

Copywriting is the creative process of writing text for advertisements or publicity material. Copywriters are the people who write the text in accordance with a brief they have been given to work to, in order to ensure the messages are delivered to the intended audience. Copywriters work in-house, for large to medium sized organisations or for a range of agencies including PR, direct marketing and consultancies.

Copywriting is used in all the main forms of advertising so outdoor media, direct mail and digital media including the internet and needs to engage the interest of the audience so that they feel positive towards your product and go to purchase it. Copywriters need to understand who the target audience is, what is their level of understanding and what do you want them to take away from your advertisement. Bowdery (2008) writes 'do you understand the customers you're trying to influence and could you pick them out in a crowd? More importantly, could they pick your ad out in a similarly crowded marketplace?'

When developing the copy it is important not to cause offence and this is especially important when the message is being used outside the country of origination and alternative concepts are needed. Where the creative concept is used overseas, complex word and local idioms must be avoided. Websites need to be carefully worded to ensure consistency and clarity of message.

Copy should be creative but clear, jargon-free and have the right tone of voice for the audience. Finally the message should be grammatically correct with no typographical errors.

SETTING MARKETING COMMUNICATION OBJECTIVES

Often accountants will suggest that promotional activity is a cost to the organisation and the counter-argument from the communications team is that it is an investment in the business. Both can be right if the communications team cannot demonstrate the benefit of the campaign or activity.

Setting objectives is important to an organisation for the following reasons:

- A method of communication and coordination between different groups with the intention that performance will be improved through a common understanding

- A guide to decision making

- A focus for decision making in the campaign

- A benchmark to measure performance against

To help organisations to set objectives, guidelines generally referred to as SMART objectives have been established.

SMART objectives require an organisation to carefully consider what the desired outcomes of the communication activity need to be. In other words, what is to be achieved, when does it need to be achieved by and who is it aimed at?

Table 11.11 is adapted from Fill (2006).

Marketing communications can have a wide range of objectives associated with them and therefore the success or failure cannot be established.

Clearly many organisations will see success as being the additional value of sales achieved and this can be measured in a number of ways, e.g. unit of sales or the value of sales. But for many organisations other measures are needed.

Table 11.11	SMART objectives (Fill, 2006)
Specific	What is the specific variable that the organisation wants to influence in the campaign? Is it sales, perception, attitude, awareness, etc.? The variable must be clearly defined and clear outcomes established.
Measurable	How is the activity going to be measured? e.g. additional sales achieved during a set period? The number of telephone calls received at the call centre?
Achievable	Objectives must be attainable, otherwise failure will simply demotivate. staff and be a waste of effort (and money)
Realistic	Objectives should be based on research or market intelligence and be relevant to the brand.
Targeted /timed	Who is the audience for the activity and over what period are the results to be achieved?

Russell Colley (1961) wanted to ensure that the advertising agencies he employed were delivering value for money and he developed the DAGMAR model. DAMGMAR stands for defining advertising goals for measured advertising results. It is suggested that advertising success or fails depending on well it communicates the information and attitudes to the right people at the right time and at the right price to the right people.

Fill (2006) summaries the hierarchy of communications as:

- *Awareness:* Customers need to be aware of the product or the brand before a purchase can be made.

- *Comprehension:* The potential audience needs to have certain information about the product and its attributes, and sometimes they need to be given specific information on the use of the product.

- *Conviction:* The customer needs to believe that the product will give them benefits not available through other the purchase of other products.

- *Action:* Thoughts need to be turned into action and the process can be facilitated through the provision of pre-paid envelopes or free-phone numbers.

THE ROLE OF MARKETING RESEARCH

Research is the collection and analysis of data from a sample of individuals or organisations relating to their characteristics, behaviour, attitudes or possessions. It includes all forms of marketing and social research such as consumers and industrial surveys, psychological investigations, observations and panel studies. Market Research Society

According to Yeshin (2006), the market research process provides the means by which the various tasks of identifying consumer needs and wants, identifying an appropriate advertising strategy, and evaluating the effectiveness of campaigns can be achieved. Market research is at the heart of an effective communication strategy.

The main purposes of the research process are:

- To reduce or eliminate uncertainty in the planning process

- Monitor the performance of the 'agreed' plan

We will see in the next section how research can achieve both objectives in practice, but organisations typically have access to a great wealth of data that can be used to support the research process. This can be internal data, from previous campaigns and activities. External data is derived from government sources as well as (for example) readership surveys, audits and Mintel, Euromonitor reports and competitor research. Organisations that are involved overseas will similarly find sources of information and in many cases there are syndicated advertising measurement services which can establish brand performance.

Research helps organisations to better understand the market through:

- *Awareness:* usage and attitude surveys will indicate the level of the brand for your own organisation and competitors.

- *Needs:* how does the existing brand(s) meet customer needs and expectations and what are the perceived gaps?

- *Attitudes:* what do customers think of existing brands, their position in the market and the benefits they offer?

- *Usage:* how often do customers buy, when and why is the product used?

EVALUATING THE EFFECTIVENESS OF MARKETING COMMUNICATIONS

We have seen the benefits of setting objectives and with SMART objectives, an evaluation of the outcomes of the marketing communication can be undertaken and lessons learnt for future activity.

Communication can be evaluated according in accordance with two criteria:

- Development and testing of messages

- Impact and effect of the communication

Research can be undertaken at various stages of the campaign to measure effectiveness.

Pre-Testing

Prior to advertising being released generally, its effectivess can be tested, and this is referred to as pre-testing, or the campaign can be measured after the advertising has run and this is referred to as post-testing. It is not unusual to undertake both activities although it should be noted that many organisations fail to pre-test and wonder why the advertising has not been as successful as they would have liked.

Pre-testing is where a concept, i.e. an unfinished advertisement, is shown to a group of people who represent the audience to obtain comment and feedback. This feedback can then be incorporated into the material prior to its release into the market. If the test suggests the material is unsuitable it can be fundamentally changed or scrapped if felt necessary. Pre-testing can also be carried out on completed advertisements to gauge customer response.

Testing can be undertaken through a variety of research methods and its purpose is to check that the material is suitable for the target audience and the objectives set for the campaign are likely to be met. Sometimes testing will be carried out on a range of advertising concepts to see which one, from the range of options developed by the advertising agency, is more likely to be successful with the target audience.

Focus Groups

Where concepts are tested, the views of the audience are generally established through the use of 'focus groups'.

A focus group typically consists of 9-11 people who are representative of the target audience. A number of groups can be selected and conducted in different parts of the country, or overseas as necessary.

A researcher will show the group the concept(s) and explore the reaction of the group through detailed questioning in order to ensure the material is suitable.

Focus groups are qualitative in nature and this means they explore people's feelings and emotions and allow for probing of comments and observations. Findings can include bias, so the selection of the group and the quality of the researcher is important. Focus groups are usually used in conjunction with other forms of research.

Consumer Juries

Consumer juries are also used to test concepts. This approach requires the audience to rank different concepts in order of merit and justify the ranking.

When an advert is ready for release, i.e. it has been completed, it can simply be released in to the market without further testing. Alternatively the finished product can be subject to additional testing in the 'live' environment.

For example if a new magazine or journal is being developed, a 'mock up' or 'dummy' version can be distributed to the potential market and their feedback obtained.

Readability Tests

Where print copy is involved, tests can be carried out for readability. Here the structure and language would be tested to check it was appropriate to the audience.

Theatre Tests

Theatre tests are used to evaluate the response to broadcast adverts and are gaining popularity within the UK having been used for a number of years in the USA.

Physiological Tests

The increasing use of the internet requires an understanding of how the webpages are laid out and how people read the messages. This can be achieved through eye tracking and tachistoscopes, which measure the ability of an advert to attract attention.

Post-Testing

Testing adverts prior to national release can be an expensive exercise, but nevertheless useful it identifies issues.

- *Inquiry tests:* are intended to measure the number of enquiries or direct responses which maybe generated by the advert.

- *Recall tests:* this tests the ability of the respondent to recall an advert which was recently screened, usually the day previously. This can be prompted or unprompted. For example, an interviewee is asked if they remember seeing an advert for dog food. If the answer is 'Yes, Oscar's dog food', this will be recorded as 'unprompted'. If on the other hand the interviewee says no, they may be asked, did you see an advert for Pedigree dog food? A positive response maybe forthcoming which is then recorded as 'prompted'. Questions are then asked about the advert and the comments are recorded verbatim.

- *Recognition tests:* here interviewees are asked if they recognise an advert and the various components such as layout and text are explored.

Other Audiences

Manufacturers will also want to test the effectiveness of marketing communication through the distribution channel to get intermediaries to stock a wider product line or test new products. In this case a retail audit can be undertaken and this is typically carried out by specialist agencies.

Other Aspects of the Promotional Mix

It is not just advertising that needs to be measured and the following summarises the different methods that could be used to evaluate the success of the particular activity. It should be noted that campaigns often involve different promotional tools and in practice this would need an evaluation of the entire campaign.

- *Personal selling:* can be measured activity or knowledge. So for example, the number of customer visits, presentations made, or prospects identified. In terms of knowledge this could relate to product knowledge or presentation skills. The key measure is the profitability of the individual or sales team and effectiveness can be measured against industry benchmarks.

- *Public relations:* can be measured in terms of column inches of editorial coverage (positive and negative), changes in attitude toward the organisation or brand.

- *Exhibitions:* Do not always generate immediate sales, so often a measure is the number of contacts made for follow up.

Figure 11.2 shows an example of an abridged communications plan.

QUESTIONS

1. What do you understand by the terms 'above-the-line' and 'below-the-line'?

2. List the key tools marketing communication tools

3. What are the main roles of advertising?

4. What are the main disadvantages when using cinema as a form of advertising?

5. Why do you think people are reading fewer printed newspapers?

6. Given the expense of personal selling, in what situation can it be justified?

7. What is the role of PR?

8. What do you understand by the term 'two way symmetrical communication'?

9. What are the advantages of sponsorship as a form of PR?

10. What activities are undertaken with Direct Marketing?

11. What do you understand by the term SMART?

Context/key issues

A major PLC currently distributes a quarterly newsletter to its 'top 1000'-business decision makers. It is used to communicate key messages cost effectively as it is distributed with the customer's monthly statement of account. The company wants to widen distribution of the newsletter to include the next tier of customers, a segment of around 3000 customers. The rationale is to reduce the influence of competitor organisations in the segment and encourage customers to continue doing business with the organisation, build loyalty and encourage additional spend.

Communication objectives 2010/2011

- To position the company as a knowledgeable and innovative player in the market and position the range of products as essential business tools which will be used in preference to other competitor products

Target audience

There are three discrete audiences to be addressed:

- Decision makers within the 'top 1000' accounts
- Decision makers in the second tier accounts which is another 3000 decision makers.
  - Research has shown that 24% of decision makers in the 'top 1000' sector read the newsletter all the way through with 60% having a brief look before putting it to one side and 16% not reading it at all.
- Gatekeepers, including administrators, secretaries and bookkeepers. They may be the recipient of the communication and can choose to ignore it and not bring it to the notice of the decision-maker, consequently the material may not reach the intended audience.

Creative and media strategy

The newsletter has been sent out to the 'top 1000' since 2004 with the monthly statement. A variety of methods including internet, email and direct mail will be used to achieve the stated objectives. Mass communication media is not appropriate.
A pull strategy will be used as we will be only be communicating with the customer.

Budget

A budget of £10,000 (inclusive of VAT) is available for this activity which will cover media, any photography, studio costs and production and distribution costs.

Phasing/Scheduling

It is envisaged that the 'top 1000' distribution cycle will continue unchanged, with the new segment receiving the first newsletter in March 2010 and quarterly there after

Evaluation

Research will be conducted 3 months after the initial newsletter has launched and additional sales will be monitored on a monthly basis.

A visual indication of the plan is shown below.

FIGURE 11.2

Abridged communications plan.

The communications plan

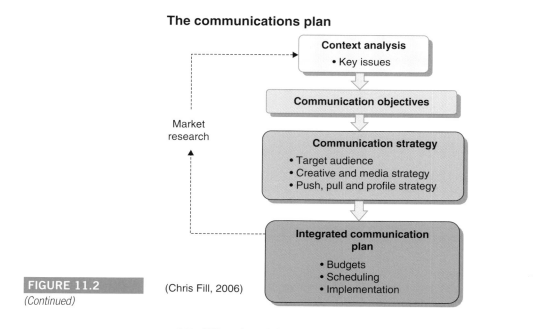

FIGURE 11.2
(Continued)

(Chris Fill, 2006)

12. What is DAGMAR?

13. What is the role of research in relation to marketing communication?

14. In what two ways can the effectiveness of marketing communication be measured?

15. What do you understand by the tem 'pre-testing'?

SUMMARY

This chapter has covered the range of communication mixes available to an organisation. Depending on the nature of the organisation, its products and the messages it wants to share with customers it must select one or more elements of the promotional mix, which should be innovative, sustainable and coordinated. As the use of online media increases, its integration with offline media becomes more important.

A range of evaluation methods has been outlined which if used will improve the effectiveness of an organisation's communication strategy by ensuring its messages are effective in terms of the messages being communicated, but also in reaching the right audience.

Effective communication needs careful planning and coordination and whilst it is tempting not to undertake pre- and post-campaign research, it is the only sure way to know exactly how well the message(s) being communicated is received.

FURTHER READING

www.cipr.co.uk

www.mintel.com

www.org.uk

www.thinkbox.tv/server/show/nav.1019

www.warc.com

www.isp.org.uk

BIBLIOGRAPHY

http://www.sponsorship.co.uk/index.html (accessed 18/12/08)

Bowdery, R. (2008) *Copywriting*. AVA Publishing SA, Switzerland.

Brassington, F. and Pettitt, S. (2006) *Principles of Marketing*. FT Prentice Hall.

Colley, R. (1961) *Defining Advertising Goals for Measures Advertising Results*. Association of National Advertisers, New York.

Fill, C. (2006) *Marketing Communications: Engagement, strategies and practice,* 4th edition. FT Prentice Hall.

Reid, A., Pullins, E.B. and Plank, R.E. (2002) The impact of purchase situation on sales-person communication behaviours in business markets. *Industrial Marketing Management*, 31(3).

Stokes, D. and Lomax, W. (2008) *Marketing: A Brief Introduction*. Thomson.

Yeshin, T. (2006) *Advertising*. Thomson.

CHAPTER 12

Agency and Agency Relationships

LEARNING OUTCOMES

At the end of this chapter you will be able to:
- **Assess the approaches to appointing agencies**
- **Examine the reporting, monitoring and measurement approaches to measure agency performance**
- **Evaluate the key information needed in managing agency relationships**

INTRODUCTION

We have seen that there is a vast choice of promotional tools available to the marketer and when combined with various media, it is clear that effective marketing not only relies on a sound planning processes, but sound execution strategies. Consider the various stakeholders and relationship networks that an organisation develops therefore the overall picture becomes complicated requiring an expert solution.

Large organisations may choose to undertake many promotional activities internally rather than employ external agencies, but increasingly much of the communication activity is given to an external agency. However, this in itself brings some choices in agency selection. What type of agency is needed (see example below), how will they will selected, which will best suit my needs?

A large UK bank had over 30 agencies on its roster. This had developed over the years as senior managers within the various divisions conducted their own pitches and appointed their own agencies. While there was an overlap in activities and knowledge this was justified on the base of the expert knowledge of each agency.

The result of an internal bank review decided that only one agency would be employed across the entire bank. The rationale was that one agency would develop a high degree of knowledge across the organisation, build synergy and reduce costs.

The newly appointed agency rapidly found that it did not have all the skills needed and initially allowed the bank to continue using previously employed agencies where they had the requisite skills.

The whole process of identifying agencies, obtaining proposals, pitching and appointment took around 12 months, and cost a substantial amount of money.

The success or otherwise of this approach is still being debated.

COMMUNICATIONS AGENCIES

An organisation has a range of agency types to choose from. Here we focus on creative agencies, of which there are four main types: full service agency, media independents, a la carte and new media.

Full Service Agency

As the name may suggest this type of agency offers the complete range of products and services which a client may need to advertise its products. Research, strategic planning, creative, media planning and buying planning.

Where the agency does not have all the skills in-house, it will sub-contact some of the work to other agencies.

Media Independents

Media independents provide specialist media services such as planning, buying and evaluation. The agency will suggest the media, the size of the advertisement, location and they provide a report on the effectiveness of the campaign.

It should be noted that media dependents will be part of a full service agency, while media independents will be separate organisations who are free to set their own direction.

A La Carte

A client may choose to select a number of agencies to carry out its communication activities. Each will be selected for its particular area of expertise, so strategic planning, media buying or creative. While this may offer the perceived advantage of specialism, it does mean that the client must take responsibility for managing and coordinating the various agencies and their activities.

New Media

This area has grown over the past few years and will continue to grow as technology continues to change the way organisations communicate with stakeholders.

Online brands, mobile communications, email and viral marketing are all growing areas which require a specialist approach. Equally the integration of on- and off-line marketing will require a greater blend of skills.

Creative Shops

The creative shop ('hotshops') is an off-shoot of the full-service agency. They have been formed by staff who have left full-service agencies to create a particular style or approach.

AGENCY SELECTION

The appointment of an agency is an important and formal process which is time-intensive. When a larger organisation changes its agency or its approach, it often generates substantial activity in the trade press. On occasions where the incumbent agency is not selected, challenges will be made, so an audit demonstrating a fair and open process is needed.

Selection starts with research. The following process assumes the organisation is undertaking the selection process on its own. However, a search of the internet will reveal that there are organisations that will assist a client in the selection, i.e. act as a consultant.

There are industry magazines and publications that list agencies according to the services offered. *Campaign portfolio* and the *Advertising Agency Roster* are useful starting points as they offer full contact information.

From the list available a number of agencies should be long listed with a view to reducing the number of agencies to a more manageable number of around 10 agencies.

Shortlist criteria:

1. Area of expertise held by the agencies

2. Quality of existing clients (need to consider any competitive issues)

3. Reputation of principals and experience of staff

4. Agency fees and methods of charging and payment

5. In-house resources

6. Geographical cover, i.e. any international contacts

It is usual to visit the agency premises to see the working conditions and have the opportunity to meet staff who may not be involved in the pitch (see below).

It may be at this stage some agencies are eliminated and not be invited to pitch. Those agencies invited to pitch will be given a brief by the client and a set amount of time to prepare it.

Table 12.1	Agency criteria
Criteria	**Explanation**
Credentials	■ Experience of industry sector ■ Positive client feedback ■ Track record of success
Creative techniques	■ Evidence of creativity and innovation in current clients' work
Staff	■ How many staff will be dedicated to the account? ■ Experience of staff ■ Have they worked on similar sized accounts? ■ How long has the team been together?
The agency	■ Is it well resourced? ■ What is the nature of the agency and will it need to outsource any activities? ■ What are its objectives? ■ How does it measure outcome? ■ What SLAs will be available? ■ What is its size? ■ Location
Specialism	■ What are the areas that the agency specialises in?
Price	■ Is the pricing structure clear and reasonable?
Legal	■ What mechanisms are in place to ensure compliance with voluntary codes of practice and regulatory requirements?
Pitch	■ Did the pitch meet the requirements of the brief?

The Pitch

All agencies should be assessed according to a set, consistent criteria. Table 12.1 offers a range of criteria which could be used.

Some criteria will be subjective: team working will be an important part of the relationship, and the staff from both the client and agency will need to be able to work effectively with each other for an agreed period of time, which could be for up to five years.

AGENCY REMUNERATION

There are four ways in which an agency can be rewarded for its efforts on behalf of its client. The three methods are listed in Table 12.2, with the fourth option being a combination of methods.

Table 12.2	Agency remuneration methods
Reward method	**Explanation**
Commission	Traditionally agencies were paid a commission in exchange for using a particular publication. Commission was paid at rate of 15%. However, different agencies received different levels and clients increasingly became concerned about agency objectivity when planning media schedules.
	Consequently the fee payment method became more popular and the concept of payment by results gained popularity.
Fees	Whatever media is chosen, payment is by a set fee for a particular activity.
	Monthly fees irrespective of the work put through the agency will be paid, known as a retainer. In addition to the retainer a fixed price will be agreed for each component of a campaign. For example, a client may agree a fixed monthly fee in addition to a menu of prices for specific activity.
Payment by Results	While popular overseas, it is used selectively in the UK. Depending on the success of the campaign different payment terms will be triggered. While many would argue the merits of the approach, an agency can argue that success is hard to define and in any event elements of the campaign maybe outside its control.

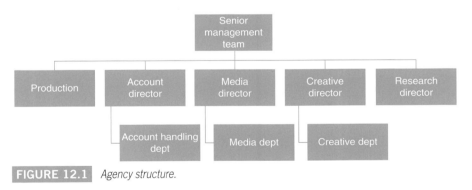

FIGURE 12.1 *Agency structure.*

AGENCY STRUCTURE

The senior management team will consist of the Chief Executive Officer (CEO), and Directors (see Figure 12.1).

The Account Director is responsible for the management of specific accounts and will have a team of Account Executives who will provide day to day support on the account dealing with routine tasks.

The production team is responsible for progress, known as managing the traffic, and also for the advertisements.

Accounts Team

Usually the Account Director will take responsibility for the management of an account or group of accounts depending on the complexity of the relationship. The Account Director will manage the relationship to ensure it is running smoothly and will also ensure its profitability.

Reporting to the Account Director will be an Account Manager or Executive who will manage the relationship on a day-to-day basis, meeting or speaking with the client to take additional commissions or manage progress on existing work. Where the client is large, then the Account Manager will also liaise with other Account Managers who will be working on other parts of the account in order to have a clear picture of the client's needs.

Planning

A senior role within the agency who works as part of the team and is responsible for planning the advertising.

Yeshin (2006) identifies five key roles for the account planner (see Figure 12.2):

1. *Defining the task:* The planner is responsible for bringing together key information from within the agency and commission research if necessary in order to clearly define the task.

2. *Preparing the creative brief:* The planner will develop the creative brief which informs the creative process.

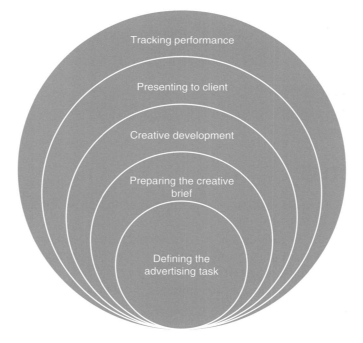

FIGURE 12.2

Five key roles for the account planner.

3. *Creative development:* The planner will input into all stages of the creative development and be the 'custodian' of the client's brand values.

4. *Presenting to the client:* The planner will join the Account handlers and present the advertising concepts to the client and answer questions regarding the rationale for the approach taken.

5. *Tracking performance:* Once the campaign is launched the planner will monitor consumer reaction and feedback to the campaign.

The Creative Team

It is the creative team that is responsible for developing for the messages used in the campaigns. It is usual for a copywriter to work with the art designer to develop the creative concept. This team will interpret the creative brief and turn it into advertising.

The Media Department

Here the team is responsible for ensuring the right material is passed to the right media at the right time. They will also take responsibility for constructing the media schedule so that the campaign objectives are available achieved through the placement of advertisements in media that will reach the target audience in an effective and cost efficient way.

The range of available media is vast and the increasing use of 'new media' means that the media team needs to consist of number of specialists in the different media.

Production

The production team is responsible for ensuring the quality of the material in terms of ensuring it is in the right format and the final appearance; font, colour, photography, all matches the brief. The traffic team is responsible for scheduling the work across the agency and ensuring that each stage of the creative process is delivered in accordance with the schedule agreed with the client.

BBH SCOOPS HEINEKEN UK

by *Noel Bussey, Campaign* 29-Jan-09

LONDON-Heineken has moved its UK advertising business out of The Red Brick Road and into Bartle Bogle Hegarty without a pitch.

The agency will now handle all of the brewer's advertising duties inside the UK market. The Red Brick Road will remain on the global Heineken roster.

BBH forced its way on to the global roster in November last year.

Source: Brand Republic, Brandrepublic.com

MANAGING AGENCIES

All agency relationships are different reflecting not only the structure of the agency, but the culture of the companies involved in the relationship (Yeshin, 2006).

It is not unusual for an agency to stay with a client for many years; equally as can be seen from the Heineken example, relationships can change quickly. Agencies must share or understand the values of the client they are working for and they must act as if they have just been appointed i.e. not become complacent, as this is will reduce their effectiveness in a highly competitive industry. As we shall see below, the consequences of changing agencies should not be underestimated. Often when a new agency is appointed there may already be some existing relationship which can be developed, however, when an entirely new agency is appointed there is a steep learning curve to be addressed, which can slow the launch of new campaigns into the market. However, there are other implications; the media may be worried that an organisation sacking an agency may be a sign of other worries, such as a slide in market share and respond badly. Equally the sacking could be seen as good news, i.e. the organisation has identified a problem and put a solution in place.

Clearly for the outgoing agency the news is generally seen as negative. However, *Campaign* (2004) suggests that clients change agencies because the agency has lost interest in the client, or is not allocating the amount of time felt warranted. In a small number of situations, organisations stated that they changed agencies as a matter of course.

Beltramini and Pitta (1991) suggest four benefits of effective relationships with agencies:

1. Agencies must have a genuine interest in meeting the needs of the client in order to demonstrate a commitment to maintaining a productive relationship. The agency must always respond to any concerns raised by the clients and it needs to be recognised that relationships can take time to build. Therefore care should be exercised by the client when considering changing agencies.

2. The relationship between the parties often requires sensitive information to be shared and consequently the agency views privileged information which offers an insight in to the nature of the client which may not be ever seen by the customer. The agency should invest time in understanding the client, its DMU and its structure.

3. Close relationships need to be maintained between the key players in the agency and the client at both the strategic and operational levels.

4. There needs to be two-way communication between the parties and the agency needs to ensure a constant flow of ideas from the client.

Where there is an international dimension, then the agency relationship will be determined by the strategies adopted for the various markets.

Where the communication is centralised, i.e. all aspects of the marketing communications process is managed from one central point, a high degree of control will be exercised across the entire process. In the situation where the decisions are taken at local level, i.e. decentralisation, more autonomy is given to the local staff. Finally some organisations choose a compromise between the two extremes and adopt a combination of both approaches. An increasing trend is to group geographical areas together that have similarities e.g. Europe or Asia.

Within the agency structure there is an account handling team and the make-up of this tries to mirror the structure of the client organisation.

Overseas agencies have additional complexity and the following outlines the issues faced in managing agencies.

Having gone through the process of selecting the agency and recognising that the relationship with the client could extend over many years, it is essential to put in place procedures to ensure the relationship runs smoothly. Often a Service Level Agreement is initiated (see Chapter 13) which specifies the minimum standards which the agency can be expected to deliver to.

Part of the selection process is to establish that the teams could work with each other together. Equally important is for the client's business objectives to be clear.

A marketing communications plan will guide the relationship and set out any budgetary or financial issues that need to be addressed.

The client needs to ensure the agency has sufficient information prior to launching a campaign. Often informal discussions will take place prior to the agency being formally given a communications brief (see Figure 12.3).

A communications agency is appointed because it is felt that it can produce better results than conducting the work in-house and it also makes better use of resources.

However, agencies must be monitored to ensure they are providing the client an acceptable level of value.

Before any campaign is launched into the market, it must undergo testing to ensure its messages are effective and understood by the audience. However, it is also import to fully evaluate campaigns that have taken place, not only for the client organisation but including their competitors.

Fill (2006) suggests that competitor strategies should be monitored for style and level of spend in addition to strategic credibility and corporate

Communication brief	
Objectives	• What objectives have been set for the campaign and how will they be measured, i.e. sales conversion of leads into prospects? • What behavioural or attitudinal measures will be used and over what timescale? • How does the activity support the overall brand promise? • Does the campaign form part of a wider campaign and if so how does it fit in?
Target audience	• Who is the audience?
Product	• Description, positioning and features • Any conditions for application? • Key competitors • Why should people buy this product? • USPs
Creative and media considerations	• Research undertaken on current creative work?
Logistical considerations	• Any media constraints?
Budget	• Exactly what does the budget cover?

Creative brief
Campaign requirement One off, or number of adverts
The target audience Demographics, lifestyle, product usage/attitudes
What is the advertising intended to achieve?
The single-minded proposition
Rationale for the proposition
Mandatory inclusions E.g. Stockists, logos, telephone/email contact
Desired brand image Friendly, professional, modern, etc.

FIGURE 12.3 *Communicating with agencies. (a) The communication brief; (b) the creative brief.*

| Table 12.3 | Example financial performance standards |

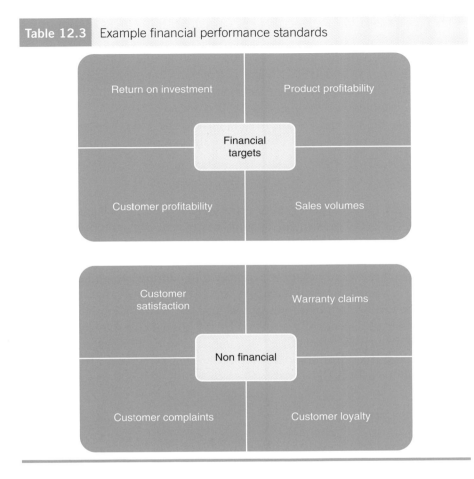

image. The objective is to improve on the quality and effectiveness of the current communications campaigns.

Pre-campaign research will suggest any changes which maybe necessary prior to the campaign launch. However, post-campaign research will establish whether or not the perceived messages were understood by the audience. It is suggested that both internal and external campaigns are addressed.

Campaigns will have a performance targets, or key deliverables set, which can be expressed in a variety of ways (see Table 12.3). Performance will be monitored on a regular basis as appropriate for the effective management of the business. An internet search engine may monitor 'hits' hourly, whereas a university may monitor student recruitment on a quarterly basis.

Achievement of the financial performance is usually relatively easy to measure as the actual performance collected through internal data is generally available. However, the data needs to be considered in the light of competitor data as this will affect.

Many organisations have developed a communications audit based around the work of Ind (1992). Here perceptions are evaluated across different media and across different divisions of the organisation in order to ensure consistency.

However, the criteria for measuring advertising effectiveness must be derived from the objects set at the outset of the campaign.

SUMMARY

The appointment of an agency takes a considerable amount of time and effort and requires a heavy investment in time, not just in evaluating the pitches, but ensuring that they are well prepared. Different agencies will bring different perspective to the client and therefore best practice needs to be implemented to find the agency that offers the right fit, culture and philosophy.

Having invested time in securing the 'right' agency, that time then needs to be further invested in ensuring that the relationship is well managed and that the agency is motivated by the thought of the client's business. Regular reviews will need to be conducted to ensure expectations are being met and that clear objectives are set so that both parties are clear on what should be delivered.

BIBLIOGRAPHY

http://www.brandrepublic.com/News/MostRead/876883/BBH-scoops-Heineken-UK/ (accessed 1/2/09)

Beltramini, R.F. and Pitta, D.A. (1991) Underlying dimensions and communication strategies of the advertising agency-client relationship. *International Journal of Advertising*(10), 2.

Campaign (2004) *Why accounts move*. 27 February 2004.

Fill, C. (2006) *Marketing Communications: Engagement, strategies and practice*, 4th edition. FT Prentice Hall.

Ind, N. (1992) *The Corporate Image: Strategies for effective Identity Programme*, revised edition. Kogan Page, London.

Yeshin, T. (2006) *Advertising*. Thomson.

Senior Examiner's Comments – Section Three

Having completed Section Three students should have a detailed knowledge of:

- The development of marketing communications strategy and objectives
- The contents and structure of a marketing communications plan
- The elements of the promotional mix and its application in different markets and organisational contexts
- Measuring the performance of marketing communications activities
- The role, management and performance measurement of agencies in marketing communications

Communication (both internal and external) is a key aspect of marketing and this is reflected by the higher weighting of this area of the syllabus (30%). To succeed, students must be able to apply the aspects of the syllabus in different organisational contexts and markets. In particular, students must be able to develop appropriate communications strategies, objectives, plans and activities that will contribute towards the achievement of organisational objectives, for example, income and profit growth; customer retention; new business acquisition; and enhanced customer satisfaction.

The market is full of examples of communications strategy 'in action'. Students are urged to supplement their study by observing and analysing what is happening in the media around them, and further afield. There are many examples daily of how organisations are successfully executing integrated communications activities, which provide excellent case studies for evaluation.

A further key aspect is measurement. Communications activities, generally, represent the highest amount of marketing expenditure for organisations. So, measurement plays a key role in 'proving' the value of marketing to the business overall.

209

Managing and Achieving Customers' Service Expectations Through the Marketing Mix

CHAPTER 13

Customer Service and Customer Care Plans

LEARNING OBJECTIVES

By the end of this chapter you will be able to:
- Examine the importance of customer service
- Assess the value, importance and financial implications of customer service
- Examine the costs involved in providing customer service

INTRODUCTION

This final section of the syllabus addresses how organisations, across a range of sectors and operating in different markets (including domestic and international), develop the marketing mix in order to meet customer service expectations.

A thorough knowledge of the extended marketing mix components is paramount. Students will then be expected to use this knowledge and apply it to different scenarios and to demonstrate, through application, a detailed appreciation of what constitutes 'service' to various types of customers.

The syllabus examines a range of tools and techniques in delivering high quality service to customers, from customer service planning, to managing key account customers and the use of SLAs (Service Level Agreements) with customers.

The key role of customer and product information, its management, storage and retrieval, is also examined. Students will be required to understand how organisations undertake these activities, and the risks and issues they face where they are not managed effectively.

THE SERVICE ECONOMY

In recent years, the UK services sector (also known as the tertiary sector) has seen considerable growth and now accounts for nearly 75 per cent of total UK output. Of course recent events in the world economy will impact on future growth, but nevertheless it is expected that services will remain a key element of the UK economy.

WHAT ARE SERVICES?

Services are referred to as being 'intangible' and consist of industries such as banking, insurance, government, education, professional services and tourism. Services embrace the not-for-profit sectors and can be intended to satisfy both business and personal customer needs.

There are many definitions of a service. Kotler et al. (1999) defines a service as 'any activity or benefit that one party can offer to another which is essentially intangible and does not result in the ownership of anything'.

Services can be split into:

- Business services

- Consumer services

Figure 13.1, adapted from Brassington and Pettitt (2006), demonstrates the difficult of classifying some services, although it is clearer at the extremes.

THE MARKETING MIX FOR SERVICES

The concept of the marketing mix (Borden, 1964) consists of four elements which when combined together create an offering for the customer. The mix known as the 4Ps (product, price, place, promotion) is not sufficient for the service sector and 3 additional Ps was proposed by Booms and Bitner (1981) which is now generally referred to as the 7Ps. The additional Ps are:

- *People:* take part in the production and delivery of the service and, as we will see later, may interact directly with the customer or be part of the support team

- *Processes:* the operational process that moves the customer from making the order through to taking delivery

- *Physical evidence:* the tangibility given to the product, so for example decor or brochures or the business infrastructure

Each of the additional Ps is discussed in more detail in Table 13.1.

Table 13.2 shows a plan to overcome service encounter issues using the marketing mix.

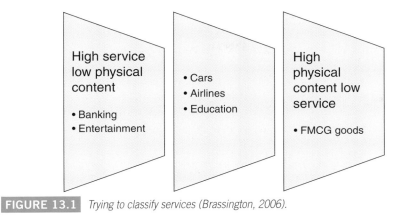

FIGURE 13.1 *Trying to classify services (Brassington, 2006).*

Table 13.1	The extra three Ps

People

Services typically require people to deliver them, often having just created them. Consequently for many customers 'people' represent the brand and where a relationship builds, it becomes difficult for a competitor to take the business away from that organisation. Clearly where there is no rapport, it is much easier for the customer to take the business to a competitor, or for the competitor to capture the business.

Processes

Processes refer to the actual delivery as well as the support in the provision of the service. In a university a new lecturer will be given guidance on how to deliver a lecture, while support teams will be providing timetables to the students and registering them for a particular module and collecting the fees, or reminding students to pay.

Physical evidence

This relates to the tangible aspects of the services. So in the example above, the lecturer will provide the students with a set of class notes. The tutor room or lecture theatre also acts as physical evidence along with the quality of the decoration.

ISSUES FOR SERVICE PROVIDERS

It can be more challenging for customers to differentiate between service providers in the same industry because they all appear to be similar. Equally it can be difficult for an organisation to manage and measure the quality of the service provided as much will depend on the customers' expectations of the service.

Marketing services presents the marketing function with some additional challenges compared with the non-service sector, particularly around the four key characteristics of services which are

Table 13.2	A plan to overcome service encounter issues using the marketing mix
Product	What is the collection of benefits that the product offers?
	Organisations offering services will still break the product into ranges. A chain of leisure centres may choose to market each one as a separate product.
	Bank accounts can be grouped into savings and current accounts and further segmented within this grouping into classic and premium current accounts.
	Airlines offer economy, premium economy, business and first class seats on some aircraft.
Price	What does our price represent are we premium priced to reflect the high quality of the product? Do we price differently for different products? Of course the nature of services makes the setting of price quite difficult and different approaches are used and even the pricing models are changing.
	Airlines historically charged a lower price as the date of the flight got closer. Ryanair and easyjet changed that and offered cheaper prices the earlier the booking was made.
	Estate agents charge a commission for selling a property and often solicitors will charge a standard fee for a particular activity.
Place	Where is the product to be delivered? Physical evidence is closely related to place and should reflect on the quality of service.
	The consumption of services can take place in hundreds of different places from the dentist's chair to high in the sky. This can limit consumption, i.e. there are only a certain number of flights per day.
	The internet is also changing the place of consumption.
Promotion	The promotional activity must reflect the positioning the product occupies in the consumer's mind based on reputation, quality and reliability.
	Also it must be able to communicate the benefits of the service.
People	Staff must be trained in the organisation's products and values. Where possible staff should be empowered to ensure customers are fully satisfied.
Processes	Processes need to be developed so that the variability in service can be reduced.
Physical evidence	This can relate to the decoration, the staff uniforms, the style of the menus, each reflecting the brand of the organisation.

- *Intangibility/ownership:* Services cannot be touched, seen, tasted, heard or smelled before being purchased, nor can they be owned. Similarly once the service has been consumed it cannot be experienced again in the same manner.

- *Inseparability:* Services cannot be stored and sold later and they cannot be separated from the provider.

- *Perishability:* As services are effectively produced and consumed at the same time they cannot be stored, so a better management of demand is necessary.

- *Heterogeneity:* The quality of the service is dependent on the person providing it, therefore it will vary.

Examples of each of these categories are:

- *Intangibility:* Create tangibility by providing some physical evidence, e.g. brochures, premises, certificates or membership.

- *Inseparability:* Developed standardised processes to maintain quality, e.g. pre-packed foreign currency, new systems and staff training.

- *Perishability:* Introduce better 'demand management' systems, e.g. low-cost airlines where flights are cheaper the further in advance seats are booked.

- *Heterogeneity:* Similar to 'inseparability', i.e. standardised processes for producing the service, e.g. in a coffee bar to ensure the same tasting coffee each time it is produced.

The challenge is for an organisation to be able to overcome the service characteristics and develop marketing approaches (Meek and Meek, 2001) which:

- Promote the advantages of non-ownership

- Make available a tangible symbol or representation of ownership

- Increase the chances or opportunities of ownership

To help overcome the perceived gaps the organisation must utilise the 7Ps of the marketing mix, as shown in Table 13.3.

Table 13.3	To help overcome the perceived gaps the organisation must utilise the 7Ps of the marketing mix
Product	What is the collection of benefits that the product offers?
Price	What does our price represent – are we premium priced to reflect the high quality of the product? Do we price differently for different product?
Place	Where is the product to be delivered? Physical evidence is closely related to place and should reflect on the quality of service.
Promotion	The promotional activity must reflect the positioning the product occupies in the consumer's mind.
People	Staff must be trained in the organisation's products and values. Where possible staff should be empowered to ensure customers are fully satisfied.
Processes	Processes need to be developed so that the variability in service can be reduced.
Physical evidence	This can relate to the decoration, the staff uniforms, the style of the menus, each reflecting the brand of the organisation.

WHAT CONSTITUTES SERVICE QUALITY?

The delivery of high-quality service is one of the most important and difficult tasks that any service organisation faces (Dibb et al., 2005); after all, customer service is an abstract concept.

Service quality is judged by the customers, not the organisation and can be defined as customers' perception of how well a service meets or exceeds their expectations.

Farrance (2002) defines service quality as 'meeting or exceeding customers' expectations at a price that is acceptable to the customer and at a return that is acceptable to the organisation'.

Gronroos (1984) argues that the quality of service, which is a series of processes, is whatever the customer perceives it to be. However, customers often see service as broad concept and an organisation must understand the basis on which customers judge service.

There are there separate elements which collectively determine service quality experience (Groonoos, 1984):

- *Technical:* e.g. waiting times. The amount of time a customer is kept waiting on the telephone, or in a queue, or having their query dealt with. The decor in the bedroom of a hotel room.

- *Functional:* how is the measurable aspect of the service deliver? For example, was the customer advised that there would be 10 minute wait, or that the decision on a customer's loan application will take 7 days?

Customers will have an expectation about the service provided, and collectively the elements of Technical quality, Functional Quality and Customer Expectation are known as the triangle of quality perception.

Clearly, for an organisation to be successful the challenge is to get the balance right because customers evaluate the service received across a number of dimensions particularly in respect of their expectations and often they experience 'gaps' in their expectations. This would suggest that there is no point in providing a service to customers that is not valued. A methodology needs to be implemented so that service quality aspects which are important to customers can be understood and processes put in place not only to meet, but exceed (delight) customer expectations.

SERVICE AND CUSTOMER LOYALTY

Service has a key role to play in building loyalty as well as generating financial benefits for an organisation through customer acquisition and retention. However, it should be noted that customer satisfaction and loyalty are not the same thing (Piercy, 2001).

Satisfaction is an attitude (how a customer feels about a company's product), while loyalty is behaviour (do they buy from us more than once?).

However, a 'zone of indifference' is often noted. The zone of indifference is where customer satisfaction ranges from satisfied to just satisfied. It is suggested there are two important conclusions to be drawn;

- The quality of the service provided must be outside the zone of indifference, i.e. it must have at least make them 'very satisfied' if they are to be expected to make subsequent purchases.

- Customers must be clearly identified as to their satisfaction levels in order for the organisation to develop the appropriate actions to build enduring relationships.

It is suggested an organisation needs to offer more than a good service and acceptable value if they are to create loyalty with customers. Piercy (2001) cites the defection rate among BA 'satisfied customers' as 13%: exactly the same as dissatisfied complaining customers.

Another important reason for building customer satisfaction is the fact that only very satisfied customers will be prepared to undertake word-of-mouth support for the organisation, which is one of the more credible communications channels when encouraging purchase. Conversely those people who have encountered poor service will be negative and act as 'terrorists', keeping people away from the product. It is an often-cited fact that each customer who has received poor service will tell at least five of their friends or colleagues. Equally, it is significantly more expensive to recruit new customers than retain existing ones.

CREATING COMPETITIVE ADVANTAGE

It has been stated previously that organisations will use service to create a point of differentiation from the competition, because good service is hard to easily replicate.

Dibb et al. (2005) suggest that a competitive advantage is 'something desired by the customer that only one company can offer'.

It is much harder to develop a competitive advantage in services, but nevertheless just like in any industry, any competitive advantage gained, must be sustainable. Otherwise any advantage gained will be lost along with the costs of the initial investment.

Key factors in developing a competitive advantage are shown in Table 13.4.

ECONOMIC EFFECTS OF CUSTOMER LOYALTY

The key benefits to be derived by an organisation when improving customer loyalty include:

- *Premium pricing:* existing customers tend to be content to pay a higher price than new customers. This can be attributed to a mutual understanding between organisation and customer.

- *Cost savings:* as seen above, once an organisation and customer understand each other, the need for expensive advertising to build that part of the relationship (brand awareness) is no longer needed and more product specific (targeted) advertising can be undertaken instead.

Table 13.4	Key factors in developing a competitive advantage (based on Dibb et al., 2005)
Key factors	**Comment**
Key sectors	What market sector(s) does the organisation need to develop?
Products	What product(s) need to be offered to the sectors identified? This should be based on market research.
Competitors	What advantages (perceived or otherwise) does the competition offer and what are their strengths?
Service gaps	Where are the service gaps between what the customer expects and what is delivered?
Sustainability	How can the advantage be maintained in the future?

■ *Income growth:* as the relationship builds (ladder of loyalty), it would be expected that the customer would place additional and on going business with the organisation with the additional income they produce.

■ *Costs of acquisition:* it is generally regarded five times more expensive to recruit a customer than it is to retain one, so the less need there is to recruit new customers the greater the savings. Equally, it can take a couple of years to recoup the costs of acquisition.

MANAGING AND IMPROVING SERVICE QUALITY

Parasuraman et al. (1985) developed a service quality model (SERVQUAL) that is used to identify the key components used in the evaluation of a service. They also developed a model of customer service gaps relating to the management perception of service quality and the tasks associated with delivering the service to the customer.

Figure 13.2 shows that customers measure the five dimensions of quality against a number of other influences which leads to an outcome on the level of service provided.

A customer maybe influenced by talking to a friend or colleague who has influenced the purchase (positively or negatively). It may well be that the customer has previously experienced the service (maybe through contacting an overseas call centre). Equally they may be experiencing the service based on an evaluation of their needs or responded to an advertisement. All of these influences when measured against the five dimensions of quality (see below) will establish the perceived level of service (seen from the perspective of the customer).

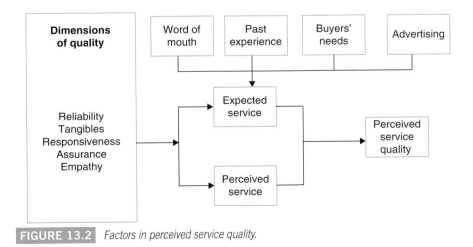

FIGURE 13.2 *Factors in perceived service quality.*

Dimensions and role of service

The components or dimensions of customer service are:

- **R**esponsiveness
- **A**ssurance
- **T**angibles
- **E**mpathy
- **R**eliability

Sometimes the components are referred to by the mnemonic RATER, or RRATE. Table 13.5 groups the components under the umbrella of the extended marketing mix.

Given that customers often view different service providers in the same industry as being the same (for example, banks), organisations are looking to differentiate themselves through the quality of their service offering. This requires a concerted effort to ensure customer needs are not just met, but exceeded (customer delight). However, the differentiation needs to be sustained, otherwise the organisation simply enjoys a short-term advantage which is quickly lost along with the investment in securing that advantage. According to Bain & Co a 5 per cent increase in customer retention can increase a company's profitability by 75 per cent.

> 'The problem really comes down to simply not understanding what things really matter most to the customer' (Piercy, 2001)

Table 13.5 The components under the umbrella of the extended marketing mix

Marketing Mix	SERVQUAL Components
Process	■ *Reliability*, the ability to perform the service, accurately, dependably consistently and in accordance with the instructions given.
People	■ *Responsiveness*, ability to offer a timely service that meets customer expectations. When there is a problem does the organisation respond quickly? ❑ *Empathy*, focus on the individual needs of the customer. ❑ *Assurance*, the ability to convey trust and confidence.
Physical evidence	*Tangibles*, look and feel of offices, cars, appearance of staff and marketing collateral.

Organisations must establish exactly what the customer wants. Take for example Vue Cinema's decision to allow adults-only to films with a lower age classification:

"These screenings have been launched in direct response to overwhelming positive customer feedback obtained from extensive research studies and trials carried out over the past year. This confirmed a significant number of cinema goers wanted to see PG, 12A and 15-rated films in screenings that could avoid unwanted disruptions that can sometimes be caused by audiences under the age of 18."

But having established exactly what the customer wants an organisation must have a clearly established service quality culture that all staff should follow.

Internal marketing is a key ingredient in improving the service encounter. There is evidence to suggest (Dibb et al., 2005) that there is a strong relationship between satisfied employees, marketing orientation and organisational performance.

It is built on communications, the development of being responsive to changing needs and a unified sense of purpose between employees.

The key steps include:

- Creating internal awareness
    - Understanding of corporate aims
- Identification of internal customer and supplier
- Communication of expectations to internal suppliers
- Internal suppliers making modification to their activities to reflect customer views
- A measure of internal service quality

But having established exactly what the customer wants, an organisation must have a clearly-established service quality culture which all staff should follow.

According to Zeithaml and Bitner (2003) in the gaps model of service (Figure 13.3), quality builds from the customer and builds the organisational tasks around what is needed to close the customer gap, i.e. the gap between what customers expect and what they receive. The central focus of gap model is the customer gap – the difference between customer expectation and perception.

GAP 1

This gap means that management perceives the quality expectations inaccurately, or, looked at another way, there is a difference between the customer expectations of the level of service to be received and the management's understanding of that expectation.

Lack of research, ineffective feedback and management being too far removed from customers can contribute to this gap.

Empowering employees when things go wrong can often close the gap.

GAP 2

A recurring theme in service companies is the difficulty experienced in translating customer's expectations into service quality specifications (Zeithaml and Bitner, 2003). This gap refers to the difference between company understanding of customer expectations and the translation into customer-driven designs and standards.

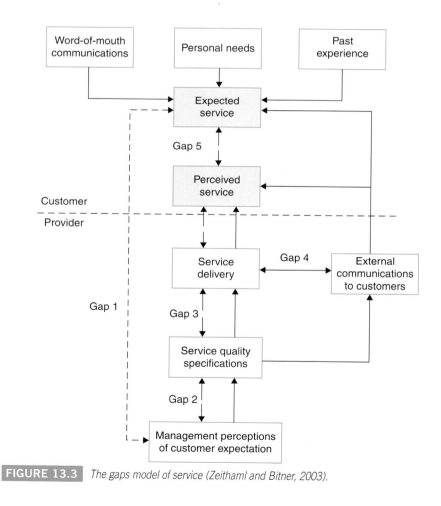

FIGURE 13.3 *The gaps model of service (Zeithaml and Bitner, 2003).*

GAP 3

This gap exists because the actual service delivery, before or after the event, has failed to meet the set standards. It can be the case that even when company guidelines exist for performing services well, employees may still fail to deliver satisfactory services. This may result from a flawed HR system, or processes.

It is important that all employees understand the standards, otherwise efficient and quality service provision may be impacted upon.

Gap 2 and Gap 3 together represent the employee gap which is a significantly important issue for the proposed organisation.

GAP 4

This gap refers to the differences between service delivery and the service provider's external communication, i.e. the levels of service are not correctly communicated or understood by the customer.

Gap 5

The service falls short of what the customer hoped for.

Do note though, it is not always possible to remove the gaps completely.

THE CUSTOMER SERVICE PROGRAMME

Having identified gaps in the level of service an organisation can take steps to address the issues. So, for example, we could try and close the gaps in the ways shown in Table 13.6.

Table 13.6	Ways of closing gaps
GAP 1	Hold regular team meetings and management briefings to ensure they are customer focused. Research in the form of customer satisfaction surveys could be undertaken to establish customer expectations and ways to exceed or delight the customers.
GAP 2	Better interaction between management and staff to establish realistic targets for staff to aspire to.
GAP 3	All customer-facing staff need to be clear on what their roles are, and what targets they are expected to achieve. Clearly internal marketing has a key role to play. It is important that staff feel valued and want to work effectively.
GAP 4	Service delivery standards need to be maintained and stronger targets set, but customers must be clear on what they can expect.
GAP 5	Clearly, if people have an expectation of what they expect, then the organisation needs to ensure the highest levels of customer service are achieved and a customer-centric approach is adopted.

Closing the gaps is, in many ways, a reactive approach. A more proactive approach is to develop a relationship marketing plan that can be based around the six markets model (discussed in earlier units) which in summary would cover:

- *Supplier markets:* building relationships with suppliers to ensure the chain is maximised and the overall quality of the customer service experience has reached its potential, and where things need to be improved there is a supplier relationship development process.

- *Recruitment:* the importance of recruiting staff with the right skills cannot be underestimated and robust procedures must be in place not only to ensure the 'right' employees are selected, but they stay with the company for a reasonable amount of time.

- *Internal markets:* companies need to create internal awareness for the corporate aims, objectives and mission, as well as determine the expectations of the internal customer. This may also cover training, systems and processes as well as change management.

- *Influence markets:* the company may need to change its perception with the media and key stakeholders.

- *Referral markets:* often new business comes through third parties, who will simply stop introducing business if it is felt that sub-optimal service is being given.

BENEFITS OF CUSTOMER ACQUISITION AND RETENTION

Most academics would agree that it costs much more to recruit a new customer than retain an existing one. It is therefore surprising that organisations still spend a disproportionate amount of time and money on the recruitment of new customers without sufficiently considering the needs of existing customers. The general feeling is that it is five times more expensive to recruit a new customer than it is to retain an existing one. Consequently the use of the marketing budget needs to be challenged where the focus is simply on new customer recruitment. Naturally some organisations are still looking for a transactional relationship, i.e. only interested in the immediate purchase, rather than the overall relationship.

Improving the acquisition process is concerned with aspects Christoper et al (2002):

- acquiring customers at a lower cost

- acquiring more customers for the same cost (or lower)

- acquiring more attractive customers
- acquiring more customers using new channels

However, this data needs to be collected at the segment level.

EXAMPLE

An organisation has identified that its customer base consists of four main segments:

Segment 1: Acquisition costs £20
Segment 2: Acquisition costs £15
Segment 3: Acquisition costs £10
Segment 4: Acquisition costs £5

Initially it would be tempting for the organisation to suggest that recruitment focuses on segment 4 because it is the cheapest channel. However, now consider the following additional information.

Population of each segment:

Segment 1: 1 million
Segment 2: 500,000
Segment 3: 100,000
Segment 4: 10,000

Is it better to have a million customers at a cost of £20 to recruit or 10,000 at a cost of £5?

This is clearly a simple example to which we would need to add additional data, such as the potential size of each segment and the profits that could be generated.

As the costs, size and potential of each segment will differ, an organisation will want to reduce the cost of recruitment while maximising revenue. Electronic channels will be an important part of the overall channel mix, and organisations, while not being able to force customers to interact through any one channel, will want to encourage customers through the most cost-effective by offering (in some cases) incentives such as an 'internet only rate'.

Banks, when launching internet banking, thought that customers would choose to use the internet and stay away from branches, supporting the branch closure period which was taking place. In fact customers saw the internet as an alternative channel which supported the branch network.

However, an important point to note is that while recruitment is the life-blood of an organisation, only profitable customers generate income. Therefore those customers who are recruited in the knowledge that they are unlikely to be profitable should be discarded.

RETENTION

Having invested in recruiting the customers to the organisation, they need to be kept! Reichheld, a professor at Harvard University, is the acknowledged expert on customer retention and his research has indicated that even a small increase in customer retention levels has a dramatic effect on profitability.

Reichheld and Sasser (1990) offer the following reasons why retention levels improve profitability:

- Customer acquisition is expensive and can take many years to recover and then generate profits.

- As customers become more satisfied and confident in their relationships with an organisation they are more likely to direct additional business.

- As the relationship develops, mutual understanding and collaboration increases which can generate efficiencies and lower operating costs. Organisations are often willing to share services to reduce costs down further.

- Satisfied customers often refer other customers to the organisation that can reduce the costs of acquisition. In some markets customer advocacy is particularly important.

- Loyal customers tend to be less price-sensitive and less likely to 'shop around' when considering a new purchase.

Improving profitability levels

Given the benefits which have been identified as a result of better customer retention, the process adopted by an organisation should be formalised and structured and not just left to chance.

The following outlines a three step process to improving customer retention (based on Christoper et al, 2002):

1. *Measure customer retention:* The customer base needs to be analysed to identify the retention rates. This will need to be evaluated for each customer segment, the product(s) purchased and a timeline established so that trends or events can be analysed. Having identified the retention levels, it is then possible to identify future trends and identify profit levels.

2. *Key service issues:* It is now necessary to understand exactly why customers stop doing business with the organisation. Often large organisations will often undertake syndicated research to

understand defection. Customers are not always totally honest and the questionnaires designed to understand may not be robust enough to extract the true reasons for defection. It may the case that the organisation is a secondary supplier and a change in policy has resulted in supplier rationalisation and consequently unless the organisation becomes the main supplier it is likely that the business will be lost.

3. *Corrective action:* Having identified trends, and obtained some ideas why customers are defecting to the competition, the final stage in the process is to put plans in place to prevent customers from leaving, or give them a reason to stay. The actions needed will depend on the reasons given for defection.

MONITORING PERFORMANCE

Monitoring the quality of the service provided is difficult because of the subjective nature of the assessment. There is considerable debate about the most effective measures of monitoring performance. So the following pathway is based on Christopher et al (2002), built on the premise that monitoring the quality of service provided is based on the organisation undertaking regular tracking studies and identifying not only current service issues but those issues which are on the horizon.

A six stage procedure is suggested:

1. *Customer service tracking studies*: The needs of customers must be clearly identified and monitored over time, so that changes can be detected at an early opportunity and action taken if necessary to address. Customers do not always know what they want from a relationship with an organisation and therefore a two-way dialogue needs to be established which enables suggestions about future improvements to be exchanged.

2. *Quality maintenance index*: The physical service environment needs to be monitored through the use of a checklist. Key areas to be measured can include lighting, decorations, accessibility, parking and cleanliness. In the virtual environment such as the internet, it is the website which becomes the physical environment and should similarly be audited.

3. *Mystery shopper*: A researcher poses as a customer and measures the service received against an agreed list of criteria which could include helpfulness of staff, length of time kept waiting, decor of the premises, stock of leaflets, etc.

4. *Staff climate monitor*: This measure looks at the customer service issue from the perspective of the member of staff and asks them where they think the gaps or issues may lie.

5. *Risk point analysis*: Analysis can identify those points in the delivery of the relationship that can cause particular problems and ensure careful monitoring.

6. *Service standards review*: Having collected all the key information, it now needs to be analysed and new service standards can be implemented in order to better match the organisation with the needs of the customer.

Moller (1988) suggested '12 golden rules' to help organisations to aid the delivery of quality service:

1. Set personal and organisational quality goals. In this way staff know what they are expected to deliver and similarly the expectations of the organisation are clearly stated.

2. Establish personal accountability. It needs to be clearly documented where responsibility for actions lies.

3. Regular checks must be made. As we have seen above, customers must be asked for their views on the level of service provided.

4. Regard the next link in the chain as your customer.

5. Avoid error. Standardised systems cut down on errors, but human error needs to be eliminated wherever possible.

6. Effective performance of tasks. Tasks need to be performed as effectively as possible within the current organisational capability.

7. Resource utilisation. Resources must be used as effectively as possible.

8. Commitment. Both the organisation and staff need to be committed to the delivery of quality service.

9. Finish. Activities started must be completed.

10. Stress. Procedures and practices need to be developed to eliminate or manage the effects of stress.

11. Ethics. Be ethical.

12. Quality. Demand quality.

CASE STUDY: ROLLS ROYCE

High above the Pacific, passengers doze on a long flight from Asia to America. Suddenly a bolt of lightning cleaves the air. Those startled by the flash and bang soon settle back into their dreams. But on the other side of the world, in Derby, in the English Midlands, engineers at Rolls-Royce get busy.

A torrent of data is beamed from the aircraft to Derby. Numbers dance across screens, graphs are drawn and technicians scratch their heads. Before the plane lands, word comes that the engine is running smoothly. The aircraft can take off on time.

Rolls-Royce's global operations room in Derby, with 24-hour news channels, banks of computer screens and clocks showing the time around the world, looks and feels like a currency-trading floor.

Rolls-Royce's fortunes are a matter of new urgency in a country that was once the workshop of the world yet seemed hell-bent on leading the way to the post-industrial age. With light-touch regulation and tax-breaks that made it an uncommonly attractive place to hire foreign talent.

Over the past couple of decades or so Rolls-Royce has transformed itself from a loss-making British firm into the world's second-biggest maker of large jet engines. In doing so, it has deliberately blurred the lines between making things and offering services. Its experience indicates that Britain can do both after all.

The country's manufacturing output has been growing over the years, but its share of GDP has been falling (as in other rich countries). Employment in manufacturing has been in decline. Only a handful of big manufacturing firms still exist. Some, such as BAE Systems, a defence company, rely on the government. And although industries such as car-making survive, they do so almost entirely in foreign ownership. Britain remains the world's eighth-biggest exporter of goods, but its share of global markets has shrunk to a little more than 3%, far behind America, China and Germany. In services it ranks second.

Export engine

The striking thing about Rolls-Royce, however, has been its success in foreign markets. Its revenues, about 85% of which come from abroad, have almost doubled in the decade since Sir John Rose took over as chief executive. About half of the latest wide-bodied passenger jets and a quarter of single-aisle aircraft rolling off the production lines these days are powered by its engines. At the Farnborough air show in 2008, its order book was swollen by almost $9.3 billion. This was half as much again as the $6 billion in sales that its two main rivals, Pratt & Whitney and GE, made between them.

In other fields it is growing even faster. Revenues from its marine operations are running at twice the rate of 2002 and its equipment is installed on 30,000 ships. In July it set up a new civil nuclear business, hoping to ride a wave of investment in new power plants around the world that it reckons may be worth some £50 billion ($75 billion) a year by 2023. It hopes to sell skills it developed on nuclear submarines built for the Royal Navy. Its defence business accounts for a fifth of its revenues, against three-fifths during the cold war.

Yet that business may provide a comfortingly stable source of cash as a slowing world economy prompts airlines to retire old jets and cancel orders for new ones. With the airline industry in trouble, Rolls-Royce has already had to cut some jobs. But because of the way in which it has melded technology and service, there is much to suggest that it will weather an economic downturn better than its rivals.

An understanding of the firm's success requires some understanding of the technology that goes into its civil-aircraft engines. This is not just Rolls-Royce's biggest business, it is also the one that both felled the company in 1971 and proved to be its salvation two decades later.

The best place to start is the surprisingly small, almost underwhelming, turbine blades that make up the heart of the giant engines slung beneath the wings of the world's biggest planes. These are not the huge fan blades you see when boarding, but are buried deep in the engines. Each turbine blade can fit in the hand like an oversized steak knife. At first glance it may not seem much more difficult to make. Yet they cost about $10,000 each. Rolls-Royce's executives like to point out that their big engines, of almost six tonnes, are worth their weight in silver – and that the average car is worth its weight in hamburger.

Turbine blades are difficult to make because they have to survive high temperatures and huge stresses.

Making the blades is merely the entry ticket to the market. Both Rolls-Royce's main rivals have also mastered the art. In such a competitive field an incremental advance by one manufacturer is usually matched by the others within a couple of years. A study by Andrea Bonaccorsi and colleagues at the Sant'Anna School of Advanced Studies in Pisa found that over about 40 years each of the three leading engine-makers has in turn taken a technological lead, but none has held it for much more than a decade.

Rolls-Royce's triumph was not to build a slightly better engine and thus earn a temporary technological edge, but to design a completely different one. It did so from a position of weakness. Until the late 1960s the market for big jet engines was dominated by Pratt & Whitney, with a share of about 90%. Rolls-Royce played a bit part, making engines mainly for European aircraft manufacturers. These were losing, bit by bit, to America's biggest aircraft-makers, which had the benefit of a much larger domestic market and substantial military orders. Rolls-Royce realised that unless it could develop a large jet engine that would fit an American-made airliner, its sales of jet engines would collapse within a decade.

It bet everything on two revolutionary technologies. The first was to use carbon composites to make fan blades (the big ones you do see) far lighter than the metal ones of the time. The second was to change the basic architecture of jet engines by using three shafts instead of two. Both tasks turned out to be harder and costlier than Rolls-Royce thought. Its composite blades shattered when hit by hail or birds. Eventually it had to abandon them for the tried and tested metal ones. And by then an embarrassing series of delays and missed performance targets had caused it to run out of cash. A Conservative government nationalised the company in 1971.

Although the new design broke Rolls-Royce, it also proved to be the base for a whole family of winning engines. These were more complex to design, build and maintain than those of rivals, but they also used fuel more efficiently and suffered less wear and tear. Much more importantly, they could be scaled up or down to fit bigger or smaller aircraft. As a result, Rolls-Royce did not have to design a new engine from scratch each time a new airliner came onto the market, allowing it to compete for sales across a far wider range of aircraft than its rivals. This was a huge advantage because the main determinant of whether a jet engine sells well is whether the aircraft it is married to sells well. Rolls-Royce can sell across the board. It is the only one of the three main engine-makers with designs to fit the three newest airliners under development, the Boeing 787 Dreamliner, the Airbus A380 and the new wide-bodied version of the Airbus A350. Of the world's 50 leading airlines, 45 use its engines.

The big pay-off from getting engines under more wings comes from selling spares and servicing them. This is because selling aircraft engines is like selling razors. The razor and engine make little if any profit; that comes later, from blades or spare parts and servicing.

The trouble with selling razors at a loss is that someone else may make the blades to fit them. And the juicy margins in engine maintenance have indeed attracted a swarm of independent servicing firms (and engine-makers after each other's business). Rudolph Hirdes, an aircraft-maintenance expert at Aviation Consultancy Holland, reckons certified spare parts for big jet engines can be had for one-third of the price charged by the original manufacturers.

This is where Rolls-Royce has melded its technology with service to make it more difficult for competitors to pinch its business. Rather than simply giving away razors to sell razor blades it has, if you will, offered to shave its clients every morning. Instead of selling airlines first engines and then parts and service, Rolls-Royce has convinced its customers to pay a fee for every hour that an engine runs. Rolls-Royce in turn promises to maintain it and replace it if it breaks down. "They aren't selling engines, they are selling hot air out the back of an engine," says an investment analyst. The idea is not unique to Rolls-Royce; the other big makers of aircraft engines do much the same. But Rolls-Royce has adopted it with greater gusto. It has been offering the service for more than a decade; more than half of its engines in service are covered by such contracts, as are about 80% of those it is now selling.

This may seem to support the theory that Britain would do better to concentrate on supplying services rather than on making things. Yet it shows instead that it is sometimes necessary to be good at making things to sell the services connected with them. At Rolls-Royce it is difficult to see where one begins and the other ends.

The operations room in Derby, for instance, continuously assesses the performance of 3,500 jet engines around the world, raising an almost insurmountable barrier to any rival that hopes to grab the work of servicing them. The data collected can be invaluable to airlines: it enables Rolls-Royce to predict when engines are more likely to fail, letting customers schedule engine changes efficiently. That means fewer emergency repairs and fewer unhappy passengers. The data are equally valuable to Rolls-Royce. Spotting problems early helps it to design and build more reliable engines or to modify existing ones. The resulting evolution of its engines has steadily improved fuel efficiency and over the past 30 years has extended the operating life of engines tenfold (to about ten years between major rebuilds). "You could only get closer to the customer by being on the plane," says Mike Terrett, the company's chief operating officer.

A further reason for its success is its wholehearted embrace of globalisation. Whereas British car firms once contented themselves with making shoddy cars for the domestic market, Rolls-Royce has transformed itself from a British firm into a global one. About 40% of employees work in countries other than Britain, compared with 7% two decades ago. About half its new engine projects are based abroad, along with the same proportion of its research and development. A side benefit is that it sets factories in different parts of the world in competition with one another for new projects, something carmakers have done for years to keep down labour costs.

Rolls-Royce can also draw on the strengths of local economies where it opens for business; those economies in turn adapt to the company's needs. It attracts suppliers and other related industries.

As much as Rolls-Royce's embrace of globalisation is both a cause and effect of its success, it also raises uncomfortable questions over the future of manufacturing in Britain. For there is much to suggest that, barring some fundamental changes at home, the shift abroad will continue to gather pace.

One reason for this is the lure of subsidies and other incentives from foreign governments. Britain has been no slouch at handing out taxpayers' money: in 2001 it lent £250m to Rolls-Royce to help develop bigger jet engines; in 2006 it agreed to give grants of £47m to a group led by Rolls-Royce to design an environmentally friendly engine. But others have been far more generous. When Rolls-Royce opened a facility in Germany recently it may have been influenced by a pledge from the state of Brandenburg to cover 30% of its capital costs. Similarly an estimated $57m in assistance from state and local governments may have helped it decide to build a factory in Virginia. "We courted Rolls-Royce for five to six years," says Liz Povar of the Virginia Economic Development Partnership, which is funded by the state.

There is no need to make a fetish of manufacturing, even when finance is in such bad way. Industrial economies such as Germany are suffering too. But the success of Rolls-Royce suggests that the world will not be neatly divided into firms (or countries) that make things and those that sell services. Flying high depends on being able to do both.

Editor's note: Simon Robertson, the chairman of Rolls-Royce, is a member of The Economist Group's board. Helen Alexander, the former chief executive of the Economist Group, serves on Rolls-Royce's board. The author of this piece did not discuss Rolls-Royce with either of them.

This article is adapted from the Economist dated 5th January, 2009, reproduced with permission from

SUMMARY

Service is an important aspect in any relationship; however, it is a difficult concept to define with certainty as different parties will have different expectations. No matter how hard an organisation may try to deliver a service that meets the needs of the customer, it is the customer who actually defines how good the service was. Ideally there should be a meeting of minds, or point of agreement about what constitutes good service and a SLA is one method of coming to mutually agreement about how good service should look. The SLA will define minimum standards of services to be delivered and outline remedies for improvements where the standards have fallen short of expectations.

As the reader will have seen in the Rolls Royce case study, there is a blurring of boundaries between product and services. While this has historically been the case for adding tangibility to a service now we are seeing service being added to a tangible product as being a key differentiator.

Services use the extended marketing mix and the reader has been introduced to this concept and how it is used in relation to the 4Ps.

QUESTIONS

1. In the Rolls Royce example why has the integration of product and service been so successful for the company?

2. What is the difference between a product and service?

3. Why is customer retention so important for an organisation?

4. Outline a process for monitoring the level of customer service provided by an organisation.

5. Draw the gaps model of service.

6. Explain the gaps model of service.

7. Why are 7Ps used when referring to the marketing mix for services?

8. Explain the additional 3Ps used in services marketing.

9. What do you understand by the term 'life time value?

10. What are the four characteristics of services?

FURTHER READING

http://www.iso.org/iso/iso_catalogue.htm28.11.08.

BIBLIOGRAPHY

http://www.bain.com/bainweb/Consulting_Expertise/capabilities_detail.
asp?capID = 102(7.11.08).

http://uk.movies.yahoo.com/07112008/5/cinema-solace-0.html(7.11.08).

Booms, B.H. and Bitner, M.J. (1981) Marketing strategies and organisation structures for service firms. In: Donnelly, J. and George, W.R. (eds) *Marketing of Services*. American Marketing Association, Chicago.

Borden, N. (1964 June) The concept of the Marketing Mix. *Journal of Advertising Research*, 23(2), 2–7.

Brassington, F. and Pettitt, S. (2006) *Principles of Marketing*. FT Prentice Hall.

Christopher, M., Payne, A., Ballantyne, D. (2002) Relationship marketing creative stakeholder value.

Dibb, S., Simkin, L., Pride, W. and Ferrell, O. (2005) *Marketing: Concepts and Strategies*, 5th European edition. Houghton Mifflin.

Farrance, C. (2002) *Managing Relationships in a Corporate Bank*. Financial World Publishing.

Gronroos, A. (1984) *Strategic Marketing Management in the Service Sector*. London, Chartwell-Brace.

Kotler, P., Armstrong, G., Saunders, J. and Wong, V. (1999) *Principles of Marketing*. FT Prentice Hall.

Meek, H. and Meek, R. (2001) *Marketing Management*. Financial World Publishing.

Parasuraman, A. et al (1985) A conceptual model of service quality and its implications for future research. *Journal of Marketing*, 49(fall), 41–50.

Piercy, N. (2001) *Market Led Strategic Change*. Butterworth-Heinemann.

Reichheld, F.F. and Sasser, W.E. (1990) Zero defections: quality comes to services. *Harvard Business Review*, Sept_Oct.

Zeithaml, V.A. and Bitner, M.J. (2003) *Services Marketing: Integrated Customer Focus across the Firm*, 3rd edition. McGraw-Hill.

Key Accounts

The learning outcomes associated with this Chapter will enable you to:

- Apply the KAM process
- Examine the value of effective KAM

INTRODUCTION

KAM is often referred to in different contexts; it is used when referring to global, national, or major corporate accounts, however as we will see below, the management of strategically important accounts overseas requires a modified approach. Often KAM is associated with an organisation's 'biggest' or 'best' customer. But it has at its heart the concept that not all customers are equal and has been used in various industries such as advertising and banking for many years.

Fill (2006) defines a key account as 'customers that, in a business-to-business market are willing to enter into relationship exchanges which are of strategic importance to the focus of the organisation'.

KAM is the process adopted by an organisation in order to provide effective management to strategically important customers which contributes directly to the organisation's business objectives. KAM seeks to achieve mutual gain between the organisations, in other words it is about building relationships with certain customers. Gone is the time when suppliers were managed at a distance, now suppliers are managed with openness and relationships built at different levels within the organisations. The concept of KAM ensures that 'key' accounts are provided with an enhanced level of service in relation to the value they offer the organisation.

While profit is usually the ultimate driver, key accounts can be selected for a number of reasons including technical expertise, image, i.e. the prestige of having a specific supplier as one of your clients, geographic proximity, or market expertise (however, this list is not exhaustive).

Equally the often-cited Pareto's Law, otherwise known as the 80/20 rule, helps us. This suggests that 80% of an organisation's income is delivered by 20% of its customers. While the actual percentages will vary across industry sectors and organisations, the rule generally holds true. The implications are clear; organisations must identify and focus on those customers delivering the income.

Not all organisations have a KAM programme in place and once the decision to implement KAM has been taken there are five stages in the process (see below) (Millman and Wilson, 1995).

However, organisations need to identify the accounts they want to embrace within the KAM programme.

Hooley et al. (2008) suggest KAM has becoming increasingly widespread as a result of:

- Increasingly levels of competition in many markets with the consequence of higher selling costs for suppliers

- Increased customer concentration as a result of mergers and acquisitions

- Growing customer emphasis on centralised strategic purchasing

- Active strategies of supplier-base reduction by larger buyers to reduce purchasing costs

Criteria for Selecting Accounts

It is well recognised that it is much more expensive to recruit new customers than to retain existing ones, so the criteria for selecting a key account has to be clear. It is of course the case that there are both 'hard' and 'soft' measures to be established when selecting key accounts.

Table 14.1 offers some suggestions as a basis for selecting key accounts.

Table 14.1	Key account selection criteria
Profitability; current and historic trends	
Potential; what is the rate of growth and in the future	
Annual turnover; does it meet the threshold now, or will it at some future point	
Brand association; does the brand convey financial or non financial benefits	
Relationship; will the status of being a key account lead to additional business or block out the competition?	

The selection criteria recognises criteria other than size and therefore it follows that key accounts are not just the 'largest' accounts and the basis for selection is vitally important.

It is often the case that having established the criteria for KAM status, not all accounts can be managed in this way because of a lack of internal resources and decisions need to be made as to the ranking given to the non-KAM accounts. Inevitability some will be 'demoted' to lower tier accounts as their potential is poor.

KEY ACCOUNT SELECTION

It is important to select those customers who would benefit from a KAM approach. The whole purpose of KAM is to build relationships with key customers and by implication this means being highly selective in the approach adopted. Cheverton (1999) developed a matrix that helps an organisation in an objective manner, seen in Figure 14.1.

There are two dimensions to be considered; *customer attractiveness* (what makes the customer or potential customer appealing to the organisation?) and *relative strength* (what makes the customer appealing to you in comparison with the competition?)

The matrix in Figure 14.1 (Cheverton, 1999) shows four categories: key account, maintenance account, opportunistic account and key development account.

Key Account

These are the accounts you have identified as the ones to build a strategic relationship with. It is highly attractive and you have significant strengths compared to the competition.

Key Development Account

Here the account is very attractive to you, but you are not the best performer in comparison with the competition. There is work to be done in developing

FIGURE 14.1 *Key account matrix.*

your strengths and making you more attractive. Depending on the number of accounts within this category, selective investment may be needed.

Maintenance Account

You have a high relative strength, but the account is not seen as particularly attractive. Here if you do not want to 'drop' the account, it must be managed effectively so that scarce resources are not wasted. The relationship could be conducted on the telephone rather than face to face, or visits could be untaken on a less frequent basis.

Opportunistic Account

Here you have a low relative strength and the customer is not attractive to you. No resources are invested, but both parties will be happy to deal with each other on an ad hoc basis.

KAM MANAGEMENT

It has been identified that KAM is concerned with long-term relationships and this can come about through gaining access to new markets, better ways of working, or through technological development. Fundamental to a long-term relationship and hence success depends on the way KAM is managed. We will see shortly the importance of people in the KAM process, but there has to be a strategic match between the needs of the supplier and the customer, otherwise frustration will develop early in the relationship. Risks to the relationship will occur when the customer demands more from the relationship and of course the other way around, when the supplier is not willing or able to provide the supplier with the relationship originally expected.

KAM relies on clear management and responsibility for relationship. A structure for managing the relationship needs to be put in place and Fill (2006) identified three possible organisational approaches to KAM which are summarised in Table 14.2.

KAM Cycle

Having identified the criteria the organisations need to satisfy, the key accounts have to be identified and a relationship built. Various commentators have developed models to reflect the various relationships and Table 14.3 is based on Millman and Wilson (1995).

All the various stages are of equal importance, however, knowing which stage a particular relationship is will determine the resources that need to be applied, or anticipated.

Table 14.2	Three possible organisational approaches to KAM (Fill, 2006)
Approach	**Summary**
Assigning sales executives	This approach is warranted in smaller organisations and is very much 'hands-on'. There is a clear point of contact, roles and responsibilities are clear and there are the added benefits of flexibility and responsiveness. However, objectivity should still be maintained in this approach. Fill (2006) alerts us to the fact that this type of relationship can offer key accounts a disproportionate level of attention.
Creating a key account division	Creating a separate division can require significant structural changes, but it has the advantage of integrating the key support functions necessary in KAM. This approach is not without additional costs as many functions will be duplicated.
Creating a key account sales force	Here the decision is made to build a dedicated KAM team who can be trained to 'higher' levels so they will offer an enhanced level of service to key accounts through a solid understanding not only of the key accounts but the markets they operate in. This approach is not without its problems as once again there is duplication of work (see above).

Table 14.3	KAM cycles (Millman and Wilson,1995)
Pre-KAM	At this stage there is no relationship and the task is to identify accounts that meet the selection criteria and have the potential to become key accounts. An important consideration here is to establish that the various parties could work with each other.
Early KAM	The relationship has started, but it is still transactional and there is an element of testing each other out. Communication channels will be formal.
Mid KAM	The relationship has now developed, the organisations are starting to understand each other and work proactively together.
Partnership KAM	The organisations recognise the importance of the other and first choice supplier status achieved.
Synergistic KAM	Both organisations see themselves as one organisation where they create synergistic value in the marketplace.
Uncoupling KAM	At this stage and for a variety of reasons, the relationship is being terminated and procedures are put in place to 'wind down' the relationship.

The transition from one stage to another differs in time and McDonald (2000) suggests the speed of transition depends on how quickly a sufficient level of trust is built. Therefore an organisation will typically have its key account portfolio at a range of stages in the cycle.

You will recall specific criteria was outlined to establish the suitability for KAM, now a profile for each key account needs to be established so that the potential to move to the next stage can be established and clear objectives and strategies set. Some accounts will 'stick' and will need to be managed accordingly, for others the growth potential may be reduced and close account monitoring will be necessary.

It needs to be recognised that in some situations the KAM relationship may need to be terminated or 'uncoupled' and procedures should be put in place for the smooth termination of the relationship.

THE ROLE OF COMMUNICATION IN KAM

KAM is concerned with building and retaining long-term relationships and people are at the heart of the relationship and this requires a 'push', communication strategy where communication is focused on the key account.

The various different KAM stages will require different communication approaches recognising the developing nature of the relationship which should be regular, high quality and personalised.

The KAM will ensure that an on-going dialogue is maintained which continually seeks to build value in the relationship. While regular communication is essential it must be coordinated so that planned and consistent messages are delivered to multiple levels across the organisations which are supportive and motivational.

Ideally the on-going dialogue supports the different KAM stages and builds trust which is essential to the success of the relationship.

In determining the most appropriate communications mix, the needs and characteristics of key accounts need to be determined which will then enable messages to be developed to reflect the purpose of the relationship and builds constructive and long term relationships.

THE ROLE OF PEOPLE IN KAM

The role of the KAM is to develop the relationship in line with the objectives set. While there is a strong sales element to the role, it is much wider and covers:

- *Problem solving:* Difficulties will be a feature of the relationship and the KAM manager must use a range of skills to ensure problems are identified and resolved quickly. Strong negotiating and implantation skills are needed along with business and project management. Creative problem solving skills are essential.

- *Relationship building:* Strong inter-personal skills are needed to build key contacts and then nurture them both professionally and socially.

- *Communicating:* Sharing key information in a open and timely manner is key to success. Often confidential information is shared to build the relationship. Trust and mutual respect having been built through personal contact. Marketing and strategic thinking skills are helpful in seeing the 'big picture' rather than focusing on the often unnecessary detail

- *Personal selling:* Negotiation, handling objections, and training support the need for managers to achieve sales targets which may ultimately drive motivation and reward. Product and technical knowledge is important to the customer as they will need reassurance that they are making the right decisions.

The key account manager is really the 'jam' in the sandwich where the role is to balance the needs of both parties to achieve mutual benefit. But the role and skills of the key account manager change with the various stages in the KAM cycle.

For example at pre-KAM the role will be to identify potential accounts and screen them. The associated skills will be communication and product or technical knowledge. As the account enters the synergistic stage, the skills needed will tend to be more along the lines of business management and the role is more concerned with coordination.

While the key account manager role may appear daunting, the tools and frameworks discussed earlier in this book help provide a sense of focus and a reminder that the tools include;

- PESTEL

- Porter's 5 Forces analysis

- SWOT

- Porter's Value Chain

Cranfield School of Management has undertaken considerable research in the area of KAM and Table 14.4 shows a brief summary of some of the research finding.

Table 14.4	Cranfield School of Management's findings on KAM

- KAM is a long-term solution and organisations need to view KAM as an ongoing relationship
- Relationships are vulnerable in the early stages of the relationship
- Not all accounts process through the cycle, some get struck
- Account teams are more effective than an account management working alone
- Key account manager is critical to the relationship and requires skills and training beyond a sales person
- GAM has additional complexity and is particularly challenging

OVERSEAS ACCOUNTS

The overseas or international aspect of KAM has been left to the end of the chapter very deliberately. Many text books as mentioned in the introduction refer to KAM as being a umbrella phrase for the management of strategic accounts irrespective of location. The syllabus requires you to apply the concept of strategic account management in the UK and overseas, so you need to be clear on the differences which are discussed below.

The nature of competition requires many organisations to operate overseas and this brings about the need to manage key accounts in a similar way to domestic accounts.

However, there are points of difference which need to be explored: first, where key accounts are located in different countries they are known as Global accounts and their management referred to as global account management (GAM), and second, there is a defined set of competencies needed to qualify for GAM.

Global accounts are large companies that operate in multiple countries, often on two or more continents, are strategically important to the supplier and have some form of coordinated purchasing across different countries (Hennessey and Jeannet, 2003).

The delivery of GAM requires three competencies (Wilson et al., 2000):

- A forum where the customer is involved and collaborates as apart of the overall process

- Clear management of the process especially with respect to the supply of information and communication

- A coordinated and globally competent supply chain

SUMMARY

The concept of KAM has been developing rapidly; organisations want long-lasting and mutually beneficial relationships with each other. Transactional relationships no longer fit with most organisation's business models as closer and open relationships are seen as more effective. The introduction of KAM between buyers and sellers marks a more professional and integrated approach where organisations work together in the pursuit of joint objectives.

Not all organisations develop a KAM approach and for those that do, as we have seen, the relationship goes through a number of stages as the organisations build and develop their relationships. Inevitably some relationships terminate because of dissatisfaction between the organisations, or the relationship is not mutually beneficial, in which case the relationship needs to be dissolved in a structured manner.

People have an important part to play in KAM and the staff selected as KAM managers need to have a specific skill set which enable them to work across the various organisations and at different levels.

We have seen that key accounts can be managed in variety of ways and that the management of key accounts located overseas is based upon KAM principles and known as GAM.

QUESTIONS

1. What do you understand by the term 'key account'?

2. What is the difference between KAM and GAM?

3. Set out the criteria for KAM

4. What three ways can an organisation structure itself to deliver KAM?

5. How does the role of the key account manager change over the KAM cycle?

6. What is the role of communication in KAM?

BIBLIOGRAPHY

Cheverton, P. (1999) *Key Account Management*. Kogan Page.

Fill, C. (2006) *Marketing Communications: Engagement, strategies and practice*, 4th edition. FT Prentice Hall.

Hennessey, D.H. and Jeannet, J. (2003) *Global Account Management: Creating value*. Wiley.

Hooley, G., Saunders, J., Piercy, N.F. and Nicoulaud, B. (2008) *Marketing Strategy and Competitive Positioning*, 3rd edition. FT Prentice Hall.

McDonald, M. (2000) Marketing management: A relationship marketing perspective. In: *Managing Key Accounts*. Cranfield School of Management, Palgrave.

Millman, T. and Wilson, K. (1995) From key account selling to key account management. *Journal of Marketing Practice: Applied marketing science*, 1(1).

Wilson, K., Croom, S., Millman, T. and Weilbaker, D.C. (2000) *Global Account Management Study Report*. The Sales Research Trust.

CHAPTER 15

Sales and Product Information and Risks

LEARNING OUTCOMES

By the end of this chapter you will be able to:

- Assess the role and value of sales and product information
- Evaluate the role of sales and product information in increasing revenue

INTRODUCTION

All customers want to feel valued and an important part of any relationship is the ability of an organisation to offer customers something of value, based on previous product purchase or knowledge of the market. However this is only possible if the organisation has detailed knowledge of its customers and the markets in which it operates. All too often organisations launch a new product into the market that simply fails to meet the needs of the customers. Similarly, ineffective marketing campaigns are launched which fail to attract the 'right' customer.

The reader will see that organisations typically collect vast amounts of information on customers, but often it is not integrated with other information so an incomplete customer or market profile is built.

It has been noted in earlier chapter that the intangible aspect of any product makes it harder for the competition to copy that aspect. Similarly an organisation that collects market information in a systematic way can also achieve competitive advantage through the information it has collected. However this, advantage can only be realised and sustained if the information is collated and made available to those people in the organisation who because of their role or position can make effective use of it. Kotler (2003) suggests that as sellers use more complex marketing approaches and face more competition, they need information on the effectiveness of their marketing tools, along with information to make timely decisions.

No matter how robust and comprehensive the information held on customers, competitors, or markets, relationships can break down in some way and the reader will be introduced to possible risks and contingency planning.

MARKETING INFORMATION SYSTEM (MIS)

Organisations typically collect huge amounts of information on customers, but often the information is not used because it is not in an accessible format, or it may just be old and no longer valid. This is a waste of resources and money. Organisations, irrespective of size, need to be able to collect useful information, store it and retrieve it in a timely manner so that it can be used to tailor offers to customers, but also measure the effectiveness of marketing activity. This activity should be measured not just against targets the organisation may have set itself as part of the planning process, but so it can be used to benchmark the organisation against the market generally.

> A typical manager reads about a million words a week.
>   A packaged goods brand manager is bombarded with 1 million to 1 billion new numbers each week. (Kotler, 2003).

Historically organisations may have collected large amounts of data on their customers. However, it was not necessarily in an accessible format, or in some cases, it just wasn't made available to the right people and opportunities to increase sales were missed, or the opportunity to build closer relations with customers lost, hence competitive advantage was lost or reduced.

Now most organisations are investing in a marketing information system (MIS) to improve data management.

> A marketing information system (MIS) consists of people, equipment, and procedures to gather, sort, analyse, evaluate and distribute needed, timely and accurate information. (Kotler, 2003)

An MIS stores and disseminates information within an organisation. In essence a MIS is a framework which allows for information to be collected from a variety of sources, both internal and external to the organisation. This information is then combined with other relevant information to produce a specific range of reports that helps the organisation manage its marketing more effectively.

Large organisations generate vast amounts of information and to be effective the MIS must be specific to the organisation. What data should be collected? How should it be collected? When and who should it be made available to?

Consider the following statement made by the Sales Director:

'Sales have increased 10% in the past six months'.

Before we can make a judgement on importance of the statement the sale directors adds some additional information:

'Competitors' sales have increased 12% in the last six months'

The initial statement doesn't look as impressive now. The point is that an MIS needs to provide individuals with the information they need to care out their role effectively. Of course MIS relies on many non-marketing systems.

Figure 15.1 shows a simple MIS which consists of three parts: external inputs, a central processing unit and outputs. It is the marketing team that should not only drive the structure of the MIS, but they also are the recipients of the information.

External Inputs

Figure 15.1 shows a range of typical information which could be specified, but it is not exhaustive, and could be supplemented with sales team information on the competition, new products being launched or planned, accounts gained by the competition and any pricing issues.

Central Processing Unit

In summary information is collected from a variety of internal sources including:

- results from market research, either primary or secondary

- sales data, margins, distribution channels, year on year comparisons, average transaction values

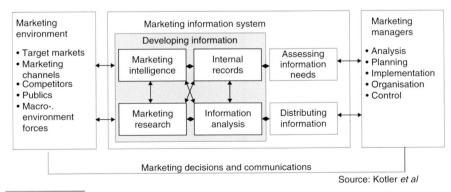

Source: Kotler *et al*

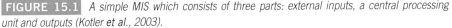

FIGURE 15.1 *A simple MIS which consists of three parts: external inputs, a central processing unit and outputs (Kotler et al., 2003).*

- key customer data covering sales, transactions and purchase frequency

- customer complaints or suggestions for product improvement

- marketing campaigns, costs and results

Marketing Intelligence

Intelligence will come from a range of sources that the organisation feels important. This can range from evaluating competitor products, to financial data, external research such as Taylor Nelson, or where overseas sales could include research from Neilsen Media.

Clearly, some information can be collected freely from the market, but it can be necessary to buy information from research organisations either in the home or overseas markets.

Organisations with large sales teams will use them as the organisation's 'eyes and ears' reporting back key data which forms part of the intelligence gathering process.

Press cuttings, audited accounts, trade bodies or associations and the internet form part of the intelligence gathering process.

Marketing Research

Research, while similar to marketing intelligence, is much more structured and proactive. An organisation will identify gaps in its knowledge and commission a research project which can be completed internally, or by appointing an external agency which may have specialist skills. Often it is not exactly clear what the cause of a problem is and exploratory research will be undertaken prior to a full research study being undertaken.

Internal Records

Most organisations are not short on internal records and collect information from literally a vast range of sources, including sales, payment terms, payment period, cash flow, stock levels, and stock turnover, etc.

Information Analysis

Separate isolated pieces of information in themselves are not of much value and need to be combined together to offer a comprehensive profile of particular segments, or individuals

Outputs

Having been analysed and refined, the data is now distributed, or made available to marketing managers in a predetermined format and agreed time.

For most organisations this information is made available to staff electronically and the marketing decision makers will usually specify the information they need, the format they need it in and the time it is required. The format of the information is usually available as a standard report, but changes can be made by respecifying the information, or, in the case in larger organisations, by staff having access to the core data and being able to manipulate it themselves.

An MIS will hold large quantities of information, therefore it is essential that the quality of the data is maintained, otherwise it simply becomes a costly exercise with no beneficial output.

Each decision maker, i.e. recipient of the information, will need to specify their data requirements, such as:

- *Format/presentation of the information:* defined report in hard or soft copy?

- *Data sources (external):* is the information from Mintel reports, company/competitor websites, annual report and accounts, industry reports, government data or economic data?

- *Data sources (internal):* key account(s), purchasing trends/patterns

- *Frequency of reports:* for example, weekly or daily?

Some organisations have moved beyond MIS and now use MDSS (marketing decision support systems) which is software that aids the decision-making process by helping managers anticipate certain outcomes based on the information available. In effect managers can interrogate the database and develop scenarios.

Given the considerable amount of data that will be held in the system it should be quick and easy to access.

Knowing the purchasing patterns of key customers allows for the effective management of them.

If they are making fewer purchases than sales forecasts suggested then knowing what they are buying, and, equally, what they are not buying, will enable a strategy to be formulated to win back sales. It may be the case that your competitors are offering promotions, and given the information you have on the customer, you can develop a counter attack.

Different divisions of an organisation will commission research or collect data from a variety of sources and as we have seen in the CPU above, it must be centralised and automated so that access to the system can be made electronically, and the database interrogated to produce ad hoc or standard reports.

REVENUE GENERATION

An MIS will help an organisation to better understand its market, so that when it comes to developing strategy and marketing plans, the organisation can set SMART objectives which will be realistic. Equally, marketing information has no value unless it is used to make informed decisions. Consequently when it is given to marketing managers it becomes an effective tool for guiding decisions which will make the organisation more profitable and build relationships with customers, through more effective targeting of customers based on an understanding of their needs. In fact the MIS is the engine which drives Customer Relationship Management (CRM).

The MIS will guide decisions to what segments of the market the organisation should be targeted and the potential income which maybe generated.

Equally, it helps in decisions about which products and channels can be made having regard to the potential and income to be generated.

> Marketing information systems have sought to address the needs of marketers who may have developed marketing campaigns based on their own initiative rather than on a solid platform of information. Customer profiles can be developed and campaigns tested for effectiveness.

While this source of data is largely invaluable it has to be used consistently and effectively and without being intrusive on the customer relationship. The customer wants to see the organisation making tailored offers which meet their needs rather than being treated to a demonstration of just how sophisticated the database is.

THE CUSTOMER RELATIONSHIP

While marketing information is necessary for any organisation who wants to compete effectively in the market, the customer journey is not always without problems. Whilst the MIS can identify potential problems there are a number if issues which may impact on the relationship and bring it to an untimely close.

The main issues which may impact on the relationship are:

- *Misconceptions:* there is a misunderstanding between the organisational and the customer, with the customer not receiving what they were expecting. This could range from an incomplete service to a service only partially delivered.

- *Inadequate resources;* caught in the desire to secure a new client or offer a competitive price, the organisation nay not be able to resource the relationship as fully as would have been expected. Staff sickness and the lack of cover can lead to service deterioration and dissatisfaction.

- *Inadequate delivery:* it is expensive to train new staff and existing staff may themselves be poorly trained leading to a disappointing service being experienced by the customer. Staff changes on both sides of the relationship can often become a friction point, each deciding to change procedures. Quality of the product may be disappointing in relation to the price and there are too many occasions where performance is below the expected level of standard.

- *Exaggerated promises:* it is often tempting for an organisation to make promises they cannot deliver on, but make the promise in order to secure the business. This can be delivery dates, availability of a specific type of hotel room, or the benefits that the product can offer which often leads to a breach of trust.

Just as products go through a life cycle it can be argued that relationships go through a similar process. The ladder of loyalty offers one view of how a relationship develops and is managed over time. Similarly the Partnership Relationship Cycle offers a similar perceptive and this is summarised in Figure 15.2.

Good customer relationships are about adding value for the benefit of both parties and therefore it is essential that relationships (as we have seen) are monitored at the various stages to ensure corrective action can be initiated when necessary.

If organisations do not have robust internal systems in place to meet the needs of customers then the relationship will be terminated early and the investment costs cost.

Porter's Value Chain analysis (Porter, 1985) offers an organisation a process which is actually a framework for establishing exactly what the customer uses the product for and then to develop an offer which fits in with the customers needs. To achieve the organisation needs to ensure that the

Partnership Stage	Initiation Stage
• Recognition of the importance of the account to the organisation • Multiple relationship contacts at all levels	• Interest generated and targets identified • Matching products to customer needs • Understanding customer needs
Consolidation Stage	**Development Stage**
• Focus on building customer loyalty • Innovation and new product development/offering	• Demonstration of organisation's ability to meet customer promises • Building resources to support the relationship

FIGURE 15.2 *Partnership relationship lifecycle.*

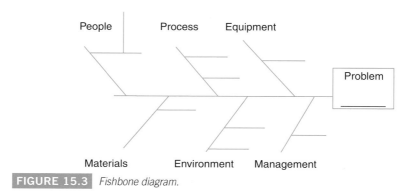

FIGURE 15.3 *Fishbone diagram.*

activities of each department are aligned and deliver value to customers. There is no benefit in a product that goes through various departments where the cost of adding the value is not compensated by the additional value perceived by the customer.

To understand where potential problems (identified above) can arise, organisations often map out the current or potential processes to identify issues or alternatives that could be used along the customer journey. The fishbone diagram is a diagnostic tool that allows companies to identify and resolve potential problems that may not be immediately obvious.

Figure 15.3 shows a fishbone diagram which offers an organisation an approach to improving service support systems and the range of value delivery sequencing.

Identifying potential problems and alternatives is a good way for an organisation to improve its offerings, but also to put contingency plans in place for when things go wrong.

OVERCOMING POTENTIAL PROBLEMS

Problems can be overcome by focusing on the needs of staff:

Staff that are motivated and happy in their work are more likely to convey positive images to the customers who in turn will be satisfied and more likely to remain as customers. Organisations can improve the service through:

Training: Service failures can often be attributed to staff who simply do not follow the existing procedures or make mistakes in carrying out a process. Sometimes it is a motivational issue; staff feel under pressure, but do not feel adequately rewarded

ACTIVITY 15.2

A customer of a major high street bank had held an account for over 25 years and was horrified to be told that a cheque had been returned unpaid with the answer 'refer to drawer'. The reason being that the bank had 'lost' the customer's signature and therefore could not pay the cheque. While on the one hand it is understandable that the bank did not want to pay the cheque, at no time did it consider the customer and how they may feel in the situation. Various calls to the banks call centre brought the standard reply that staff were only 'following procedure and that the cheque would need to be reissued '.

Following the bank's instruction, the customer duly issued the cheque gain, only to face exactly the same problem as the bank had not thought to address the actual issue.

What do you think the bank could have done to help the customer and prevent the same situation happening again?

Fishbone analysis could be used to identify all the customer contact functions and seek to improve customer/staff interaction. It could also review the remuneration package to ensure it is appropriate for the level of responsibility involved. Staff need different skills to undertake the various roles within an organisation which simplistically can be broken down into visible and non-visible staff. Visible staff are those who have a direct or indirect involvement with the customer. For example where a member of staff interacts with the customer on the telephone they will need a good telephone manner, but they can dress very casually. On the other hand staff who meet customers face to face will not only need a pleasant manner, but will need to dress appropriately.

Where staff are not performing to an acceptable standard, the organisation will need to consider developing an appropriate training course an appropriate training course, or sending staff on a course delivered externally.

Productivity: We have looked at the measurement of service in an earlier chapter and the difficulties identified. Where the levels of productivity are perceived to be below that acceptable to the organisation or the industry average, processes should be put in place to address, but the underlying cause needs to be identified.

An organisation wanted to improve efficiency and wanted to automate the process of fulfilling orders. It introduced a system where customers handwrote the order, which was then scanned onto the system for processing. Initially the rejection rate was over 90% as the customer needed to use black ink and write within the boxes on the order form, although that wasn't made clear on the form.

Once staff were alerted to the problem, they monitored the completion of the order form to eliminate the problem.

Technology: Increasingly technology is being used to improve the customer experience. The major supermarkets are introducing self-service tills along with a number of High Street stores in an effort to improve the customer experience. If we need a regular prescription from the doctor, we can now collect from the pharmacy without the need to see the doctor.

Customer interaction: Increasingly we are moving to a team-based solution to customer needs rather than an individual one. Banks have 'account teams', doctors have Group Practices; individual shops have migrated to department stores or supermarkets. With a team approach the likelihood of service failure is reduced as another member of staff should be trained and available to deal with the issues. We are also used to customer interactions taking place at lower levels of an organisation as staff become empowered to deal with complaints.

> A customer who regularly stayed with a large hotel chain was given the wrong room. The receptionist was empowered to offer a 50% reduction and a free stay next time. The customer accepted the gesture and remained loyal to the hotel chain.

Align supply and demand: Supermarkets use sophisticated stock management systems to ensure minimum stock levels are kept to eliminate 'stock outs'. In the past the customer would have simply accepted that there was a likelihood that stock may not always be available.

> The busiest time of days for banks is at lunch time, so it was not surprising customers got annoyed at having to queue for a long time because bank staff were at lunch themselves. The introduction of technology linked with changing staff rotas reduced the problem to acceptable levels.

COMMUNICATION

The role of people is critical to the customer relationship, but communication is also important to the relationship, the challenge is to balance cost and frequency. The relationship between people and effective communication is fundamental to the success of the client relationship. Staff must be well trained, informed and their role valued.

Each stage of the relationship will require a different blend of the communications mix to ensure that every opportunity to maintain and build on the client relationship is taken and maximised in terms of client satisfaction and organisational profitability. This is a key area and the effectiveness of the communications will have a direct impact on the effectiveness of the client relationship and its resilience to future challenges and threats potentially from competitor activity.

A wide variety of communications channels exist, from face to face through to use of paid for media. Each channel should be explored to understand what role it can play in achieving effective communication with the client. A key element of this will be a sustainable communication message and everyone involved in doing business with the client should be aware of what the message is and what his/her role is in communicating that message. The importance of front line customer-facing staff must be understood here and their role in presenting a consistent and meaningful message to the client is critical to the sustainability of long-term profitable relationships with clients.

Organisations must be open to new technologies which many customers prefer to use when doing business with organisations, such as social networking and text messaging which are the preferred communications channels in some important and growing customer segments.

It is important to have key points of accountability for communications throughout the organisation ensuring that there is vertical integration from the senior account manager though to the administrative and support staff. The client relationship will rely heavily on a single, integrated communications message that everyone understands. Conflicting messages do not create confidence in the minds of clients who want to see a single cohesive and integrated organisation in their dealings with it.

The role of information in relation to effective communications is also important. Clients must be able to identify who to contact, how, when and by what means. Any changes must be communicated to clients in a timely and effective way in order to ensure continuity and maximise customer satisfaction.

Effective communication is two-way and within the client relationship there should be every opportunity for the client to communicate with the organisation in order to have a positive view of the relationship. This applies at every level from simple transactional information through to contact about significant issues. Clients must be able to access the organisation in ways and times that are convenient to them and not solely determined by the organisation's needs.

Effective channels of communications can be critical to the relationship with the client particularly in times of crisis when the client needs to be able to obtain instant and easy access to somebody they know and trust in a timely way. This is particularly the case in relation to complex high value services such as banking where clients expect a knowledgeable, informed point of contact who knows them and has sufficient authority and autonomy to act quickly. It is of less importance in relation to simple transactional relationship such as retail purchases where clients, in the main, have lower expectations.

When the client relationship is under threat from competitor activity, the value of effective relationships supported by sound two-way and responsive communication will prove critical in defending relationships against aggressive competitors. It is much more difficult to steal business from a competitor if the client feels valued, well informed and able to access key people they know and trust.

Many organisations now recognise the importance of communications in developing and maintaining long-term profitable relationships that can lead to referrals for new business from clients who have progressed up the loyalty ladder to become effective advocates. This is recognised in the investment that those organisations are now making in corporate communications which sustain and support relationship management at account level.

QUESTIONS

1. Why is service quality difficult to measure?
2. What do you understand by the term MIS?
3. What role does an MIS fulfil?
4. What are the key components of a MIS?
5. What are the key areas that can contribute to problems arising in a relationship?
6. Give examples of how staff can be used to overcome potential problems in a relationship.
7. Identify the key components of the Partnership Relationship Cycle.
8. How can the use of a MIS develop revenue for an organisation?

SUMMARY

An effective MIS can offer an organisation significant advantages over its competitors who do not enjoy a similar system. Information collected from a wide range of internal and external sources are brought together, analysed and given to key functional areas within the organisation in order to maximise key resources and offer customer a more tailored product offering. New products can be launched at competitive prices or prices that the market is prepared to pay and positioned against or away from the competition.

Relationships with customers do not always run smoothly and contingency plans need to be developed and effective communications must be established to overcome problems in the relationship.

BIBLIOGRAPHY

Kotler, P. (2003) *Marketing Management*. Prentice-Hall.
Porter, M.E. (1985) *Competitive Advantage*. The Free Press.

Senior Examiner's Comments – Section Four

On completion of Section Four students should have a detailed understanding of the:

- Meaning of 'service' to different types of customers and in various organisational contexts

- Development and implementation of customer service plans and customer care programmes

- Identification, management and development of 'key account customers'

- Management and use of information in the development of customer relationships

- Determination of service standards and measuring levels of customer satisfaction

Students must be able to apply marketing tools and techniques, especially the marketing mix, in the context of delivering service to customers. To do this effectively, students must understand how customers' service needs can first be ascertained and how these can then be met through the appropriate adaptation of the marketing mix elements and other marketing approaches.

Students also need to be able to make the connection between the execution of an outstanding customer service proposition and the attainment of critical marketing objectives, in particular customer retention, high levels of customer satisfaction and strong customer loyalty. Through these, important benefits will flow, including the achievement of differentiation and competitive advantage as well as the generation of additional revenue growth from cross-sales activities.

Exceeding customers' service expectations is key in the development of long-term customer relationships, which in turn is vital to achieving sustainable future business growth. It is especially important that students understand how organisations identify their 'key account customers' and develop (and execute) plans for their long-term development.

259

Index

Index

Index